Joyce/Lowry

Joyce/Lowry

Critical Perspectives

Patrick A. McCarthy
and Paul Tiessen
Editors

THE UNIVERSITY PRESS OF KENTUCKY

Publication of this volume was made possible in part
by a grant from the National Endowment for the Humanities.

Scholarly publisher for the Commonwealth,
serving Bellarmine College, Berea College, Centre
College of Kentucky, Eastern Kentucky University,
The Filson Club Historical Society, Georgetown College,
Kentucky Historical Society, Kentucky State University,
Morehead State University, Murray State University,
Northern Kentucky University, Transylvania University,
University of Kentucky, University of Louisville,
and Western Kentucky University.

Editorial and Sales Offices: The University Press of Kentucky
663 South Limestone Street, Lexington, Kentucky 40508-4008

01 00 99 98 97   5 4 3 2 1

Library of Congress Cataloging-in-Publication Data
Joyce/Lowry : critical perspectives / Patrick A. McCarthy and Paul Tiessen,
    editors.
        p.   cm.
    Includes bibliographical references and index.
    ISBN 0-8131-2002-0 (alk. paper)
    1. Joyce, James, 1882-1941—Criticism and interpretation.
    2. Lowry, Malcolm, 1909-1957—Criticism and interpretation.
    3. Modernism (Literature)—England. 4. Modernism (Literature)—
Ireland. I. McCarthy, Patrick A., 1945- . II. Tiessen, Paul.
PR6019.09Z667   1997
823'.912—dc20   96-43475

Contents

Acknowledgments

The editors wish to thank Joanne Buehler-Buchan at Wilfrid Laurier University for her assistance and support in the production of this volume. Others at Wilfrid Laurier for whose help we are grateful include Ed Jewinski, Giselle Lavalley, Sandra Wallace, and Carol Weller. We wish to acknowledge, also, the encouragement offered by the staff of the University Press of Kentucky and the advice provided by the Press's readers, Morris Beja and Morton P. Levitt, and the copyeditor, Gloria Thomas Beckfield.

A Note on References

References are incorporated parenthetically within the text of each essay. Unless otherwise noted, references to James Joyce's and Malcolm Lowry's works are to the editions cited below and are prefaced by the following abbreviations. All other sources are included in the lists of works cited for individual essays.

Works by James Joyce:

CW   *The Critical Writings of James Joyce,* edited by Richard Ellmann and Ellsworth Mason. New York: Viking Press, 1966.

D   *Dubliners: Text, Criticism, and Notes,* edited by Robert Scholes and A. Walton Litz. New York: Viking Press, 1969.

FW   *Finnegans Wake,* 8th printing, with the author's corrections incorporated in the text. New York: Viking Press, 1958. [Citations are given by page and line number.]

LJJ   *Letters of James Joyce,* 3 vols., edited by Stuart Gilbert (vol. 1) and Richard Ellmann (vols. 2 and 3). New York: Viking Press, 1966.

P   *A Portrait of the Artist as a Young Man: Text, Criticism, and Notes,* edited by Chester G. Anderson. New York: Viking Press, 1968.

SH   *Stephen Hero,* edited by Theodore Spencer, 1944. New edition, including additional manuscript pages, edited by John H. Slocum and Herbert Cahoon. New York: New Directions, 1963.

U   *Ulysses: The Corrected Text,* edited by Hans Walter Gabler. New York: Random House, 1986. [Citations are given by chapter and line number.]

Works by Malcolm Lowry:

CML   *The Cinema of Malcolm Lowry: A Scholarly Edition of Lowry's "Tender Is the Night,"* edited by Miguel Mota and Paul Tiessen. Vancouver: University of British Columbia Press, 1990.

CP   *The Collected Poetry of Malcolm Lowry,* edited by Kathleen Scherf, with explanatory annotation by Chris Ackerley. Vancouver: UBC Press, 1992.

DG   *Dark as the Grave Wherein My Friend Is Laid,* edited by Douglas Day and Margerie Bonner Lowry, with a preface by Douglas Day. New York: New American Library, 1968.

Introduction

Patrick A. McCarthy

In an age that has become increasingly skeptical about literary canons, James Joyce remains one of the few undeniably canonical modernist writers: *Finnegans Wake* is probably more often admired than read, but *Dubliners, A Portrait of the Artist as a Young Man,* and *Ulysses* are among the works most frequently studied by critics and assigned to students of twentieth-century literature. Malcolm Lowry's status is less secure, but the posthumous publication in recent years of many of his works, along with an increasingly substantial body of biographical and critical studies, indicates a level of scholarly interest that Lowry's fiction only briefly attained during his lifetime, following the 1947 publication of *Under the Volcano*. If Joyce is one of the avatars of high modernism, Lowry speaks for the next generation, those writers who came of age in the thirties. Despite numerous differences, the works of these two expatriate writers have much in common, including verbal richness, experimentation with narrative structure and perspective, a fascination with cultural and historical forces as well as with the processes of artistic creation, and the inclusion of artist figures who are in varying degrees ironic self-portrayals.

In assembling this set of original critical studies our intent has been to use theoretical perspectives or comparative, contextualized readings of the works to focus attention on Joyce's and Lowry's relationship to one another and to broader issues in the study of literary modernism and its aftermath. The essays are not primarily concerned with influence, an issue that Lowry himself addressed and that several critics have explored elsewhere. Lowry could not have influenced Joyce, since the only book he published during Joyce's lifetime was *Ultramarine,* a 1933 *Künstlerroman* that was forgotten soon after its publication (much to the relief of its author). Indeed, there is no evidence that Joyce ever read anything by Lowry, although he might at least have seen his name, since both authors contributed to the Spring 1931 issue of *Experiment,* which was published at Cambridge University by Lowry's friend Gerald

Noxon.[1] Otherwise, it is unlikely that Joyce would have heard of Lowry, despite Lowry's story that he once "encountered" Joyce "in the Luxembourg Gardens," as he put it casually in 1951 (*SC* 2:413). Lowry elaborated on that story the following year, telling David Markson that he and Joyce had "spent the day together," but Markson perceptively notes that the details of this meeting were "lost to the usual digressions" (Markson 228). Well might they be lost, for it is almost certain that this meeting, like some of Lowry's stories of childhood blindness and persecution, occurred only in his imagination.

The question of Joyce's influence on Lowry is another matter altogether. When Lowry began writing seriously in the late 1920s, Joyce was already a prominent fixture in modern literature, and the highly allusive nature of *Ultramarine* and *Under the Volcano*, as well as their experiments with narrative technique, made it inevitable that many early reviewers of Lowry's fiction would regard him as one of Joyce's imitators. In his letters, Lowry often defended the originality and authenticity of his work by denying that he was at all influenced by Joyce, had much in common with him, or even had more than a passing acquaintance with *Ulysses*. Replying to a 1947 review of *Under the Volcano* in which Jacques Barzun complained about what he called its "long regurgitations of the material found in *Ulysses* and *The Sun Also Rises*," Lowry admitted the widespread influence of Joyce and Hemingway on modern writers but denied that he had derived his "materials" from either of them, adding that he had "never read *Ulysses* through" (*SC* 2:51, 2:52). In 1950, a year before he began claiming to have met Joyce, Lowry wrote to Downie Kirk that he disliked Joyce (*SC* 2:205), presumably because of the many references to *Ulysses* in reviews of *Under the Volcano*. As late as 1952 we find Lowry telling Albert Erskine, his editor, that he had only recently read "*Ulysses* through—essentially—for the first time" (*SC* 2:581).

Despite Lowry's claim that he had not read *Ulysses,* or at least had not read it carefully, there are references in other letters that indicate greater familiarity with Joyce's work. In 1950 (as Tiessen reveals in his essay in this collection), Lowry actually sang its praises, and in 1951 he told Markson that Joyce "had a superstition . . . about the name Lowry, which occurs in the funeral scene" (*SC* 2:413). Evidently Lowry had at least read *Ulysses* up to the point in the "Hades" chapter where Bloom skims the obituaries in the *Freeman:* "Mr Bloom's glance travelled down the edge of the paper, scanning the deaths: Callan, Coleman, Dignam, Fawcett, Lowry, Naumann, Peake, what Peake is that? is it the chap was in Crosbie and Alleyne's? no, Sexton, Urbright" (*U* 6.157-59). The suspicion that Lowry was more familiar than he was willing to admit with Joyce's work in general, and with *Ulysses* in particular, is reinforced by

Clarissa Lorenz's recollection that Lowry took *Ulysses* with him when he went to Spain in 1933, and read it there (Lorenz 150).

Richard Hauer Costa has described Lowry's fear of being categorized as a Joycean writer, arguing that "all his writing life that aspect of the Lowry *persona* which emerges from the limited published works seemed to be trying to exorcise even the idea of James Joyce from its soul" (Costa 335). Lowry's many declarations that his art had not been shaped by Joyce's, even that he did not like Joyce very much, may reveal the anxiety of influence to which Costa alludes. The same dread of over-involvement with Joyce might also lie beneath one of the diary passages from "Through the Panama": referring to the convoluted relationship between art and life in his autobiographical novel, which seems to have taken over the life on which it was originally based, Sigbjørn Wilderness writes that his work is a "story of a man (Man himself no less) Joyced in his own petard" (*HL* 41).[2] The writer described by this ambiguous allusion is simultaneously threatened by his own potentially destructive work (his own petard) and by the overwhelming influence of a writer like Joyce.

Joyce's relationship to Lowry has gone largely ignored in critical studies of Joyce, apart from an occasional passing reference such as William York Tindall's inclusion of Lowry among the "important novelists" who "have drawn freely upon Joyce" (Tindall 3). On the other hand, affinities and distinctions between Joyce and Lowry have been explored by several Lowry scholars and by critics of the modern novel generally. These comparisons range from investigations of specific parallels between *Under the Volcano* and *Ulysses* by David Markson[3] and Anthony R. Kilgallin to R.M. Albérès's description of Joyce, Lowry, and Michel Butor as authors who invite the reader to decipher a palimpsest-like or labyrinthine text.[4] There is, however, no consensus about the Joyce-Lowry relationship, which is sometimes taken too much for granted and sometimes denied altogether. Thus George Stade describes *Under the Volcano* as "an attempt to take in and take over ... the modernist methods, moods, and themes that had received their classic expression in *Ulysses*" (Stade viii), while Michel Zeraffa regards the two novels as fundamentally opposed in vision and design.[5]

Perhaps the best-known comparison of Joyce and Lowry appears in Stephen Spender's introduction to the 1965 Lippincott edition of *Under the Volcano*, which has been reprinted in subsequent American editions. Unlike such modernists as Joyce, Eliot, and Pound, Spender says, Lowry was a romantic who sought to express rather than to escape personality; while the modernists employed mythic analogies and symbolism in an attempt to get outside the historic moment, Lowry used similar techniques toward the opposite end, "to exemplify 'the times,' to describe the Consul as illustration almost" (Spender xii). Costa, on the other hand, regards Lowry as Joyce's inheritor (albeit at one remove) rather than as his antithesis. Costa argues that Lowry makes extensive use of Joycean techniques in his presentation of dialogue and consciousness, but he contends that Lowry absorbed these methods from Conrad Aiken's *Blue Voyage*, which was itself influenced by *Ulysses*, instead of deriving them directly from Joyce.

Ronald Binns's position falls somewhere between these poles. Although he argues that in *Under the Volcano* (and in Virginia Woolf's *Mrs. Dalloway*) "the forces of modern history . . . rupture the liberal-humanist values which Joyce chose to celebrate" in *Ulysses*, Binns regards Lowry's novel as a "re-telling" of Joyce's and cites a number of specific parallels between the two works (Binns 43, 55). More recently, suggestive comparisons have been made by Andreas Höfele, who contrasts Joyce's use of Daedalus as a model of the self-liberated artist with Lowry's figure of the artist as Laocoön, and by Thomas Petruso, whose study of novelistic characterization since Joyce and Proust includes some sharp observations on the relationship between Lowry's experience and that of his autobiographical characters.[6]

The present collection of essays embraces a variety of approaches to the works, but in general each contributor has attempted to place Joyce and Lowry in some larger context and, by setting the works of one against those of the other, to arrive at insights that would not have been so readily apparent to a reader of only one of these writers. Three contributors either have previously written a comparative study of Joyce and Lowry or have examined these two writers, and others, within a more general argument. Chris Ackerley first studied the operations of coincidence in *Ulysses* and *Under the Volcano* in a 1980 essay. In the essay published below he returns to the subject from a different angle, this time considering how the main characters' response to coincidence is related to the concepts of artistic design that inform the two novels. Martin Bock's *Crossing the Shadow-Line*, a study of estrangement in nineteenth- and twentieth-century literature, treats Joyce's work and Lowry's in separate chapters, but in this volume he places them together to examine the manifestations in their works of the relationship between bodily and mental illnesses. In *The Blinding Torch*, Brian Shaffer demonstrates how several modern novelists, including Joyce and Lowry, engage in a critique of the discourses of modern civilization; here he narrows his focus to one aspect of that critique, the way *Ulysses* and *Under the Volcano* portray the relationship between nationalism and anti-Semitism.

Along with Ackerley and Shaffer, four other contributors are concerned primarily with connections between *Ulysses* and *Under the Volcano*, but their approaches to the works vary widely. Sherrill Grace examines Joyce's parodic use of expressionism in *Ulysses* and Lowry's more serious application of expressionist technique in *Under the Volcano* as a means of contrasting the tragicomedy of Joyce's ironic, depersonalized art with Lowry's tragic vision of a world, and a self, on the path to destruction. Joseph Voelker also turns to issues of narrative perspective and the representation of the self in an essay that examines the roles Geoffrey Firmin and Stephen Dedalus play in "carnivalesque skits that reenact their misery, replay their family romance." Richard Cross argues that *Ulysses* and *Under the Volcano* are fundamentally concerned with demonstrating both the necessity and the difficulty of loving, an issue that in each case involves a negotiation between spirit and flesh, the desire to merge with the loved one and the desire to sustain and develop the individual self. In her study of manuscript revisions in the construction of Molly Bloom and Yvonne Firmin, Sue Vice discerns an "authorial transvestism" that holds "accepted gender roles, voices, and behavior patterns" up to question.

The remaining essays address various aspects of the Joyce-Lowry nexus. In a parallel reading of *Ultramarine* and *A Portrait of the Artist as a Young Man*, Suzanne Kim shows that an examination of Lowry's style as a means of authorial identification calls attention to a similar relationship between form and content in Joyce's novel. A concern with the ways in which the authors' lives and minds are reflected in their fiction also underlies not only Bock's investigation of mental and physical illness, which follows Kim's essay, but also my own study of the related images of the world as a book and the book as a machine. I argue that a contrast between their handling of these tropes reveals a basic distinction between Joyce's ironic detachment from his art and Lowry's agonized entanglement with his works.

The last two essays study aspects of the relationship between literature and cinema. Paul Tiessen maintains that Lowry's involvement with cinema was an attempt to reopen a dialogue between literary and cinematic art, which modernist writers had briefly embraced in the 1920s but had abandoned, in part because of Joyce's (and his critics') lack of interest in film. Finally, Rebecca Hughes and Kieron O'Hara move away from literature into a direct consideration of film as they compare John Huston's cinematic versions of *Under the Volcano* and "The Dead." Rather than judging these films on the basis of their success in reproducing the effects of fictional works, Hughes and O'Hara emphasize the way each film reveals not just the strengths and limitations of cinema in general but the specific aesthetic aims that run throughout Huston's career.

The volume thus begins with a consideration of Joyce and Lowry as practitioners of expressionist art and concludes with an essay on the way their works have served as material for another artist's work. Often divergent in their approaches (and at times in their conclusions), these eleven essays provide evidence that the relationship between Joyce and Lowry is richer and more complex than the simple issue of influence or imitation. As different as they are in many ways, James Joyce and Malcolm Lowry remain among those writers whose works most clearly bear testimony to their authors' struggles with questions that are fundamental to modern life and modern art.

Notes

1. *Experiment* no. 7 (Spring 1931) contained, among other items, a draft of the Willingdone Museyroom episode from Joyce's *Work in Progress (Finnegans Wake)*, reprinted from the inaugural issue of *transition*; "A Footnote to *Work in Progress*," by Stuart Gilbert; and Lowry's story "Punctum Indifferens Skibet Gaar Videre," later revised and included as part of *Ultramarine*. My thanks to Paul Tiessen for pointing out this occasion on which Joyce and Lowry appeared in the same table of contents; I am also indebted to him for other ideas that appear in this introduction and in my own contribution to the present volume.

2. A version of the phrase also appears in a letter to Albert Erskine, Lowry's editor, this time apparently referring to an overly elaborate style (*SC* 2:458). Lowry is alluding to Hamlet's description of the engineer who is "hoist with his own petar[d]" (*Hamlet* 3.4.207)—i.e., blown up with his own bomb.

3. Markson developed his Homeric/Joycean reading of *Under the Volcano* first in his Columbia University master's thesis, then in his essay "Myth in *Under the Volcano*," and finally in his book *Malcolm Lowry's "Volcano."*

4. "For Joyce, for Butor, for Malcolm Lowry, it is necessary in effect that the reader be invited to *decipher* the novel, to see in it a palimpsest or a labyrinth, whereas the traditional novel, where everything is explained, transformed into descriptions and masterly analyses, does not demand the same effort in reading, holds no mystery, and does not correspond to real life, in which we must also *decipher* reality." Albérès also finds in Lowry "the same attachment as Joyce for a secret order, for a secret structure of the novel" (Albérès 124, 128; my translations).

5. "*Under the Volcano* has in common with *Ulysses* only its being enclosed in one day: the human condition seen by Joyce is opposed on all points to the one Lowry understands. Bloom's itinerary is a progression, the Consul's a regression" (Zeraffa 343, my translation).

6. See also Victor Sage's "Art of Sinking in Prose," which contrasts some rhetorical features of *Ulysses* and *Under the Volcano* and comments on differences between Lowry's and Joyce's use of "knowledge" in their works (Sage 43-45). Many other books and essays on Lowry either invoke brief comparisons with Joyce or—as in the case of Victor Doyen's "spatial reading" of Lowry's novel—use a reference to Joyce's work as a point of departure for their studies. For a physician's view of the role of alcohol in the lives and works of Joyce and Lowry, see Lyons's essays.

Works Cited

Ackerley, Chris. "'After Lowry's Lights': Coincidence in *Ulysses* and *Under the Volcano*." In *The Interpretative Power: Essays on Literature in Honour of Margaret Dalziel*, edited by C.A. Gibson. Dunedin, New Zealand: Univ. of Otago Press, 1980.

Albérès, R.M. *Métamorphoses du roman*. Paris: Éditions Albin Michel, 1966.

Barzun, Jacques. "New Books." *Harper's Magazine,* May 1947. Excerpted in *Malcolm Lowry, "Under the Volcano": A Casebook*, edited by Gordon Bowker. Basingstoke: Macmillan Education, 1987.

Binns, Ronald. *Malcolm Lowry*. London: Methuen, 1984.

Bock, Martin. *Crossing the Shadow-Line: The Literature of Estrangement.* Columbus: Ohio State Univ. Press, 1989.

Costa, Richard Hauer. "*Ulysses,* Lowry's *Volcano,* and the *Voyage* Between: A Study of an Unacknowledged Literary Kinship." *University of Toronto Quarterly* 36.4 (July 1967): 335-52. [Reprinted with minor revisions in his *Malcolm Lowry* (New York: Twayne, 1972).]

Doyen, Victor. "Elements Towards a Spatial Reading of Malcolm Lowry's *Under the Volcano.*" *English Studies* 50 (Feb. 1969): 65-74.

Höfele, Andreas. "Daedalus-Laocoön: Self-Representing in Joyce and Lowry." In *Anglistentag 1989 Würzburg: Proceedings*, edited by Rüdiger Ahrens. Tübingen: Max Niemeyer Verlag, 1990.

Kilgallin, Anthony R. "Eliot, Joyce and Lowry." *Canadian Author and Bookman* 41.2 (Winter 1965): 3-4, 6.

Lorenz, Clarissa M. *Lorelei Two: My Life with Conrad Aiken*. Athens: Univ. of Georgia Press, 1983.

Lyons, J.B. "Portraits of Alcoholism by James Joyce and Malcolm Lowry." In *"What Did I Die Of?": The Deaths of Parnell, Wilde, Synge, and Other Literary Pathologies*. Dublin: Lilliput Press, 1991.

———. "The Drinking Days of Joyce and Lowry." *Malcolm Lowry Review* nos. 31 and 32 (Fall 1992 and Spring 1993): 112-21.

Markson, David. *Malcolm Lowry's "Volcano": Myth, Symbol, Meaning*. New York: Times Books, 1978. [Incorporates material previously published in Markson's "Myth in *Under the Volcano,*" *Prairie Schooner* 37 (Winter 1963-64): 339-46, and "Malcolm Lowry: A Reminiscence," *Nation* 202 (7 Feb. 1966): 164-67.]

Petruso, Thomas F. *Life Made Real: Characterization in the Novel since Proust and Joyce*. Ann Arbor: Univ. of Michigan Press, 1991.

Sage, Victor. "The Art of Sinking in Prose: Charles Jackson, Joyce and *Under the Volcano*." In *Malcolm Lowry Eighty Years On*, edited by Sue Vice. New York: St. Martin's, 1989.

Shaffer, Brian W. *The Blinding Torch: Modern British Fiction and the Discourse of Civilization*. Amherst: Univ. of Massachusetts Press, 1993.

Spender, Stephen. Introduction to *Under the Volcano*. Philadelphia: J.B. Lippincott, 1965.

Stade, George. Introduction to *Six Contemporary British Novelists*, edited by Stade. New York: Columbia Univ. Press, 1976.

Tindall, William York. *James Joyce: His Way of Interpreting the Modern World*. New York: Scribner's, 1950.

Zeraffa, Michel. *Personne et personnage: Le romanesque des années 1920 aux années 1950*. Paris: Éditions Klincksieck, 1971.

one

Midsummer Madness and the Day of the Dead: Joyce, Lowry, and Expressionism

Sherrill Grace

Since the publication in 1947 of Malcolm Lowry's masterpiece, *Under the Volcano*, it has been critically de rigueur to call Joyce's *Ulysses* (1922) an influence or even a seminal precursor.[1] After all, the two texts have stunning similarities, not the least of which being that they are both "family romances" that take place in a single day. But *Volcano* also parallels *Ulysses* in details of relationship and event: in each an essentially noble, middle-aged husband (the one a Jew, the other significantly mistaken for a Jew) is betrayed by his wife; in each the hero is haunted by his past sins, failures, and guilts; in each a younger male is involved in the hero's life while pursuing his own independent, rather self-indulgent, goals; and in each the wife is a symbol of eternal woman.

Such thematic parallels only scrape the surface of similarity between *Ulysses* and *Volcano*, however, for both texts are complex, multilayered, polyphonic narratives with a multitude of shared allusions (Dante, Goethe, Shakespeare, and Homer, for example) and motifs (dogs, drink, whores, Good Samaritans, riderless horses, etc.). And both texts create, at once, highly symbolic and self-reflexive textual worlds tenaciously rooted in time and place, in history and myth. Both can be boring and fascinating, sad and funny, and both are elaborate *stagings* (or *re*-stagings), before a reader / spectator / voyeur, of the human imagination, consciousness, or soul. Despite their pervasive similarities, however, *Ulysses* and *Volcano* are very different works, so different that, in the last analysis, influence studies break up and founder on the Scylla and Charybdis of comparison. Stephen Spender summed up the situation precisely in his introduction to the 1965 edition of *Volcano* by concluding that "the

9

aims and methods of Lowry are the opposite of those of Joyce and Eliot" (xii) and that "Lowry has borrowed from Joyce [but] turned his symbolic devices upside down" (xiii).

At the bottom of this difficulty in bringing Lowry into alignment with Joyce is the concept of modernism itself and how we have come to understand and use the term. As long as we think of the modern period as the age of Joyce and of the modernist novel as Joycean (specifically after *Ulysses*), then we narrow unjustifiably our perspective on an enormously complex and varied movement. In the interests of unity and order we take the part, albeit an important part, for the whole. Recent developments in postmodernist art criticism and theory, however, are forcing us to reassess modernism.[2] A crucial element in this reassessment is our increased awareness of the contribution made to modernism by German expressionism and of expressionism's overlap with futurism, vorticism, dadaism, cubism, and surrealism. It is my contention, in what follows, that the profound difference between Joyce and Lowry *as modernists* can be illuminated by examining the response of each to expressionism. Without doubt there are a number of other ways of approaching the Joyce/Lowry question, but a discussion of the expressionist *Aufbruch* (awakening) in *Ulysses* and *Under the Volcano* throws an interesting light on the matter.

Expressionism flourished in all the arts in Germany between 1905 and the mid-1920s. If literary scholars in the English-speaking world know less about it than they might, this is in part because Hitler made every effort to destroy all traces and artifacts of the movement and in part because the movement came to be seen as exclusively Germanic; with very few exceptions, it did not catch on in France or England. The centers for its activity were Berlin, Munich, and Vienna, with considerable expressionist/dadaist activity in Zürich during World War I. The expressionist artist was revolutionary in his aesthetics and, to one degree or another, in his politics, and he defined himself against the preceding modes of realism and impressionism on the one hand and against the materialism and dehumanization of an increasingly "bourgeois" patriarchal society on the other.

The result of this ferment and revolt was the intense subjectivity (what Kandinsky called "innere Notwendigkeit" [Kandinsky 26]) of the expressionist *Vision* expressed in violent outbursts *(Schrei)* from the suffering or inspired poet/individual that led, in turn, through *Aufbruch* to *Erlösung* (deliverance). The violent outbursts were in the form of highly distorted and abstracted presentations of reality or lurid projections of passionate feelings in externalized, objectified forms. Several pictorial images of this *Vision* come to mind (from the portraits of Oskar Kokoschka

Fig. 1. *Geschrei (The Scream)*, lithograph by Edvard Munch, 1893. Photo: Munch Museum, Oslo. Reproduced by permission of the Munch Museum.

or Ludwig Meidner), but the key icon (and iconic sign) in expressionist semiotics is Edvard Munch's *Geschrei (The Scream,* 1893). The screaming face in Munch's painting and lithograph (see fig. 1) had become a visual cliché by 1930—a point I shall return to—prefiguring its marketing on T-shirts and inflatable plastic "dolls" in the 1990s.

In the theater, the smooth, hypotactic structures of well-made plays gave way to paratactic forms, staccato language, and the objectification of soul states; the modeling, perspective, and representation of previous painting gave way to violent non-naturalistic colors, a rejection of light modulations in favor of planes of solid pigment, and the distortion of recognizable forms. In expressionism, metaphors were literalized, and the more grotesque they were, the better; hence, Gregor Samsa *becomes ein Ungeziefer* in Kafka's *Die Verwandlung,* a tree *becomes* a cross in Georg Kaiser's *Von Morgens bis Mitternachts* (1919), and the jungle *becomes* the primitive Soul of the hero in Eugene O'Neill's *Emperor Jones* (1920). What the expressionist never lost sight of was Man, and even when the artist eschewed any direct political engagement, his *Vision* (as Kaiser called it) embraced the redemption and rejuvenation of humanity. Most expressionists were romantic, anthropocentric, and deeply humanist, even when (as is the case with certain dramatists and fiction writers) they employed heavy irony and satire.[3]

The case for Joyce's or Lowry's knowledge of, let alone affinity with, expressionism is an interesting one. Several critics argue that Joyce was contemporaneous or parallel with expressionism or even, himself, a direct influence on the German expressionist novel.[4] More recently, however, Ira Nadel has suggested that Joyce had firsthand knowledge of expressionism through the paintings and plays of the Austrian Oskar Kokoschka and through his Zürich contacts between 1915 and 1920, when he was working on *Ulysses*. These contacts included Max Reinhardt's famous expressionist production of Georg Büchner's *Dantons Tod* and August Strindberg's *Totentanz*, although, as Richard Ellmann notes, Joyce found Strindberg's plays to be little more than "hysterical raving" (Ellmann 412).[5]

Moreover, in a brief discussion of Joyce and Conrad Aiken, Charles McMichael and Ted Spivey note Joyce's keen interest in Aiken's *Coming Forth by Day of Osiris Jones* (1931) and describe *Osiris Jones* and *Finnegans Wake* (which Joyce was working on when Aiken's poem was published) as "expressionistic."[6] Although the description of *Finnegans Wake* as expressionistic strikes me as inaccurate, Nadel's more general claims are, I think, conclusive. Nevertheless, it is important to remember that James Joyce was no expressionist. If he used expressionism, he did so in the form of parody—parody that served his larger, and different, purposes.[7]

With Lowry the case is more cut and dried. Not only did Lowry know German expressionism well—from the plays of "Gay-org Kaiser" to the famous Ufa films of Robert Wiene, F.W. Murnau, and Fritz Lang—he was an aficionado of O'Neill's early expressionist plays and continued to speak favorably of expressionism (likening it to jazz) throughout his life.[8] Equally relevant here is the fact that Lowry was profoundly influenced by Aiken and that in his November 28, 1951, letter to Seymour Lawrence (the letter that was written for the special issue of *Wake* devoted to Aiken) he tells the story of Joyce "almost up to the very point that great man died . . . looking for, trying everywhere to purchase, expecting to receive indeed, Conrad Aiken's masterly dramatic poem, 'The Coming Forth by Day of Osiris Jones'" (*SC* 2:461). Then, just to make the filiation as clear as possible, Lowry explicitly links Aiken's sensibility "with expressionist painters, such as Munch" (*SC* 2:465). Munch, of course, was no stranger to Lowry, nor was the Munch/Aiken/Joyce/Lowry nexus a new idea for him in 1951: included with his September 1931 letter to Aiken, written in Oslo, is his sketch (après Munch) of "The Shriek!" (see fig. 2 and *SC* 1:111).

Elsewhere I have argued that *Volcano* is a profoundly expressionis-

THE SHRIEK!

Fig. 2. Drawing by Malcolm Lowry in a September 1931 letter to Conrad Aiken. Conrad Aiken Collection (AIK 2497), Huntington Library, San Marino, California. Reproduced by permission of the Huntington Library.

tic vision of the modern world (Grace 163-84), but for the present purpose it will suffice to concentrate upon a few salient aspects of Lowry's expressionism that highlight his difference from Joyce. If Joyce parodies expressionism and Lowry uses it seriously, how do they do this and, more importantly, why?

Speaking of "Circe" in *The Odyssey of Style in "Ulysses,"* Karen Lawrence remarks that here "impressionism [has been] replaced by expressionism. . . . Whole landscapes and situations symbolically express feelings and sensations. . . . Nighttown is both the literal setting of the plot of the chapter and the expressionistic equivalent of the feelings of guilt and trespass that are experienced by the characters" (Lawrence 148-49). "Circe," in fact, stages, in a heightened and exaggerated form—

even for expressionism—almost all the features of expressionist plays. It is set in or near a brothel at midnight and peopled by a collection of grotesques, from "real" prostitutes to dogs, ghosts, hallucinations, and talking, inanimate objects; everything swarms with life and is distorted by a mauve or greenish-yellow light (Joyce listed mauve as the key color in "Circe," but green is equally strong). The two dominant figures of the play, Bloom and Stephen, are obsessed by their families—unfaithful wives, dead children, unforgiving mothers, chastising fathers—and their own sexuality, but each man moves through an apparent *Aufbruch* (Bloom by besting Bello Cohen, Stephen by smashing the light with his Siegfriedian ashplant) towards an apparent *Erlösung* (signaled by Rudy's appearance at the end).

The rhetorical and structural device for the chapter is parataxis: our sense of logical order or linear sequence is disrupted as one ordeal (of accusation, arrest, trial, haunting, etc.) rapidly follows another without explanation, and conventional dialogue explodes into hectic babble, long monologues, and fragmented, staccato outbursts: "Keep to the right, right, right. If there is a signpost planted by the Touring Club at Stepaside who procured that public boon? I who lost my way and contributed to the columns of the *Irish Cyclist* the letter headed *In darkest Stepaside*. Keep, keep, keep to the right. Rags and bones at midnight. A fence more likely. First place murderer makes for. Wash off his sins of the world" (*U* 15.231-36).

All the same features occur in *Under the Volcano*, where, it is safe to say, the entire objective world teems with an appalling, threatening vitality when it is perceived through the Consul's alcohol-inspired eyes. Chapters 2 through 12 are, indeed, the replaying / restaging, exactly one year after his death on November 2, 1938, of the last twelve hours in Geoffrey Firmin's life.

There are several expressionistic high points in Lowry's text, from Geoffrey's drunken, hallucinatory search for tequila in his ruined garden of chapter 5 to his terrifying ride on the Máquina Infernal in chapter 7, where he is literally emptied out, stripped of his identity, to the *excusado* scene in chapter 10, where, as in "Circe," all the voices from earlier in the day (or in the book) babble at Geoffrey as he struggles to wipe himself, to read the schedules and advertisements proliferating on the bathroom walls, and to achieve some understanding of his soul's agony. But the chapter that bears closest comparison with "Circe," and that also brings Geoffrey to his tawdry climax and tragic death, is chapter 12, which is set in the bordello-cum-bar known as El Farolito, at the foot of Mount Popocatepetl: under the volcano.

Here Geoffrey drinks the fatal mescals, reads Yvonne's lost letters, is seduced by the prostitute María, is harangued, harassed, plucked at,

babbled at, insulted, exhorted, mocked, and warned by a host of grotesque figures swarming in the smokey gloom or projected from his cwn
inner state. Finally, he is arrested by the fascist military police, who take
him for an anarchist, an Antichrist, a Jew, and a spy. As the clock strikes
seven and Geoffrey accuses the police—"You stole that horse"—he is
murdered: "'I blow you wide open from your knees up, you Jew chingao,'
warned the Chief of Rostrums. . . . 'I blow you wide open from your
knees up, you cabrón . . . you pelado'" (*UV* 373). The Farolito, like
Nighttown, functions as the setting for the action, as a symbol of the
dark climax towards which the protagonist moves, and as the expressionist projection (or literalized metaphor) of his guilt, terror, lust, and
self-loathing.

Several features of "Circe" indicate that here Joyce aims at a parody
that repeats *with difference* the familiar features of expressionist drama
while moving towards a mockery of expressionism and the expressionist protagonist. In general, the obvious absurdity of the episode, its raucous hilarity and extreme exaggeration—a pulling out of *all* the stops—is
typical of parody and of Joyce's parodic efforts elsewhere in *Ulysses*. But
more importantly, nothing untoward results from the events in
Nighttown; nothing is unequivocally destroyed or changed, unless it be
Madame Cohen's lamp. Joyce's critics have argued that, at best, Bloom
and Stephen are redeemed and prepared to enter the new Bloomusalem
of "Nostos," and that, at worst, we cannot be certain about anything in
"Circe" except that there is no "recoverable truth."[9] If the latter, more
cautious, reading of "Circe" is correct (and it is certainly more consistent
with what I see as Joyce's parodic intentions), then why has Joyce created this extravagant spoof?

Before attempting to answer this question, I want to examine one
specific example of Joyce's parody at work. Towards the end of "Circe,"
and just before Private Carr punches Stephen, an apocalyptic note that
we have heard before is struck once more:

DISTANT VOICES
Dublin's burning! Dublin's burning! On fire, on fire! [*U* 15.4659-60]

This is followed by a long, increasingly scrambled stage instruction describing the apocalypse in a string of the most melodramatic expressionist clichés imaginable: "(*Brimstone fires spring up. Dense clouds roll past.
Heavy Gatling guns boom. Pandemonium. Troops deploy. Gallop of hoofs. Artil-
lery. Hoarse commands. Bells clang. Backers shout. Drunkards bawl. Whores screech.
Foghorns hoot. Cries of valour. Shrieks of dying. . . .*)" (*U* 15.4661-65). According
to the stage instruction, the scene climaxes in a black mass celebration

of fertility. When the dialogue reappears, however, instead of any serious, conscious registering of disaster, the damned chant "D-O-G" while the blessed chant "G-O-D" "in strident discord" (*U* 15.4717). Nothing of any consequence has happened because of this apocalypse, and it is impossible to *place* it as merely one character's hallucination or as an event in the plot. And this decentering brings us to the point of Joycean parody in "Circe."

At the same time as he repeats and exaggerates the familiar forms of expressionist drama (scenes of chaos and violence on a cosmic scale; lurid urban settings; a style replete with fragmentation, parataxis, and synecdoche; tag words such as "cries" and "shrieks"; and the themes of suffering, death, and punishment),[10] Joyce denies the raison d'être of such scenes and language—a suffering central consciousness, the source for what the Germans spoke of as the *Ausstrahlungen des Ichs* (emanations of the ego). Moreover, he has stripped the event of any symbolic referent or validating context by refusing to anchor it in the plot or in the otherwise densely realist fabric of the diegesis. Once more Karen Lawrence is on the right track when she notes that the basic paradox of "Circe" "is that we do not move beneath convention to the 'real' original selves of the characters or through the rhetoric to 'sincerity'" (Lawrence 158-59). What we encounter is convention, the melodramatic conventionality of the unconscious, of the inner passions of the soul acted out, of metaphor literalized—of expressionist drama. What we as readers/ spectators are invited to recognize in Joyce's parodic tour de force is that there is *no expressive origin* free of all traces of the socially, linguistically, and textually constructed Self. Joyce, I am suggesting, has exposed the "expressive fallacy,"[11] with its metaphysics of presence and its privileging of the inner, subjective reality as Truth, and in so exposing it he ridicules, debunks, and defuses the central expressionist paradox and dilemma, thereby freeing his unheroic, most un*übermenschlich* twosome for their homecoming and comedic end.

In *Under the Volcano*, however, Lowry portrays the inevitable fate of the expressionist Man in his Consul, who subscribes uncritically to the "expressive fallacy." Geoffrey's agony results from what Hal Foster has described as the typical expressionist double bind of alienation: "Such is the pathos of the expressionist self: alienated, it would be made whole through expression, only to find there another sign of its alienation. For in this sign the subject confronts not its desire [for meaning, identity, psychic wholeness] but its deferral, not its presence [nor that of the Logos] but the recognition that it can never be primary, transcendent, whole" (Foster 62).

Lowry presents Geoffrey's life as a pathopoesis from which he cannot escape because, to the end, he strives to believe (as Lowry also did) in "a content beyond convention, a reality beyond representation" (Foster 63). Geoffrey believes that María is the literal sign of his damnation because she is not Yvonne, and he is killed for being the Jew, spy, *pelado* that he is not. His life, as he recognizes in a moment of terrible insight, is one of constant deferral and fragmentation: "He was surrounded in delirium by these phantoms of himself, the policemen, Fructuoso Sanabria, that other man who looked like a poet, the luminous skeletons, even the rabbit in the corner and the ash and sputum on the filthy floor—did not each correspond, in a way he couldn't understand yet obscurely recognized, to some faction of his being?" (*UV* 361-62).

Like "Circe," chapter 12 of *Volcano* also ends with an apocalyptic vision towards which the narrative has been moving from the start. But the differences from "Circe" are instructive. As the dying Consul is lifted and thrown into the barranca, he hears "the world itself . . . bursting, bursting into black spouts of villages catapulted into space, with himself falling through it all, through the inconceivable pandemonium of a million tanks, through the blazing of ten million burning bodies, falling, into a forest, falling—" (*UV* 375). Even Lowry's use of a single word such as "pandemonium" acquires a different intertextual quality from Joyce's when it occurs within the rhythmic, cumulative repetitions of Lowry's prose, and the power of the word (which is sharply undercut in Joyce's context) is further intensified for us as readers because we know the historical reality of Geoffrey's prophetic vision.

What we also *hear* is the Consul's dying Munch-like *Schrei*, which is presented before us in a typically Lowryan narratological simile—*as if* before our eyes on a huge screen—in sharp contrast to the self-consciously bracketed stage instruction employed by Joyce: "Suddenly he screamed, and it was as though this scream were being tossed from one tree to another, as its echoes returned, then, as though the trees themselves were crowding nearer, huddled together, closing over him, pitying" (*UV* 375). Here the analogical ambiguity of "it was as though" and "then, as though" creates the pathopoetic blurring of the Consul and his world (much as do the lines around the central head in Munch's lithograph). Lowry's wider point (further stressed by the extra-diegetic warning facing the reader on the last page of the text—*¿Le gusta este jardín?*) is that we must all learn from Geoffrey's example: learn to act, to love, and to resist, if possible, the "expressive fallacy."

One could explain Lowry's darker vision with recourse to biography and temperament, or to the historical moment (*Under the Volcano* was written during World War II by a man peculiarly sensitive to world history and politics), but such explanations account for little; Joyce was writing *Ulysses*, after all, during World War I and was at least equally sensitive to world affairs. The fact remains, however, that *Ulysses* is a tragi-*comic* text and Bloom's ordeal in "Nighttown" is, as Poldy describes it, "midsummer madness," whereas *Volcano* is a comi-*tragic* text set on the November Day of the Dead and on the eve of the outbreak of a war in a world so heinous that it would die of remorse if it should sober up.

Lowry's modernism is deeply infused with romanticism, the ideals of endless voyaging, of individualism and brotherhood. More particularly, his modernism demonstrates the romantic qualities of expressionism in sharp distinction to the highly objectified, depersonalized (as far as the artist's personality is concerned) modernism of Joyce and Eliot. Where Joyce's vision is ahistorical, synchronic, his stance ironic and his style parodic, Lowry's is deeply historical, diachronic, his stance prophetic and pathopoetic and his style kinetic. Where Joyce's vision is centripetal and comic, Lowry's is centrifugal and tragic; where Joyce stages an expressionist parody of the alienated Self, Lowry anatomizes that Self on the stage of this world.

Where Joyce aspires to myth, Lowry aspires to allegory, and the parameters of the modernist novel, of modernism itself, contain them both. In *Under the Volcano*, Lowry reaches back into the expressionist roots of early modernism to explore the causes of alienation, solipsism, and anguish in his hero, and *perhaps* to exorcise them in himself. In *Ulysses*, Joyce remains *hors de combat*, mocking and exposing the failings of Bloom's uneventful life and of our own expressionistic Self-stagings.

Notes

1. Among the first of Lowry's critics to address the Joyce/Lowry question were Stephen Spender, in his 1965 introduction to *Under the Volcano*, and David Markson, in *Malcolm Lowry's "Volcano."* Richard Hauer Costa has argued, in *Malcolm Lowry* (28-44), that Lowry absorbed Joyce's influence through the mediation of Conrad Aiken, whose fiction and poetry were a source of direct and important influence and stimulus for Lowry. See also Malcolm Bradbury's useful essay "Lowry as Modernist" in *Malcolm Lowry: Under the Volcano*.

2. In *The Modes of Modern Writing*, David Lodge explores the variety within the field of modernist fiction. Two especially interesting explorations of the relationship between modernism and postmodernism are those by Andreas Huyssens and Hal Foster, but Ihab Hassan was among the first to tackle the problem.

3. For a detailed discussion of German expressionism, see Bronner and Kellner, Patterson, Sokel, and Willett. I have discussed Munch's *Geschrei* and contemporary parodies of it in *Regression and Apocalypse*.

4. Breon Mitchell argues in "Expressionism in English Drama and Prose Literature" (181-92) that Joyce influenced Alfred Döblin (among others). See also Weisstein's comments in the same volume (15-28, 29-44).

5. Since Frank Budgen's early disclaimer of any influence on Joyce from the visual arts, critics have tended to dismiss the possibility of such influence, but in *The Ruin of Representation in Modernist Art and Texts*, Jo Anna Isaak makes a convincing case for interartistic comparisons based, in part, on Joyce's awareness of contemporary developments in the arts.

6. According to McMichael and Spivey, "both works are expressionistic: *Osiris Jones* is the form of expressionistic poetic drama, and *Finnegans Wake* represents probably the height of English expressionistic prose" (65).

7. Joyce's parody in "Circe" conforms to the conventional understanding of the technique as one of repetition with difference that tends towards mockery rather than tribute (see Linda Hutcheon), and it provides a fine example of what Gérard Genette classifies in *Palimpsestes* as hypotextuality.

8. See Lowry's enthusiastic praise for Georg Kaiser in a 1951 letter (*SC* 2:374). In an unpublished letter to Robert Giroux of 11 January 1952, Lowry writes that jazz "isn't music perhaps so much as a form of expressionism . . . more analogous to literature or poetry, than music" (cited in Grace 182).

9. In *Joyce's Moraculous Sindbook: A Study of "Ulysses"* (200-202), Suzette Henke argues that by the end of "Circe" there has been a revolutionary alteration in consciousness for Bloom and Stephen. Her argument rests on the claim that Joyce is responsible for the "expressionistic dramas" that expose the shadow selves of Bloom and Stephen. By contrast, Hugh Kenner insists that *Ulysses* is all a surface of style and voice on which it is impossible to distinguish subjectivity from objectivity, that there is no "recoverable truth" (Kenner 91-93).

10. The apocalypse passage from "Circe" might be compared with a number of expressionist texts for similarities in image, syntax, punctuation, and general exaggerated effect, but the following outburst from Georg Kaiser's Cashier suggests the parallel Joyce had in mind: "Here I stand. I stand above you. Two are too many. There's space for only one. Loneliness is space; space is loneliness. Coldness is sun. Sun is coldness. The fevered body bleeds. The fevered body shivers. Bare fields. Ice spreading. Who can escape? Where is the way out?" (Kaiser 72).

11. In *Recodings*, Hal Foster describes the double bind of what he calls the expressionists' "expressive fallacy" as a "paradox: a type of representation that asserts *presence*—of the artist, of the real" (60).

Works Cited

Bradbury, Malcolm. "Lowry as a Modernist." In *Malcolm Lowry: Under the Volcano*, edited by Gordon Bowker. London: Macmillan, 1987.

Bronner, Stephen Eric, and Douglas Kellner. *Passion and Rebellion: The Expressionist Heritage*. London: Croom Helm, 1983.

Costa, Richard Hauer. *Malcolm Lowry*. New York: Twayne, 1972.

Ellmann, Richard. *James Joyce.* New York: Oxford Univ. Press, 1983.

Foster, Hal. *Recodings: Art, Spectacle, Cultural Politics.* Seattle: Bay Press, 1985.

Genette, Gérard. *Palimpsestes.* Paris: Éditions du Seuil, 1982.

Grace, Sherrill. *Regression and Apocalypse: Studies in North American Literary Expressionism.* Toronto: Univ. of Toronto Press, 1989.

Hassan, Ihab. *The Dismemberment of Orpheus: Toward a Postmodern Literature.* Madison: Univ. of Wisconsin Press, 1982.

Henke, Suzette. *Joyce's Moraculous Sindbook: A Study of "Ulysses."* Columbus: Ohio State Univ. Press, 1978.

Hutcheon, Linda. *A Poetics of Postmodernism: History, Theory, Fiction.* New York: Routledge, 1988.

Huyssens, Andreas. *After the Great Divide: Modernism, Mass Culture, Postmodernism.* Bloomington: Indiana Univ. Press, 1986.

Isaak, Jo Anna. *The Ruin of Representation in Modernist Art and Texts.* Ann Arbor: UMI Research Press, 1986.

Kaiser, Georg. *From Morn to Midnight.* In *German Expressionism: Plays Volume One—Georg Kaiser,* translated by B.J. Kenworthy, Rex Last, and J.M. Ritchie. London: John Calder, 1985.

Kandinsky, Wassily. *Concerning the Spiritual in Art,* translated by M.T.H. Sadler. New York: Dover, 1977.

Kenner, Hugh. *Joyce's Voices.* Berkeley and Los Angeles: Univ. of California Press, 1978.

Lawrence, Karen. *The Odyssey of Style in "Ulysses."* Princeton: Princeton Univ. Press, 1981.

Lodge, David. *The Modes of Modern Writing: Metaphor, Metonymy, and the Typology of Modern Literature.* Ithaca: Cornell Univ. Press, 1977.

Markson, David. *Malcolm Lowry's "Volcano": Myth, Symbol, Meaning.* New York: Times Books, 1978.

McMichael, Charles T., and Ted R. Spivey. "'Chaos-hurray!-is come again': Heroism in James Joyce and Conrad Aiken." *Studies in the Literary Imagination* 3 (Oct. 1970): 65-68.

Mitchell, Breon. "Expressionism in English Drama and Prose Literature." In *Expressionism as an International Literary Phenomenon,* edited by Ulrich Weisstein. Paris: Didier, 1973.

Nadel, Ira. "Joyce and Expressionism." *Journal of Modern Literature* 16 (1989): 141-60.

Patterson, Michael. *The Revolution in German Theatre, 1900-1933.* New York: Routledge & Kegan Paul, 1981.

Sokel, Walter H. *The Writer in Extremis: Expressionism in 20th Century German Literature.* Stanford: Stanford Univ. Press, 1959.

Spender, Stephen. Introduction to *Under the Volcano.* Philadelphia: J.B. Lippincott, 1965.

Weisstein, Ulrich, ed. *Expressionism as an International Literary Phenomenon.* Paris: Didier, 1973.

Willett, John. *Expressionism.* New York: McGraw-Hill, 1970.

two

Clown Meets Cops:
Comedy and Paranoia
in *Under the Volcano* and *Ulysses*

Joseph C. Voelker

At the Salón Ofélia, Geoffrey Firmin asks Cervantes for a mescal: "To drink or not to drink.—But without mescal, he imagined, he had forgotten eternity, forgotten their world's voyage, that the earth was a ship, lashed by the Horn's tail, doomed never to make her Valparaiso. Or that it was like a golf ball, launched at Hercules' Butterfly, wildly hooked by a giant out of an asylum window in hell. Or that it was a bus, making its erratic journey to Tomalín and nothing. Or that it was like—whatever it would be shortly, after the next mescal" (*UV* 287).

Under the Volcano resembles a figure-ground ambiguity, like the image in the psychology textbook that is either a goblet or two identical faces smiling at one another. In other words, the novel implies two opposed categories of reader. The "symbolist" reader apprehends the novel as primarily tragic, accepts the portentous linkage of Geoffrey Firmin's demise with the onset of World War II, and downplays alcoholism as a mere symptom of a larger spiritual illness. This reader collaborates with Geoffrey Firmin, explicating the arcane meanings that he thinks the world as symbolic forest provides. Reading the passage above, the symbolist notes an echo of Hamlet's suicide soliloquy, and realizes that there are cabalistic possibilities in "Valparaiso," the Valley of Paradise.

Let's say that the symbolist reader sees the goblet—and certainly at Lowry's encouragement. Both in his "Letter to Jonathan Cape" of January 1946, and later in the preface to the French edition of *Under the Volcano,* Lowry described the book's construction in terms of a discrete stratification of meanings, borrowing his palimpsest metaphor most likely from Eliot's *Waste Land,* with its authorial footnotes to Grail legend and Hindu doctrine, or from Joyce's *Ulysses* and Stuart Gilbert's guidebook, where Joyce hinted at the structural role of metempsychosis, Odysseus karmically recycled as Bloom. *Under the Volcano* is thus very much the child of high modernism in its author's willingness to make quasi-mystical claims for his text.

The other reader looks at the passage quoted above and sees the smiling faces. The scene in which Geoffrey concocts his mad analogies becomes a comic authorial doubling. After all, whose invention falls short here? Whose poetic motor runs out of fuel—is it that of Geoffrey Firmin, spinning similes, or Malcolm Lowry, author of this text? Inspired by mescal, this sequence of comparisons reels and totters on the edge of incomprehensibility, then stops short miraculously just before it falls, like a clown on a platform, fifty feet above a tiny bucket of water. The passage achieves cosmic hyperbole by exploiting Lowry's favorite trope: *cat-achresis*, or overextended metaphor. The Greek word *katakhresis*, this second reader notes, means "excessive use." How apt.

We'll call this second reader "carnivalesque," after Jonathan Arac's Bakhtinian study entitled "The Form of Carnival in *Under the Volcano.*" Instead of ordered strata, Arac sees in *Under the Volcano* a Menippean breakdown of genres, incorporating "scandalous scenes" and "eccentric behavior" and wielding a "boldness of invention and fantasy" (Arac 483). He sees in the very public aspect of the Mexican Day of the Dead an opportunity for Lowry to pursue a vision of life "the wrong way 'round. . . . What seems improper and unseemly under ordinary circumstances is now the rule of the day" (Arac 487). Perhaps most insightfully, he links the carnivalesque quality of the novel to its metaphoric, rather than metonymic, tendencies: "In *Under the Volcano* many elements make most sense if we see them in relation to one another, rather than going outside the work to 'realistic' referents" (Arac 488).

Lowry encouraged this reading of *Under the Volcano* as well, calling the book "an authentic drunkard's story": "It can be regarded as a kind of symphony or opera, or even as something like a cowboy film. I wanted to make of it a jam session, a poem, a song, a tragedy, a comedy, a farce. It is superficial, profound, entertaining, boring, according to one's taste" ("Preface," 15, 14). The carnivalesque reader is a Bergsonian, a member of a crowd, fairly intolerant, using the head more than the heart, and wearing the untinted glasses of collective common sense. This reader withholds sympathy for Geoffrey, finding his letter to Yvonne maudlin, his cries of abandonment in bad faith, his pretensions to magicianship paranoid, his reading of symbols Quixotic. And the carnivalesque reader has surrogates within the text, voices that shout from windows: "*You-are-a-man-who-like-much*-Vine!" and "Borracho!" (*UV* 56, 337).

Most importantly, the carnivalesque reader finds the text of *Under the Volcano* to be performative, a theater with no delimitation of its stage area, in which Geoffrey Firmin, very much like Leopold Bloom in the "Circe" episode of *Ulysses,* acts as Master of the Revels. He initiates a series of skits that turn himself and the other characters inside out, transform them into burlesques of themselves, and then bring them to a comic confrontation in that delusional place that Shakespeare designated as "a wood outside Athens" or "The Boar's Head Tavern," and that Joyce called "Mrs Cohen's" (see Bell 154-70). Lowry located this space in several bars and brothels, most important among them the Salón Ofélia and the Farolito.

Its alcoholic sources determine that this is a dark, even terrifying, variant upon traditional comedy. As in Joyce's "Circe," the author exploits his own paranoid impulses to produce a world without privacy, in which the characters at all times know or suspect that they are under surveillance, a land of espionage, peopled by "espiders." In every instance, knowing they are seen, the characters in this kind of fiction mug for the camera—in a word, they *clown.*

Finally, for the carnivalesque reader, alcoholism is no mere symptom. Rather, it is the source of the taxonomy of the narrative text, like a map of Spain drawn in a puddle of tequila. Joyce's "alshemist" wrote from his own bodily excretions: Lowry's transforms alcohol into ink. The next mescal will indeed tell us what the world is like. The very mode of the novel's telling makes narrative tropes of alcoholic blackout, hallucination, paranoia, vertigo, dyslexia, nausea, loss of inhibition, aggression, egocentric elation, and even hiccups. The principle behind the book's narrative language is *everything in excess: where walking might suffice, roller skate on your hands.* Consider the performative quality of what has to be the novel's most dazzling sentence: "'Do you really like it?' M. Laruelle asked him, and the Consul, sucking a lemon, felt the fire of the tequila run down his spine like lightning striking a tree which thereupon, miraculously, blossoms" (*UV* 215). Another principle evidently governed Lowry's selection of narrative centers of consciousness, as if he wrote himself a memorandum that said: "If the chapter does not belong to Geoffrey, choose someone who will be drinking." The novel displays no interest in narrating a mind in a sober state. Is there another book that provides a reading experience that more closely parallels what it is like to be drunk? Whose narrative lurches through so vividly immediate a sequence of *nows*?

In one significant way only, *Under the Volcano* remains more realist, and less performative, than Joyce's "Circe": the text never entirely abandons its literal level (Binns 25). Lowry cleaves technically to the "initial style" of the first six chapters of *Ulysses;* he employs an arranger / narrator who is privy to a character's interior monologue, and he does not blur the attribution of psychological as opposed to literal content. If a hallucination occurs, it is attributable to a single character, and the reader sees it, as it were, through his eyes. On the contrary, by chapter 15, *Ulysses* has lost its sense of obligation to its realist donnée. While Bloom and Stephen somehow preside over the chapter's surrealist events, those events are more an extravaganza, or pantomime (Herr 98-99), than fabrications of an individual character's psyche. In "Circe" gas jets and kisses, soap and goats talk directly to the reader, who occupies the sole perspectival space, equivalent to the throne of Louis XIV in Molière's theater. Lowry's text, while more conventionally novelistic than "Circe" in terms of point of view, announces its performative aspect in at least two ways. First, there are its alcoholic tropes, its linguistic excess, its dizzying technique. Second, there is its penchant for comedic allusion: the novel locates Geoffrey Firmin in predicaments that recall the tradition of comic representations of drunkenness and delusion, from Rabelais, Shakespeare, and Cervantes to Lewis Carroll, Samuel Beckett, and, most proximately, James Joyce.

Once a year, the town of Killorglin, in County Kerry, Ireland, elects a goat to be mayor for a day. November 2, 1938, is Geoffrey Firmin's lucky day in Mexico. The primary marker of his role as the novel's Lord of Misrule is his little goatee, an ambiguous signifier marking lechery and cuckoldry on the one hand, but on the other, the pretension to intellect and dignity that accords so comically ill with Geoffrey's inability to wear socks or a belt with his tuxedo, or with his habit of lying down in roads, or losing his car, or vomiting Bay Rum and Clam Magoo, or spending twenty-three pages of his novel in the bathroom, twelve of them seated on a toilet. Leopold Bloom, said to be the first character in modern fiction to be so placed, remains for a mere page and a quarter.

Lowry, in a comic piling-on of identities, makes a game of linking Geoffrey, by allusion, to other goateed figures. A brief census indicates what a patchwork construction he is and gives us a notion of what he's supposed to look like. The most repeated allusive association is with Don Quixote (and since Lowry cites the work of Gustave Doré [*UV* 6], we are possibly to recall the engraving of the Hidalgo seated in his study, sword in the air, surrounded by his sick fantasies of romantic rescues à la Amadis de Gaul). Jacques Laruelle, in whose brain the whole novel may be unfolding for us (McCarthy 70), wants to write a film based on *Dr. Faustus* featuring a figure like Trotsky (McCarthy 47). Mephistopheles typically is represented as having a goatee; Trotsky's was often caricatured in political cartoons of the thirties, attached beneath the unkempt hair and wild eyes of the political fanatic. One can also consider the devil holding a pitchfork on the Anís del Mono label, the little Mexican mailman with the "tiny goatee beard" (*UV* 192) who seems to be replicated infinitely in Quauhnahuac (Geoffrey himself plays mailman in Jacques's house), and the painting of the Spanish surgeons with goat faces at Dr. Vigil's (*UV* 137). There are other literary sources: for instance, Geoffrey's elvish namesake, Chaucer, with his divided goatee, who composed numerous fabliaux concerning cuckolds, most of whom are delusional, some of whom fall. From Shakespeare, there is Falstaff—another Master of the Revels in taverns and brothels, who also drank prodigiously and was responsible for the deaths of soldiers in his charge, and Prospero, who magically lures his enemies to his isle. In short, the book frequently flashes distorted replications of Geoffrey's face; we are invited to imagine him as a composite of them.

Like Bloom, who is Chaplinesque with his "flat spaugs and the walk," and his bowler "high grade ha," Geoffrey, with his beard, his Taskersonian uprightness overcorrecting a wibberley-wobberley walk exacerbated by a limp, and his ad hoc Britishism, is a clown. To read the text as performative is to bring this aspect into high relief. Consider an otherwise insignificant moment—Geoffrey in the shower: "First to wash. Sweating and trembling again, he took off his coat and shirt. He had turned on the water in the basin. Yet for some obscure reason he was standing under the shower, waiting in an agony for the shock of cold water that never came. And he was still wearing his trousers" (*UV* 148). This has what is known in the Catskills as *timing*—like a well-told joke, or a scene from a silent film comedy. We sense that, despite the agony, Geoffrey appreciates it, and is sorry for the want of an audience.

Like Bloom, Geoffrey knows when he is being seen, and therefore makes a public spectacle of himself. There is, for example, his fall in the Calle Nicaragua (*UV* 77). Given his spiritual aspirations as author of the future volume *Secret Knowledge,* Geoffrey's propensity for pratfall is Quixotic, in that Quixote is repeatedly brought to terrible suffering in consequence of his efforts to translate noble delusions into earthly action (McCarthy 101-2). Geoffrey also replays the misadventures of a derivative of Quixote, Lewis Carroll's White Knight, who dreams of inventions, such as a new way to jump over fences. When his horse moves, the knight falls off; but his thought is uninterrupted: "'What does it matter where my body happens to be?' he said. 'My mind goes on working all the same'" (Carroll 304). Geoffrey, face down in the road, embarks upon an elegant monologue to his brother, who is, palpably, not there. And he maintains the White Knight's bravado. In reflecting on his adventure in the street, he says that Yvonne "knew nothing whatever of

what all too recently he had gone through, his fall in the Calle Nicaragua, his aplomb, coolness, even bravery there—the Burke's Irish whiskey! What a world" (*UV* 85). This jauntiness characterized his response
to the very English gentleman who nearly ran him over in his motor car
and then, helping him up, asked, "Are you sure there're no bones broken or anything, old man?" (*UV* 80), directly echoing Alice, who "said in
an anxious tone, as she picked him up, 'I hope no bones are broken?'"
(Carroll 301). The stoicism of both Geoffrey and the knight has a streak
of British satire, but it points to a philosophical parable as well, for these
figures belong to the type Hugh Kenner has named the "Cartesian Cen-
taur" (Kenner 117-32), a tenuous amalgam of intellect and body in which
both are perfectible as machines, one following the laws of logic, the other
the laws of mechanics, but in which they have stunningly little to do with
one another. Stephen Dedalus in *Ulysses* is another dualist clown: he eats
nothing and lives on "spirits," while practicing what Lynch calls "porno-
sophical philotheology. Metaphysics in Mecklenburgh street" (*U* 15.109).
    Chapter 5, in which Geoffrey does a vaudeville turn entitled "Katzen-
jammer" for his unimaginative American neighbor, Quincey, is the most
unapologetically comic sequence in the novel, playing out the same debate of values found in the confrontations between Malvolio and Sir
Toby Belch, or Crazy Jane and the Bishop. Lowry adapts Geoffrey's point
of view and his style of diction, declaring his delirium tremens "an inconceivable anguish of horripilating hangover thunderclapping about
his skull" (*UV* 126). Geoffrey discovers, as he is lurching through his
garden in search of a tequila bottle, that Quincey is watching: "The other
gazed at him a moment with the cold sardonic eye of the material world"
(*UV* 132). Geoffrey instinctively chooses to clown, seeing the moment as
an opportunity to be brilliant, admired, or even loved. Sockless and
beltless, he replies to Quincey's informing him that his fly is down,
"*J'adoube,*" elegantly mimicking a chess player's indication that he
touches his piece only to make a minor adjustment. Already falsely accused of having been sick over the fence ("hicket"), Geoffrey wittily re-
assures Quincey that he intends no real move with his "piece"—that he
will not pee on his flowers. He playfully puns in Latin and Greek on
Quincey's cat, then feeds his stolid neighbor easy straight lines about
tigers and snakes, all the while keeping himself upright in the manner of
Abraham Taskerson. And he even alludes self-consciously to the
performative aspect of the encounter: "The Consul laughed, his laughter having a humourless sound, as though the part of his mind that knew
all this essentially a burlesque of a great and generous man once his
friend knew also how hollow the satisfaction afforded him by the performance" (*UV* 135).

It is at such moments of incipient depression throughout the novel that the comedy turns paranoid. At any moment alcohol can cause Geoffrey's awareness of his own foolish visibility to aggravate itself into delusion. Here he sees Dr. Vigil in Quincey's garden, wonders if Vigil has been summoned in order to catch him retrieving the tequila bottle, and then suspects that Dr. Vigil's newspaper contains a story of his public trial for the deaths of the German officers on the *Samaritan*. (Lowry may be deliberately echoing Bloom's mock trial in "Circe," which seems to grow from a similar concern—at being *seen* in the brothel district.)

Alone and unseen in his garden, Geoffrey would not be so broadly funny. Quincey (and Vigil briefly) is the surrogate for the comic reader's eye. Quincey does not hear the contrapuntal fugue of Geoffrey's brilliant thoughts, but only his nearly nonsensical speech. He cat-alytically allows Geoffrey to be apprehended from outside and inside simultaneously, a double perspective, informing us that, while Geoffrey may be a brilliant fool, he is a fool nonetheless. "Mr. Quincey glanced at him over the top of the watering-can as if to say: I have seen all this going on; I know all about it because I am God, and even when God was much older than you are he was nevertheless up at this time and fighting it" (*UV* 132). Lowry, in the years he devoted to writing *Under the Volcano*, even as he drew closer to his alcoholic hero (Binns 28), saw that Geoffrey was untenable as a tragic figure, and that the adaptation of traditional comic tropes, such as this confrontation, offered him the opposing vision that would render the story in its multiple tonalities.

A third definitive act of foolish self-display—and another instance of Cartesian clowning—takes place in chapter 7 at the carnival, when Geoffrey rides the "Máquina Infernal"—the "huge looping-the-loop machine" (*UV* 221). (Like Beckett's clowns, who get their testicles caught in bicycle spokes, Geoffrey is not good with machines: he has almost been run over by a car, he has lost his own car, and for unexplained reasons, he keeps his lawn mower in Hugh's bedroom.) Extraordinarily intoxicated at this moment, Geoffrey is having enough trouble hanging onto the earth, which, in fact, opens the chapter by invoking terms of planetary mechanics: "On the side of the drunken madly revolving world hurtling at 1:20 P.M. toward Hercules' Butterfly" (*UV* 194). Geoffrey's walk is now so vertiginously unsteady that a parade of children has formed behind him, recalling the file of mocking newsboys that follow Bloom in "Aeolus." Partly to evade the children and partly in Quixotic response to the challenge the machine's name implies, Geoffrey enters the little "confession box" of the loop-a-plane. He is hurled and held upside down above a gathering crowd of amused spectators, where he discovers that "this was not amusing" (*UV* 222). Such Britannic understatement is the verbal equivalent to the film image of Buster Keaton's face as his ship revolves a full 360 degrees.

Curiously, as Geoffrey endures what must be an intolerable sensation, given all he has drunk, and as all his possessions fall from his pockets onto the pavement below, his Cartesian brain continues with admirable detachment, as he attempts to be the symbolist reader of his own scene: "And it was scarcely a dignified position for an ex-representative of His Majesty's government to find himself in, though it was symbolic, of what he could not conceive, but it was undoubtedly symbolic" (*UV* 222). Upon his departure from the Máquina Infernal, he cuts the silliest figure of any moment in the novel as he lurches about drunkenly and dizzily on the ground, observed by a crowd: "And yet it was not over. On terra firma the world continued to spin madly round; houses, whirligigs, hotels, cathedrals, cantinas, volcanoes: it was difficult to stand up at all. He was conscious of people laughing at him but, what was more surprising, of his possessions being restored to him, one by one" (*UV* 223). As Geoffrey sees himself through the eyes of his Mexican witnesses, we imagine what he must look like. The performance has been so good that they pay him for it with his own possessions. As always, he reverts to his Britishness as a source of dignity, and, attempting to recover, "He replaced his dark glasses, set his pipe in his mouth, crossed his legs, and, as the world gradually slowed down, assumed the bored expression of an English tourist sitting in the Luxembourg Gardens" (*UV* 223).

Admittedly, Geoffrey Firmin is not always in public. In fact, on November 2, 1938, the pattern of his travels makes a kind of chiaroscuro, a shuttling between sunlit public spectacle and shady, furtive hiding-out. He lurches and reels for an audience in the town square one moment; the next he's hunkered down in the dark with Señora Gregorio. Geoffrey, immobile and in solitude, still clowns—for his own and the reader's amusement. Driven by his insatiable appetite for alcohol, he performs acts of mental acrobatics, rationalizations as dizzying as his physical performance in the Máquina Infernal. One thinks of Quixote's airtight explanation to Sancho: an enemy sorcerer can easily disguise giants to look like ordinary windmills. Or Falstaff justifying thievery on the grounds that "tis no sin for a man to labour in his vocation." Or Beckett's Molloy: "I can't help it, gas escapes from my fundament on the least pretext, it's hard not to mention it now and then, however great my distaste. One day I counted them. Three hundred and fifteen farts in nineteen hours, or an average of over sixteen farts an hour. After all it's not excessive. Four farts every fifteen minutes. It's nothing. Not even one fart every four minutes. It's unbelievable. Damn it, I hardly fart at all, I should never have mentioned it. Extraordinary how mathematics help you to know yourself" (Beckett 30).

Geoffrey employs the same relativity of scale to defend his collapse in the Calle Nicaragua: "Just like the Taskersons: God bless them. He was not the person to be seen reeling about in the street. True he might lie down in the street, if need be, like a gentleman; but he would not reel" (*UV* 85). Or take his arguments that his impotence is evidence of his fidelity to Yvonne, and has kept him free of venereal diseases, and that alcohol—the cause of his impotence—is both an aphrodisiac and a food: "How can a man be expected to perform his marital duties without food?" (*UV* 92). And Geoffrey employs mathematics. Counting drinks is a vocation of sorts, one that he labors in throughout the day, at one point even attempting to estimate total bottles consumed since Yvonne's departure. Like a crooked accountant, he keeps two sets of books: the number of drinks he's had, and the number he's been seen to have (McCarthy 62; Hill 136). He engages in logical proofs: "He thought: 900 pesos=100 bottles of whiskey=900 ditto tequila. Argal: one should drink neither tequila nor whiskey but mescal" (*UV* 77). In the morning, his "pleasant and impertinent familiar" tells him: "You . . . have already fought down this temptation have you not you have not then I must remind you did you not last night refuse drink after drink and finally after a nice little sleep even sober up altogether you didn't you did you didn't you did we know afterwards you did you were only drinking enough to correct your tremor a masterly self-control she does not and cannot appreciate!" (*UV* 69).

The clown is a regressive signifier: he re-presents his audience's needs and aspirations in infantile figures (Willeford 117-23), performing the intensity of his desires free of adult restraint. To some extent, Malcolm Lowry constructed Geoffrey Firmin out of Freudian lumber. Richard Cross, in a psychoanalytic reading of the novel, explains the Consul's arrangement of his day in terms of family romance. He finds in the death of Geoffrey's mother, followed by his father's disappearance into the Himalayas and the subsequent death of his stepmother, a psyche traumatized by abandonment. Geoffrey is a man, according to Cross, who compulsively reenacts his orphanhood. On the Day of the Dead, 1938, Geoffrey sees reunited the players in the story of his adult betrayal. He requires of his wife and the two men with whom she has slept that they take roles in the improvised drama of his lonely death in the Farolito (Cross 45). But prior to that third-act event, he arranges a feast of defeat, a holiday of misery-making. ("Drink all morning," he says; "drink all day, this is life.") Geoffrey's purpose is thus to stage a primal scene, to force himself to witness—at least in symbolic terms—his own cuckold-ing. A paranoia in which Lowry may have been expert via his own alco-holism generates the strangely surveillant world of *Under the Volcano*, with its lurking figures in sunglasses, its police watchtowers, observa-tion planes, Mr. Quinceys, miradors, Spaniards who see with their eyes closed, hostile sunflowers gazing through windows, all of which doubles Geoffrey's own Oedipal need to see.

The novel's most uncanny effects of this kind result from the merged identities of Geoffrey and the book's arranger/narrator. Geoffrey sus-pects that he has magical powers over Yvonne, Hugh, and Jacques (see for instance *UV* 210). That suspicion is a metaphor within the fiction for a fascinating fusion of artist and protagonist deep in the unconscious levels of the creative process, where it is not entirely susceptible to analy-sis, similar to Shakespeare's examination of his own theatricality in the person of Prospero. *Under the Volcano* echoes a Shakespearean, and an-ticipates a postmodern, trope: Hugh and Yvonne and Jacques are *under control* because Lowry is writing them. Seeing the emotional collabora-tion of Lowry and his Consul is a little like entering a train compartment in which a pair of Siamese twins are seated, only to realize that one of them is a fiction.

The paranoiac effect is perhaps most powerful in chapter 4, the ac-count of Hugh and Yvonne's horseback outing. At the end of chapter 3, Geoffrey falls asleep "with a crash." The narrative lurches to a garbled telegram that we eventually learn is being read by Geoffrey's brother, Hugh, with whom it then stays. Oddly, this narrator who now occupies Hugh's brain (a) is hostile to Hugh for reasons that are Geoffrey's (Binns 28-29), and (b) transforms traditional third-person point-of-view narra-tive into unabashed espionage. In other words, a surrogate for Geoffrey, the narrator keeps an eye on Hugh and Yvonne that is metaphorically represented in the paranoiac landscape. A prison watchtower, housing the police and their binoculars, sweeps in and out of view. At one point in their ride, Hugh wonders, "Could that white dot down there be Geof-frey himself? Possibly to avoid coming to a place where, by the entrance to the public garden, they must be almost directly opposite the house, they trotted into another lane that inclined to their right" (*UV* 105).

The word "possibly" in that sentence is problematic. One could maintain that it is Hugh's word, and marks his uncertainty about his own motives. But it can as easily be read as a speculative gesture made by a being very close to Geoffrey Firmin. There are other such instances of malice. Hugh offers explanations for his absurd cowboy get-up. The narrator tells us that "he was secretly enormously proud of his whole outfit" (*UV* 96). And "'My God. Horses,' Hugh said, glancing and stretching himself to his full mental height of six-feet-two (he was five feet eleven)" (*UV* 104).

And there is the goat that follows Hugh and Yvonne on their ride. Ackerley and Clipper have pointed out that Geoffrey, with his chin whiskers, calls himself "cabrón," which means both "goat" and "cuckold" (Ackerley and Clipper 108; *UV* 69). He bitterly plays on "camarones" ("shrimp") when he is with Jacques, calling them "cabrones"—an allusion to his cuckolding by the Frenchman. The goat in chapter 4 regards Hugh and Yvonne with "patriarchal contempt" (*UV* 99)—a suggestive term since Hugh calls Geoffrey "Papa." Six pages later, he is still on their tail, and lifts toward them "a Machiavellian eye" (*UV* 106). Lowry may have had *Ulysses* in mind here, since in "Lestrygonians" Bloom remembers that a nanny goat saw him and Molly embracing on Howth Head (*U* 8.911-12).

Not content simply to watch them, the goat finally charges, driving Yvonne into Hugh's embrace. By doing so, the animal seems to act as surrogate (or familiar) for Geoffrey, helping him to revisit the emotion of sexual betrayal. It acts for Geoffrey as Ariel does for Prospero (who also falls asleep). The descent from airy spirit to beady-eyed farmyard animal is a comically rueful measure.

In any case, while Geoffrey is asleep, an eye is most unnervingly open, and it is that of the novelist/arranger. The blurred identities of Consul and narrator create a tear in the firmament above Hugh and Yvonne, through which a godlike eye is felt—but not seen—to be peering. The uncanny effect resembles the "Wandering Rocks" chapter in *Ulysses*—a novel equally fraught with espionage. ("We know that,' as Martin Cunningham takes pleasure in saying, "in the castle"[*U* 12.1636-37]). "Wandering Rocks" is a chapter that can be played as a board game on a map of Dublin and that employs surveillance from a vertical perspective as its narrative metaphor. Curiously, as with chapter 4 of *Under the Volcano*, the narrative presence is somewhat hostile, manifest most fully in the first section, the travels of Father John Conmee. Novelistic surveillance keeps tabs not only on his whereabouts, but also on his private thoughts, which reveal him to be sanctimonious, insincere, and self-regarding to a fault. As the game continues, we glimpse clay feet on Simon and Stephen Dedalus, Tom Kernan, even the young Patrick Aloysius Dignam, until Dublin is revealed to be peopled primarily by the venal.

Where in chapter 4 Geoffrey's surveillance is magical, in chapter 7 we return to his point of view as he succeeds in his infantile quest to witness his own betrayal. Again, the landscape is salted with the imagery of observation: binoculars, police on a tower, the view across the ravine, the observation plane. Invited to Jacques's home for a drink, Yvonne and Geoffrey are doubly aware of the awkwardness of the social situation, as only they two know that Yvonne is now in the home of one man with whom she has betrayed Geoffrey, while in the company of the brother with whom she has also betrayed him. Yvonne escapes, and Geoffrey lingers in one of Jacques's two towers, where, after an impressive exercise in mental gymnastics, he empties everyone's glass and the cocktail pitcher as well, and descends to the living level of the house. There, as he sits waiting, he sees Jacques naked and successfully bears witness to the instrument of his cuckolding (rendered in an appropriately exhibitionistic prose): "But the abominable impact on his whole being at this moment of the fact that that hideously elongated cucumiform bundle of blue nerves and gills below the steaming unselfconscious stomach had sought its pleasure in his wife's body brought him trembling to his feet. How loathsome, how incredibly loathsome, was reality" (*UV* 207). Geoffrey then begins his walk into town with Jacques, on his way to the bus stop. In the high road before Jacques's house, Geoffrey sees across the ravine to where Yvonne and Hugh are viewing the Rivera murals, and he hears Jacques call them a "formidable couple" (*UV* 212). Shortly thereafter, Jacques fades out of the scene, Geoffrey takes his ride on the Máquina Infernal, and then he glimpses Hugh and Yvonne again, in a moment that he seems to have choreographed for his own chagrin:

> The Consul felt a clutch at his heart and half rose. He had caught sight of Hugh and Yvonne again at a booth; she was buying a tortilla from an old woman. While the woman plastered the tortilla for her with cheese and tomato sauce, a touchingly dilapidated little policeman, doubtless one on strike, with cap askew, in soiled baggy trousers, leggings, and a coat several sizes too large for him, tore off a piece of lettuce and with a consummately courteous smile, handed it to her. They were having a splendid time, it was obvious. They ate their tortillas, grinning at each other as the sauce dripped from their fingers; now Hugh had brought out his handkerchief; he was wiping a smear from Yvonne's cheek, while they roared with laughter, in which the policeman joined. What had happened to their plot now, their plot to get him away? Never mind. [*UV* 224-25]

We sense how Geoffrey deliberately frames and shoots this vignette, loading it with the invidious message so familiar today, thanks to television advertising. *This couple is perfectly happy; they have something you do not.* The handkerchief wiping away the tomato sauce from the perfect cheek is a self-consciously banal version of what Geoffrey wants his surveillance to uncover. Like Laruelle's penis, he finds it somehow disgusting. It justifies his improvised performance at the Farolito, where, in a sequence of increasingly mad acts of buffoonery, he will succeed in getting himself killed, thereby, at least, avoiding the mother of all Katzenjammers.

For the carnivalesque reader, *Under the Volcano* is "autobiographical" in the sense that Geoffrey Firmin is a version of his author as clown. Likewise, at least in the intoxicated chapters of *Ulysses*, and especially in "Circe," that relation holds between Joyce and the two comic refractions he made of himself in Stephen and Bloom.

Geoffrey and Stephen Dedalus certainly hold much in common. Both are poets manqués, whose achievements are peculiarly laughable in light of their ambitions. Both claim to be *poètes maudits*, occupants of a personal hell that they have rationalized to be the punishment inflicted by unjust deities for their peculiar brands of courage and integrity. And on the single day in which their fates unfold for the reader, both get stinking drunk.

But the more remarkable similarity between Geoffrey and Stephen Dedalus lies in their role as improviser of a sequence of carnivalesque skits that reenact their misery, replay their family romance. Geoffrey Firmin and Stephen Dedalus both impose a two-step emotional sequence that provides a kind of crisis and climax to their day. First, in a state of extreme drunkenness, they confront and bitterly reject the solicitude of a beloved woman. In Bella Cohen's brothel in the "Circe" chapter of *Ulysses*, Stephen, having invoked the ghost of his mother, rejects both her solicitude for his well-being and her exhortations to submit to the Roman Catholic God or be condemned to hell. In the Salón Ofélia, after a number of mescals, Geoffrey confronts Yvonne with the hypocrisy of her solicitude, her self-serving efforts to "save" him. By staging these scenes, both Geoffrey and Stephen cut themselves loose from all spiritual obligation to others, and make a bitter proclamation of their absolute aloneness.

In the second step of this sequence, having rejected love, both Stephen and Geoffrey confront the public realm of force symbolized for them by the police and the military. They both engage in a perversely improvised self-victimization. Geoffrey baits the Unión Militar—fascist paramilitary police whose official status is dubious and who have evidently just murdered a bank courier. Stephen likewise insists on inciting two British soldiers, whose presence in Ireland naturally strikes a similar note of unjustifiable force.

The sequence is thus from private emotional life—where they inflict pain—to the public realm of power—where it is inflicted upon them. Because the texts here are more performative than psychological, no clear motivation in the characters for their staging of these scenes is traceable.

Perhaps their guilt becomes acute in the aftermath of their rejection of
the beloved woman, and they confront the authorities to get themselves
punished. Or, having failed to respond to human affection, perhaps both
feel a sudden need to disassociate themselves from the cold brutality of
the human race. Or perhaps alcohol makes them behave gratuitously.
The principle is Napoleonic: *"On s'engage, et puis, on voit"* (One acts, and
then one sees).

One can also argue that psychic separation from the mother (and
Yvonne is demonstrably Geoffrey's mother-surrogate) ejects these two
figures into a pronouncedly un-maternal realm. Having denied love,
Geoffrey and Stephen respond to an internal need to make a gesture
against "history"—to prove it is a violent and meaningless tale by pro-
voking it to strike at them.

Stephen's famous utterance that history is "a nightmare from which
I am trying to awake" is echoed in Geoffrey's confrontation with Yvonne
and Hugh in the Salón Ofélia:

> "Read history. Go back a thousand years. What is the use of interfering
> with its worthless stupid course? . . . What in God's name has all the heroic
> resistance put up by poor defenceless peoples all rendered defenceless in
> the first place for some well-calculated and criminal reason . . . to do with
> the survival of the human spirit? Nothing whatsoever. Less than nothing.
> Countries, civilisations, empires, great hordes, perish for no reason at all,
> and their soul and meaning with them, that one old man perhaps you never
> heard of, and who never heard of them, sitting boiling in Timbuctoo, prov-
> ing the existence of the mathematical correlative of *ignoratio elenchi* with
> obsolete instruments, may survive." [*UV* 310]

Certainly the solipsism of Geoffrey and Stephen renders suspect their
contempt for collective action. Geoffrey the magician fancies himself in
the role of that philosopher. Likewise Stephen—who in *Portrait* had refused to sign the petition for universal peace unless MacCann paid him—
tells Private Carr: "But this is the point. You die for your country. . . . But
I say: Let my country die for me" (*U* 15.4471-73).

Geoffrey and Stephen see their private destinies not as a portion of
some larger collective process, but rather as of prior importance and
related to the collective exclusively via metaphor. When Hugh says
Geoffrey can't distinguish *War and Peace* from *Anna Karenina*, he lodges
the same weighty objection that MacCann had made when he said, "Minor poets, I suppose, are above such trivial questions as the question of
universal peace" (*P* 197). Geoffrey and Stephen share particularly acute
feelings of contempt toward those who aspire to reform the world. Hugh,
with his socialism and obsession with Spain, and Bloom, the fuzzy-

headed meliorist who wants to inspect brothels and move cattle on tram lines, annoy Geoffrey and Stephen. When Hugh makes a gesture toward saving the murdered Indian, Geoffrey says, "Never mind, old boy, it would have been worse than the windmills" (*UV* 248). And Stephen curtly interrupts Bloom's disquisition in the cabman's shelter on the obligation of every Irish citizen to labor with, "We can't change the country. Let us change the subject" (*U* 16.1171).

Geoffrey's egotism does not allow him to make the distinction between private and public, personal and historical. He sees no difference in importance between "war's senseless Titus Andronicus" (*UV* 248) and the thundering of his own familiars. It is all just mental theater, what Joyce called "the Pageant of Past History worked up . . . by Messrs Thud and Blunder" (*FW* 221.18-21). Geoffrey metaphorically fuses—or confuses—Hugh's attempts to interfere in Spain's history with Hugh and Yvonne's attempts to interfere in his life. "You're all the same, all of you, Yvonne, Jacques, you, Hugh, trying to interfere with other people's lives" (*UV* 312). The parallel moment in *Ulysses* occurs when Stephen Dedalus conjures the ghost of his mother. She exhorts him to return to the Catholic fold or suffer the pains of hell, to which Stephen shouts, "No! No! No! Break my spirit, all of you, if you can! I'll bring you all to heel!" (*U* 15.4235-36). Then he swings his ashplant and cries *"Nothung!"*

Both Geoffrey and Stephen, as solipsists and drunkards, try to stage their acts of defiance against a cosmic backdrop. Stephen, for instance, in striking his blow with the ashplant, inspires the following apocalyptic stage directions: *"Time's livid final flame leaps and, in the following darkness, ruin of all space, shattered glass and toppling masonry"* (*U* 15.4244-45). Similarly, just before Private Carr strikes Stephen, the stage directions tell us that *"brimstone fires spring up,"* followed by battles and the dead arising from their graves (*U* 15.4661ff.). Geoffrey, likewise, insists upon the cosmic import of his own death after he is shot: "No, it wasn't the volcano, the world itself was bursting, bursting into black spouts of villages catapulted into space, with himself falling through it all, through the inconceivable pandemonium of a million tanks, through the blazing of ten million burning bodies, falling—" (*UV* 375). Geoffrey's single demise enjoys a status equal to that of the total deaths in World War II, which it somehow adumbrates. It limits our sympathy to know that for him apocalypse is a wholly personal matter. As he prays in chapter 9, "Let me be truly lonely, that I may honestly pray. Let us be happy again somewhere, if it's only together, if it's only out of this terrible world. Destroy the world!" (*UV* 289).

But Geoffrey's and Stephen's authors deny their protagonists' solipsistic claims by acknowledging their overblownness. Even at their most desperate, Geoffrey and Stephen are clownish. For instance, Geoffrey indignantly rises from the table at the Salón Ofélia, tells Hugh and Yvonne that their souls stink, and notices that "a glass, *fortunately empty*, fell to the floor and was smashed" (*UV* 313, my italics). And he acknowledges his own infantilism when he deliberately confuses Yvonne with his mother: "Mummy, let me go back to the beautiful brothel!" (*UV* 313). And we learn on the next page of "Circe" that what Stephen destroyed was not all time and space but a lamp chimney on Bella Cohen's chandelier that Bloom haggles down to sixpence.

Then Geoffrey and Stephen go find the police and the military for a vaudeville episode of "The Cop and the Anthem" or "Quixote Meets the Holy Brotherhood." The manner in which they bring acts of violence down upon themselves is nearly identical. First, both engage in obscure allusions, taking drunkards' delight in their own brilliance while infuriating their interlocutors. Geoffrey insists against the evidence that his name is not Firmin, but William Blackstone. At the moment that he gets himself killed, he mixes public provocation with impenetrably private reference: "You poxboxes. You coxcoxes. You killed that Indian. You tried to kill him and make it look like an accident"; "if you'd only stop interfering, stop walking in your sleep, stop sleeping with my wife, only the beggars and the accursed" (*UV* 371-72). Stephen taunts Privates Carr and Compton with the same semi-comprehensible mélange: "You are my guests. Uninvited. By virtue of the fifth of George and seventh of Edward. History to blame. Fabled by mothers of memory" (*U* 15.4370-72). With the gesture that finally brings about the blow, Stephen invokes William Blake, ensuring that the subtlety will be lost. Pointing to his brain he says, "It is in here that I must kill the priest and the king" (*U* 15.4436-37).

The British soldiers differ only in local habitation and name from the Mexican fascists. "I blow you wide open from your knees up, you Jew chingao" (*UV* 373) is the same speech-act as "I'll do him in, so help me fucking Christ! I'll wring the bastard fucker's bleeding blasted fucking windpipe!" (*U* 15.4720-21). As Stephen says, "Will someone tell me where I am least likely to meet these necessary evils? *Ça se voit aussi à Paris*" (*U* 15.4575-76).

There are also parallels in the sufferings of Geoffrey and Stephen, after one is shot, the other merely struck. In Geoffrey's death, alongside the apocalyptic vision, there is a more moving moment for the reader, for it reintroduces the not-quite-closed possibility of compassion: "Then a face shone out of the gloom, a mask of compassion. It was the old fiddler, stooping over him. 'Compañero—' he began. Then he had vanished" (*UV* 374). Stephen is more fortunate in having at his side the Good

Samaritan that Geoffrey could neither find nor be. But it is richly comic
that Stephen, in his delirium, sings Yeats's "Who Goes with Fergus?"
inviting young men and women to leave "history" and enter the solipsistic world of poetic vision, only to have Bloom misunderstand this
perversely persistent expression of the urge for transcendence and think,
"Ferguson, I think I caught. A girl. Some girl. Best thing could happen
him" (*U* 15.4950-51).

From such fatuous errors Bloom stitches the multicolored garment of
survival. In "Circe," he too arranges a play in which he will witness the
act of his betrayal, confront his faithless wife, and get himself arrested
and tried, convicted, and punished—but on a level of pure inconsequence.
While Stephen suffers his theatrical turns in "Circe" in a spiritual agony,
and Geoffrey's fascist-baiting is based in suicidal misery, Bloom takes a
pure delight in being on stage. There is a redundancy to his theatrics: he
plays many scenes, each scene tending toward an ultimate explicitness,
as if he were having too much fun to stop.
      When he acts out the coming-to-grips with his wife's adultery, the
necessary mental act that he sidestepped in "Sirens," Bloom, like Geoffrey,
does so in graphic terms. But where Geoffrey expresses a fussy Dedalian
disgust at the sight of Laruelle's penis, Bloom engages in a masochistic
romp, as he and a number of other witnesses (there is no private space in
"Circe") watch Molly and Boylan engage in intercourse:

                              BOYLAN
(*to Bloom, over his shoulder*) You can apply your eye to the keyhole and play
with yourself while I just go through her a few times.

                              BLOOM
Thank you, sir. I will, sir. May I bring two men chums to witness the deed
and take a snapshot? (*he holds out an ointment jar*) Vaseline, Sir? Orangeflower
. . . ? Lukewarm water . . . ?
· · · · · · · · ·

                          LYDIA DOUCE
(*her mouth opening*) Yumyum. O, he's carrying her round the room doing it!
Ride a cockhorse. You could hear them in Paris and New York. Like mouth-
fuls of strawberries and cream.
                              KITTY
(*laughing*) Hee hee hee.
                          BOYLAN'S VOICE
(*sweetly, hoarsely, in the pit of his stomach*) Ah! Godblazegrukbrukarchkhrasht!
[*U* 15.3787-810]

Aided by his masochism, Bloom confronts the material world that
Geoffrey and Stephen reject, the Land of Phenomenon in its brutishness,
and he transforms it into play.

Seen from this perspective, Geoffrey is an amalgam of Stephen and
Bloom. Although he suffers perversely, like Stephen, he also reveals a
ludic spirit, remaining, even to his dying moment, *homo rhetoricus*. At
the Salón Ofélia, he accuses Hugh and Yvonne of having played "bubbies
and titties" and rises to Othello-like heights of jealous eloquence with
playfulness in excess of the task at hand: "But even if Hugh makes the
most of it again it won't be long, it won't be long, before he realises he's
only one of the hundred or so other ninneyhammers with gills like codfish and veins like racehorses—prime as goats all of them, hot as mon-
keys" (*UV* 313). Admittedly, one senses a greater degree of horror at
human appetite in Geoffrey than there is in Bloom, but that horror knows
its limits. It can still be exploited for its theatrical potential.

And both Joyce and Lowry indulge in such stylistic excesses in depicting the moment of their cuckolding. As Bella tells Bloom: "He shot
his bolt, I can tell you! Foot to foot, knee to knee, belly to belly, bubs to
breast! He's no eunuch" (*U* 15.3140-41). Pain be damned, both Bloom
and Geoffrey play the cuckold with gusto. Both will mug an indignation
they do not entirely feel. Geoffrey speaks for both when, after insulting
Yvonne, he observes that "the queer thing was, he wasn't quite serious"
(*UV* 314).

Actually, Bloom's confrontation with his unfaithful spouse in "Circe"
is emotionally undercharged, marking the extent to which he has already come to terms with his altered situation. An unrepentant Molly,
dressed in harem clothes and walking a camel, says in the aftermath of
her adultery: "So you notice some change? *(her hands passing slowly over
her trinketed stomacher, a slow friendly mockery in her eyes)* O Poldy, Poldy,
you are a poor old stick in the mud! Go and see life. See the wide world"
(*U* 15.328-30).

In "Circe" Bloom, too, gets arrested. The parallels are so close that
one could suspect that Lowry went to Joyce for his model. Geoffrey gives
a false name to the Mexican police; Bloom tells the Watch that he is "Dr
Bloom, Leopold, dental surgeon," a cousin of "von Blum Pasha" (*U*
15.721-23). The Mexican police find the telegraph to Hugh Firmin in
Geoffrey's pocket and thus by mistake determine rightly that Geoffrey's
name is Firmin; the Watch see the card fall out of Bloom's hat and mistakenly conclude that he is Henry Flower. Sanabria tells Geoffrey, "I am
afraid you must come to prison" (*UV* 370); the Watch tell Bloom, "Come
to the station" (*U* 15.756). Geoffrey claims that he is not a journalist but a
writer on economic matters, and the Chief of Rostrums replies, "Wrider?

You antichrista. Sí, you antichrista prik" (*UV* 370). Bloom claims he is an author-journalist (*U* 15.802), and later Dowie calls him Antichrist.

But because "Circe" has left the literal level of the fiction behind, Bloom is able to expand the moment of his arrest into a skit in which he is tried for sexual voyeurism. He flatters the police and behaves sycophantically throughout his trial, which leads of course to his masochistic fantasy punishment—a whipping at the hands of the leading socialites of Dublin. And later in "Circe," when Bloom does "die"—or is reduced to a smoking cinder—he springs back to life as in an animated feature, where violence is by convention inconsequential. The realism of *Under the Volcano* obviates these antics. Geoffrey's death is irreversible and cannot be argued away. Yet, for the carnivalesque reader, his last scene still possesses a performative aspect. Geoffrey's muddled expression of indignation toward the police is no more heartfelt than his rage at Yvonne. He is deliberately acting up in the Farolito—drunkenly swinging that machete, making a public spectacle of himself that will lead to his ritual expulsion. As Lord of Misrule, or Master of the Revels, he must be dethroned at day's end. His detachment from his own pain, expressed in the phrase "this is a dingy way to die," seems to connect the realist and the ritualistic levels of the narrative. And, finally, in the novel's "preposterous" structure (Arac 481), in which chapter 1 occurs after chapters 2 through 12, we have only to turn back to the novel's first page and re-enter Jacques's mind to begin remembering the holiday all over. Carnival is beyond historical contingency, enjoying a fixed place on the calendar. Once a year—or each time we reopen *Under the Volcano*—the cuckold has to cross paths with the cops. It is how we explain our own sense of expulsion.

Mr. Finn will always be fined again. We come to count on it.

Works Cited

Ackerley, Chris, and Lawrence J. Clipper. *A Companion to "Under the Volcano."* Vancouver: Univ. of British Columbia Press, 1984.

Arac, Jonathan. "The Form of Carnival in *Under the Volcano.*" *PMLA* 92 (1977): 481-89.

Beckett, Samuel. *Molloy*, in *Three Novels by Samuel Beckett*. New York: Grove, 1965.

Bell, Robert. *Jocoserious Joyce: The Fate of Folly in "Ulysses."* Ithaca: Cornell Univ. Press, 1991.

Binns, Ronald. "Materialism and Magic in *Under the Volcano.*" *Critical Quarterly* 23 (Spring 1981): 21-33.

Carroll, Lewis. *The Annotated Alice: "Alice's Adventures in Wonderland" and "Through the Looking Glass,"* edited by Martin Gardner. New York: Bramhall House, 1970.

Cross, Richard K. *Malcolm Lowry: A Preface to His Fiction.* Chicago: Univ. of Chicago Press, 1980.

Herr, Cheryl. *Joyce's Anatomy of Culture.* Urbana and Chicago: Univ. of Illinois Press, 1986.

Hill, Art. "The Alcoholic on Alcoholism." In *Malcolm Lowry: The Writer and His Critics,* edited by Barry Wood. Ottawa: Tecumseh Press, 1980.

Kenner, Hugh. *Samuel Beckett: A Critical Study.* New ed. Berkeley and Los Angeles: Univ. of California Press, 1968.

Lowry, Malcolm. "Preface to a Novel." In *Malcolm Lowry: The Man and His Work,* edited by George Woodcock. Vancouver: Univ. of British Columbia Press, 1971.

McCarthy, Patrick A. *Forests of Symbols: World, Text, and Self in Malcolm Lowry's Fiction.* Athens: Univ. of Georgia Press, 1994.

Willeford, William. *The Fool and His Sceptre: A Study in Clowns and Jesters and Their Audience.* Chicago: Northwestern Univ. Press, 1969.

three

"Well, of course, if we knew all the things": Coincidence and Design in *Ulysses* and *Under the Volcano*

Chris Ackerley

> All the events in a man's life would accordingly stand in two funda-
> mentally different kinds of connection: firstly, in the objective, causal con-
> nection of the natural process; secondly, in a subjective connection which
> exists only in relation to the individual who experiences it, and which is
> thus as subjective as his own dreams. . . . Both kinds of connection exist
> simultaneously, and the selfsame event, although a link in two totally dif-
> ferent chains, nevertheless falls into place in both, so that the fate of one
> individual invariably fits the fate of the other, and each is the hero of his
> own drama while simultaneously figuring in a drama foreign to him.
>
> —Schopenhauer

To begin with an absurdity: one of Jung's more extreme examples, from
his celebrated essay "Synchronicity," the account of M. de Fortgibu and
the plum-pudding:

> A certain M. Deschamps, when a boy in Orléans, was once given a piece of
> plum-pudding by a M. de Fortgibu. Ten years later he discovered another
> plum-pudding in a Paris restaurant, and asked if he could have a piece. It
> turned out, however, that the plum-pudding was already ordered—by M.
> de Fortgibu. Ten years later M. Deschamps was invited to partake of a plum-
> pudding as a special rarity. While he was eating it he remarked that the
> only thing lacking was M. de Fortgibu. At that moment the door opened and
> an old, old man in the last stages of disorientation walked in: M. de Fortgibu,
> who had got hold of the wrong address and burst in on the party by mistake.[1]

According to Jung, the odds against this being purely fortuitous are
804,622,222 to 1 (how, precisely, he ascertained the figure remains a
mystery). Yet making allowance for an uncertainty principle at work in

both this figure and Jung's interpretation of it, one might accept his premise that such coincidences sometimes seem to pile up in a most impressive way, acknowledge the strangeness of this demented particular, the figuring of M. de Fortgibu in the drama of M. Deschamps, and derive from it one of two incompatible conclusions:

(a) That there exists in the universe a principle of recurrence, a pre-established harmony, perhaps,[2] whereby particulars unconnected in time and space are nonetheless linked by some acausal force. This, essentially, is Jung's position, the position of two of Lowry's favorite theorists, J.W. Dunne and Peter Ouspensky, and that of Paul Kammerer, the Austrian biologist, whose *Das Gesetz der Serie* argues that the single coincidences we see are isolated manifestations of a universal principle operating independently of physical causation—an acausal force that acts to bring similar configurations together in space and time, and that correlates by affinity.[3] This, he points out, makes coincidence rule to such an extent that the concept of coincidence is itself negated—a notion that Lowry found quite congenial—so that random events form minor mysteries that are in turn pointers toward a greater one (Ackerley, "After Lowry's Lights," 116).

(b) That such coincidences are simply apparent; that "affinity" is a quality of the mind perceiving (constraints of time and space conceptually suspended) rather than the object perceived; and that "coincidences" tend to be foregrounded disproportionately because the human mind, in making sense of things, selects from the infinitude of random events only those impulses that it is predisposed to find significant. For every one such instance of a M. de Fortgibu and the plum-pudding, skeptics would suggest, there could be at least 804,622,221 like configurations that go unobserved. Who would have noticed, for instance, that the name Lowry not only occurs in the list of those dead in "Hades" (*U* 6.158) but is also that of Beckett's stationmaster in *Watt* (Beckett 25)?

This essay attempts the incommensurable: to reduce the respective worlds of *Ulysses* and *Under the Volcano* to microcosms small enough to permit a scrutiny of their fundamental particles; and to establish for each, yet with respect to the other, a meaningful tension between a deterministic universe and the apprehension of coincidence by the central characters. This necessarily entails simplifications and a paradigmatic approach to the two novels that permits significant differences to be examined. I propose, therefore, to look at the way each of the major characters (Bloom, Stephen, and the Consul) perceives and structures his subjective world. I begin with *Ulysses* and examine some passages in which Bloom's sense of coincidence is set against the wider causal drama of his interaction with Stephen, as perceived by the reader; and that in turn against what might be termed "the incertitude of the void" (*U* 17.1014-15). I then contrast with Joyce's design Lowry's sense of the universe as an "infernal machine," and consider the drama of choice and determinism as it acts within the equally infernal mechanism of the Consul's mind. A tentative conclusion may then perhaps be drawn.

At the beginning of "Lestrygonians," Bloom is given a throwaway by "a sombre Y.M.C.A. young man." This action, apparently inauspicious, assumes significance as the day unfolds. Bloom's initial reaction is one of considerable confusion (*U* 8.8-9):

> Bloo . . . . Me? No.
> Blood of the Lamb.

The misapprehension fixes the phrase in his mind and triggers off an immediate chain of associations centering about blood and sacrifice: "Birth, hymen, martyr, war, foundation of a building, sacrifice, kidney burntoffering, druids' altars" (*U* 8.11-13). The kidney, apparently thrown casually into the sequence, is not a chance occurrence, because Bloom is recalling an earlier incident of the day, the burning of his breakfast, and binding in one image the experiences of past and present. A little later, Bloom having talked to Josie Breen about Mrs. Purefoy's troubled labor, images of birth mingle with the now composite image into a further synthesis (*U* 8.480-83): "One born every second somewhere. Other dying every second. Since I fed the birds five minutes. Three hundred kicked the bucket. Other three hundred born, washing the blood off, all are washed in the blood of the lamb, bawling maaaaaa." The phrase apparently bothers him no more after this, yet in some transformation it reappears time and again: the silken ribbons (lustrous blood) to be washed in rainwater (*U* 8.620-24); rawhead and bloody bones in the Burton (*U* 8.720-30); the bloodless pious face of the fellow going in to be a priest (*U* 8.1112-13); the vision of the New Bloomusalem, in the shape of a huge pork kidney (*U* 15.1549), with an appropriate prayer: "Kidney of Bloom, pray for us" (*U* 15.1941); and the muddled comment to Stephen: "It's in the blood. . . . All are washed in the blood of the sun. Coincidence . . ." (*U* 16.889-90). The mysteries of blood, food, belief, life, and death have become intricately entangled in these variations rung upon a chance theme that, having entered Bloom's consciousness, has in subtle ways conditioned his thought and emotion. Perhaps the climactic moment of the series is Bloom's epiphany at the end of chapter 15, when he sees in Stephen something of Rudy, the dead child of his blood, who appears to him with a white lambkin peeping out of his waistcoat pocket (*U* 15.4967).

This is but one of presumably thousands of similar motifs that together constitute Bloom's consciousness and pattern his world: acoustic knots, correlating by affinity and uniting particulars otherwise unconnected ("Bloom" and "blood") within the serial universe of the mind. And yet this notion of an "acoustic knot" implies a coincidence, one born from the necessary double articulation of language, whereby a small number of phonemes form (and reform) an indefinitely larger number of words in such a way as to make correspondence at the higher level unavoidable. To isolate the pattern in this way is, of course, artificial, and it would be fair to say that after the first impression the "blood of the lamb" motif functions in Bloom's mind beneath any threshhold of significant awareness. Yet it works to synthesize his experience and render intelligible his world. At times such "knots" become more conscious, for Bloom has the habit of deliberation and often uses set phrases to clinch his thought. For instance, having bought his kidney, he silently responds to the porkbutcher's words (*U* 4.185-87):

> —Thank you, sir. Another time.
> A speck of eager fire from foxeyes thanked him. He withdrew his gaze after an instant. No: better not: another time.

The phrase "another time," used by the butcher as to be of future service, has been invested by Bloom with the additional sense of (perhaps later) acknowledging a common Jewish background. The ambiguity is creative and is typical of the way in which Bloom's mind brings together in common dialogue different aspects of his experience. In like manner, trying to avoid M'Coy's talking head and to glimpse a lady's silk stockings, he can respond to a comment about Paddy Dignam's death yet express his frustration at missing the flash of an ankle (*U* 5.136): "Yes, yes, Mr Bloom said after a dull sigh. Another gone." The common theme of a lost opportunity is iterated through a similarity of phrasing. Again, a principle of double articulation is at work: a word or phrase established as a set piece, but able to relate to a number of possible contexts and thereby to correlate them.

It is doubtful that such motifs and verbal repetitions should be called coincidence, for in terms of Bloom's awareness they would not register as such. Certainly, Bloom does not possess the kind of linguistic sophistication that would enable him to understand the principle of double articulation, and to recognize that whenever a smaller number of elements are required to "articulate" others at a higher order of complexity, then some such correspondence is inevitable. Yet, in terms of noting such accidents, and for the reader in particular, it is more a question of degree than of kind, for the same principles are at work when Bloom, skeptic though he is, draws attention to what he calls coincidence. Four such moments are typical:[4]

1. "Fifteen yesterday. Curious, fifteenth of the month too" (*U* 4.415). This could be taken as an intimation of a serial universe: a correspondence between Milly's age and the day of the month. Yet that apparent connection is no more nor less inevitable than that between her previous birthday and the fourteenth of the month, or her next birthday and the sixteenth, for when two such series interact coincidence is a mathematical certainty.[5] That Bloom notes it says more about the analogical cast of his mind than about the event itself.

2. "And there he is too. Now that's really a coincidence: second time. Coming events cast their shadows before. With the approval of the eminent poet, Mr Geo. Russell" (*U* 8.525-27). Although Bloom's perception of George Russell strikes him as a striking coincidence, his previous thought of Russell was quite some time earlier (*U* 8.332), and was then, as now, prompted by the reply to his advertisement from Lizzie Twigg. Moreover, Bloom has just commented about a similar "apparition" of John Howard Parnell shortly after thinking of his more famous brother: "Haunting face. Now that's a coincidence. Course hundreds of times you think of a person and don't meet him" (*U* 8.502-4). That thought of Charles Stewart Parnell was only a little earlier (*U* 8.462), but the echo of Russell is more distant, and in the meantime Bloom has indeed thought of many persons whom he has not met. It is also possible that the one apparent denial of coincidence (the Parnells) is in part responsible for the later assertion of it (Russell). Finally, as Bloom is ironically aware, such foreshadowings would indeed have the approval of the oracular George Russell. The structure of this coincidence has a complex reality.

3. "*Martha* it is. Coincidence. Just going to write" (*U* 11.713). It indeed appears to be a coincidence that Bloom should be writing to Martha Clifford just as Simon Dedalus is about to sing an aria from Flotow's *Martha*, but it is perhaps more interesting to consider how far the intensity of Bloom's ensuing epiphany arises from a sense of his personal engagement with the song. The name Martha is not uncommon, and the aria was a popular one, so the constraints of probability are not violated: to put it another way, two separate series (Bloom's preoccupations, and the world of popular song) have come into accidental contact, and Bloom has responded to the conjunction. Another woman, or another aria, and any effect upon Bloom might not have registered.

4. "The stick fell in silted sand, stuck. Now if you were trying to do that for a week on end you couldn't. Chance. We'll never meet again" (*U* 13.1270-72). As with the coincidence of *Martha*, another way of looking

at the apparently significant happening is to consider it as just a special case of the thousands of similar chances during the day that equally might have happened but in fact did not occur. Stephen's abstract speculation, "was that only possible which came to pass?" (*U* 2.52), is here illustrated in practical terms: a given event as but one actualization of the many possible, and the apprehension thereof by the human mind as the constituting of "reality."

The point of these four very ordinary examples is that the apparent coincidence is readily explicable in more mundane terms, essentially as the serial interaction of elements simultaneously acting in a different order from that perceived. Joyce has presented Bloom not so much as one abnormally conditioned by coincidence but as one whose mind is responsive to possible relations between what he sees as causally unrelated events. There is a careful balance, in other words, between his sense of coincidence and the "real" world (of accepted probability) in which he lives. This is true of even the major coincidence that seems to haunt him all day: the specter of Blazes Boylan. From the moment he sees the "bold hand" of the letter to "Mrs Marion Bloom" (*U* 4.244), mundane particulars register unusually on his mind in a way they normally would not: the kettle is "boiling" (*U* 4.264); he thinks about "seaside girls" (*U* 4.442-43); he recalls Boylan entering Drago's shop (*U* 4.488: "Queer I was just thinking that moment"); he registers innuendo (*U* 5.153: "Who's getting it up?"); and he sees Boylan everywhere, though he tries to avoid the thought (*U* 6.201-2: "The nails, yes. . . . Worst man in Dublin") and certainly any meeting (*U* 8.1168: "Straw hat in sunlight. Tan shoes. Turnedup trousers. It is. It is").[6] It is not so much the details themselves as the attribution of significance to them that shapes Bloom's actions, notably when he sees from afar Boylan's gay hat on the jaunting car, and comments: "It is. Again. Third time. Coincidence" (*U* 11.302-3). Yet to the reader that coincidence is readily explicable: Boylan's presence at the Ormond Hotel has an entirely rational explanation, albeit one hidden from Bloom, for Lenehan has arranged an appointment at four (Bloom is very conscious of the hour) to interest Boylan, a theatrical "organiser," in Tom Rochford's new invention (the underlying "mechanism of events"[7] is displayed in chapter 10, pp. 189 and 191). Bloom, caught in his own drama with Boylan and unable to appreciate the wider drama of events, does not understand the causality but notes only the affinity, which he calls "coincidence" (Ackerley, "After Lowry's Lights," 118).

This paradigm of apparent coincidence is of importance to any "reading" of the central action of the novel, the meeting of Stephen and Bloom. Stephen, attempting to read the signatures of all things, is confronted with a crucial ambiguity in his meaning of the word "read": does it imply the world as given, a book or object, its signatures there to be understood; or does it have the more active sense of to constitute meaningful interpretation? The difference is, broadly speaking, one between the analogist and the skeptical inquirer, and rather than suggest that Stephen is one or the other I would underline the dramatic nature of his reading, which draws attention to the very problem. Stephen is conscious that the day is (could be?) one of crisis for him, and at a critical moment at the end of chapter 9 he finds himself on the library steps where he had been earlier (*P* 224), and at a similar moment of decision, conscious of the augury of the birds (*U* 9.1197-225). There, feeling the presence of one behind him, he stands aside to let Bloom pass. He recalls the dream he had the previous night and hears Mulligan's mockery of Bloom, which he finds offensive. For the reader this moment is of immense potential signification, coming as it does at the virtual midpoint of the novel, and intimating the future "union" of Stephen and Bloom as well as suggesting that the answer that Stephen is seeking may be implicit in the scene.

Yet such mystical intimations have a realistic underpinning. The meeting of Bloom and Stephen, as most readers of *Ulysses* are aware, will be of crucial importance to Stephen's aesthetic development: an act of kindness that may (in time) humanize an arrogant artistic credo, break through psychological and creative blockages, and lead (perhaps in ten years) to the writing of *Ulysses* itself. Since such figural significance is present in this moment of incipient epiphany it is the more important to appreciate why Stephen should be disposed toward the later acceptance of Bloom, who is in almost every way very different from him. The answer is deceptively simple: to Stephen, Bloom's presence here may be an accident (a coincidence in time and place), but Mulligan's mockery fixes (at whatever level of consciousness) the image of Bloom in his mind, and thereby prepares him for such acceptance. I here use the word "image" in Pound's sense of an intellectual and emotional complex presented in a moment of time (an epiphany in miniature), and would comment briefly upon three of the elements that make up that complex:

1. In Stephen's mind, Mulligan is associated with Photius and the brood of mockers who cast doubt upon the consubstantial nature of father and son (*U* 1.656-57). Mulligan's mockery of Bloom and the suggestion of unnatural lust is therefore the more resented. Earlier, when Stephen was talking of the family lives of famous men and the mystical estate of fatherhood (*U* 9.838), he noted Bloom's entry. Later he extended his dramatic performance: "Mr Magee, sir, there's a gentleman to see you. Me? Says he's your father, sir" (*U* 9.819-20). The Wordsworthian parody was then associated with Bloom, as Stephen recalled Mulligan's earlier words: "He knows your old fellow" (*U* 9.824 and 9.614). The suggestions of

anti-Semitism and unnatural lust in that earlier exchange ("O, I fear me he is Greeker than the Greeks") have thus conditioned the later moment on the steps.

2. Stephen's image of Bloom is expressed in terms of another private motif, the black panther: "A dark back went before them, step of a pard" (*U* 9.1214). Again, the association subconsciously intimates Bloom as a possible father figure by blending him into an existing complex of private symbolism (again, one that involves a theological speculation upon the nature of fatherhood). Stephen will not be aware of the "Leo" in "Leopold," but he has registered that Bloom, too, is in black. For the reader, and Bloom, that detail will later be accentuated when Zoe Higgins[8] asks Bloom, "You're not his father, are you? . . . You both in black" (*U* 15.1290-95).

3. Stephen's dream ("Street of harlots after. A creamfruit melon he held to me" [*U* 9.1207-8]) has a predictive force, and is certainly a factor in his later acceptance of Bloom's hospitality. There is an uncanny similarity between that dream and Bloom's Eastern vision (*U* 4.84-98), and such likeness intimates reconciliation. Yet there is more than simply a superstitious faith in dreams coming true or the mystical notion that the dream of each may be fulfilled somehow in that of the other. There is a simple explanation for both dreams, and for their similarity, in that both Stephen and Bloom have seen recently the pantomime *Turko the Terrible* and that performance has left its mark. If the wider scheme of events is considered ("Well, of course, if we knew all the things" [*U* 8.50]), apparently analogical relations might be seen from a mechanistic perspective; and it is my argument that the structure of *Ulysses* invites precisely that possibility.

That perspective is important because, for the reader, there must be a simultaneous appreciation of the subjective dramas of the two major characters and that of the interaction between them. The drama of that interaction seems to demand a spatial or analogous reading, in which elements (words, images, motifs) articulated in one series correspond with others of a different order. One of the considerable pleasures of (re)reading *Ulysses* is the appreciation of the verbal echoes between the scenes with Stephen and those with Bloom—echoes that bind the dramas together and intimate the "great goal" toward which the action moves, the meeting of the two. A number of such may be heard at the beginning of chapter 4, recapitulating details from chapters 1 to 3:[9]

"Cup of tea soon. Good" (*U* 4.14): Buck Mulligan is, almost at that moment, about to make tea (*U* 1.357).
"Height of a tower" (*U* 4.29): the reference to the opening of the novel is obvious.

"the jug Hanlon's milkman had just filled for him" (*U* 4.36): there is perhaps an echo of the visit of the old milkwoman to the tower in "Telemachus."

"They shine in the dark" (*U* 4.41): an absurd and teasing suggestion of a link between Bloom's [non-Siamese] cat and Stephen's recollections of the delicate Siamese student, faintly beating feelers, tranquil brightness (*U* 2.67-76), and a darkness shining in brightness (*U* 3.409-10).

"his lost property office secondhand waterproof" (*U* 4.67): Stephen is wearing "secondleg" breeks (*U* 1.116).

"the latchkey" (*U* 4.72): the key to the tower is a major concern for Stephen in chapter 1, and a similar "innuendo of home rule" (*U* 7.150), that is, Boylan's "usurpation" of certain "key" rights, will greatly influence the course of Bloom's day.

There are others too numerous to recite. Such details suggest an interpenetration of the two dramas, the fate of the one individual fitting into that of the other, and there can be little doubt that such parallels, both the significant (the latchkey) and the absurd (the cat's whiskers), are intended. Yet it is curious to note that, of those listed above, several (the cup of tea, "height of a tower," the milk jug, and the word "second-hand") were not included in the first published version of the text in the *Little Review*. In his various later revisions Joyce took pains to increase the parallels, and by pushing more plums into the pudding considerably thickened the mixture. Add to this the Homeric correspondences, the associations between each chapter and an organ of the body, and various other schemas (Art, Color, Symbol, Technique), and the result is an analogist's delight, as Valery Larbaud early recognized: "As we arrive at this conclusion, all sorts of coincidences, analogies, and correspondences between these different points come to light; just as, in looking fixedly at the sky at night, we find that the number of stars appears to increase. We begin to discover and to anticipate symbols, a design, a plan, in what appeared to us at first a brilliant but confused mass" (Larbaud 259-60). In like manner, others such as Joseph Frank and A. Walton Litz have stressed the need to read *Ulysses* spatially, the entire pattern of internal references apprehended as a unity (Frank 230), and with the sense of the work as one vast static Image (Litz 57). With such arguments there can be no broad disagreement. My intention here is simply to suggest that such a spatial reading must also coexist with a narrative one, which recognizes the dramatic interaction of different levels; and that the text of *Ulysses* embodies its own critique of spatial principles, for when the anticipated meeting of Stephen and Bloom arrives, the narrative techniques adopted make it impossible, in both practice and principle, to determine the significance of the encounter. We may

also be reminded that one of the first lessons of modern astronomy and
relativity ("what's parallax?" [U 8.578]) is to render uncertain any such
notion as "the number of stars" making up a fixed design or plan: change
the perspective, and the constellations disappear. I shall discuss two examples only:

1. As Fritz Senn has noted, the opening sentence of "Eumaeus" ("Preparatory to anything else Mr Bloom *brushed* off the greater bulk of the
shavings and handed Stephen the hat and ashplant and *bucked* him up
generally"—Senn's italics) echoes the opening of the novel, but in such a
way as to impose upon it an additional layer of gratuitous correspondence (Senn 45). "Eumaeus" is full of such "imposters," ranging from
the dubious etymological association of Bloom as Stephen's "companion" as they pass the bakery (U 16.61) to the appearance of W.B. Murphy
(U 16.452).[10] These have the effect of casting doubt upon all they touch,
so that at the moment the reader most needs certainty any such assurance is denied.

2. The epiphany at the heart of "Ithaca" is at best imperfect: the lo-
cus classicus of meaningful interpretation takes place when Bloom and
Stephen share a moment of apparent communion with "Epp's
massproduct, the creature cocoa" (U 17.369-70). Many have shared
Goldberg's distrust of Tindall's "surely excessive faith in cocoa"
(Goldberg 28, with reference to Tindall 222), without being able to deny
the hints of the mass and creation (creativity?) implicit in the phrasing.
Yet any attempt to overread this detail should be qualified immediately
by the following one: Bloom's suppressed contemplation of the fissure
in the right side of his guest's jacket, with its ludicrously inappropriate
connotation of the wound in the side of Christ (Ackerley, "After Lowry's
Lights," 119). Joyce seems here to be deliberately inviting his reader to
symbolic speculation and then, equally deliberately, mocking that very
impulse. A similar juxtaposition of resonant meaning and absurdity may
also be found in "Araby" (D 29), where the description of the wild garden and its central apple tree (so reminiscent of Eden) is followed immediately by that of the rusty bicycle pump (a reductio ad absurdum of the
Holy Spirit?). My suggestion is, very simply, that such juxtapositions
may be seen as paradigms of Joyce's realism in that they subject unavoidable analogy to immediate skeptical inquiry.

In like manner, the ga*lactic* pun of the "uncondensed milky way"
(U 17.1044) mocks the very efforts of the conscious rational animal to
impose significance upon the incertitude of the void. Yet we may perhaps be reminded of Joyce's comment to Frank Budgen to the effect that
the Holy Roman Catholic Church was built on a pun, and that should be
good enough for him (Budgen 347). One could even consider the central

action of *Ulysses* as not simply an Image, as Litz has suggested, but as a giant pun: the coincidence, in a brief "parenthesis" (*U* 17.1055), of time and space, of two essentially different individuals, whose momentary union through an act of kindness asserts their kinship.[11] As Stephen and Bloom depart, perhaps never to meet again, each hears different echoes of the bells of the church of St. George: by Stephen, *"Liliata rutilantium. Turma circumdet. Iubilantium te virginum. Chorus excipiat"*; by Bloom, *"Heigho, heigho, Heigho, heigho"* (*U* 17.1228-34). Nowhere is the difference between them so ironically accentuated, and yet somewhere in the distance tolls John Donne's bell, reminding us all that no man is an island.

The universe of *Ulysses* reflects a vision of analogy and uncertainty bound in a complex dualism. So far I have tried to indicate this by looking first at Bloom's structuring of his experience through language (elements of one order of experience inevitably constituting coincidence at another) and by considering some of the ways in which Joyce has dramatized the complex interaction of word and world. I then chose a moment at the end of chapter 9 when Stephen, attempting to read the signatures of his world, constructs a complex image that includes the figure of Bloom, and indicated how the apparent figural significance of that moment may be seen simultaneously as being constructed of causal elements functioning in different serial orders. I looked next at the problem of the reader to understand the individual dramas of Stephen and Bloom and the more complex one of their interaction, given that the text asserts apparently significant analogy yet confounds any attempt to interpret it definitively. The dualism of structure and uncertainty at the heart of *Ulysses* constitutes what I would define (perhaps uncritically) as Joyce's sense of realism. And yet in *Ulysses* there is also the beginning of that tendency to push more plums into the mixture that would lead eventually to the method of *Finnegans Wake*, with its lack of a direct human and dramatic context and its tendency to let words behave increasingly in a substantive manner freed from the restrictive constraints of place and time—perhaps one reason why Nabokov, with an unwitting nod toward M. de Fortgibu, was to criticize that work as "a cold pudding of a book" (Nabokov 71). But that is another matter. *Ulysses* remains the work in which Joyce expressed most powerfully his vision of both the absurdity of existence and the power of the human imagination to transform that meaninglessness into significant shape and form; and it is that vision that will form the point of departure and contrast for Malcolm Lowry's similar but very different work.

Lowry's deeper acquaintance with *Ulysses* is a matter of conjecture: though he claimed that his first "intelligent and complete reading" was

not until 1952 (*SC* 2:581), his throwaway line ("Le gusta esta Dujardin")
and a number of references in the short stories (notably, in "Through the
Panama") and earlier letters (*SC* 1:321, 1:506; *SC* 2:51, 2:205, 2:413) suggest a wider awareness than he was willing to acknowledge. And he
was clearly impressed, as he indicated to David Markson, by the coincidence of "his" name in Joyce's list of the dead (*SC* 2:413, with reference
to *U* 6.158). While one might agree broadly with Richard Hauer Costa's
contention that Lowry absorbed Joyce through Aiken, particularly with
respect to the handling of interior monologue in *Ultramarine*, there are
nevertheless specific details in *Under the Volcano* that probably have their
origins in *Ulysses:* the biographical division of himself into the Consul
and Hugh, as Joyce had done with Bloom and Stephen; the Consul's
"change of worlds" (*UV* 53) as an echo of Martha Clifford's "I do not
like that other world" (*U* 5.245); his smashing the lightbulb (*UV* 92) in
imitation of Stephen at Bella Cohen's (*U* 15.4243); Hugh's charity to the
seagull (*UV* 151) as analogous to Bloom's (*U* 8.73-76); the Consul's use
of the word "Agenbite" (*UV* 218) as an unmistakable echo of Stephen's
remorseful "Agenbite of inwit" (*U* 1.481); possible similarities between
the Consul's nightmare in chapter 10 and Joyce's Nighttown. And given
Clarissa Lorenz's direct statement that Lowry was reading *Ulysses* in
Spain in 1933 (Lorenz 150; Bowker 150), Lowry's bald claim to Jacques
Barzun that he had never read *Ulysses* through (*SC* 2:52) seems (to mix
the metaphor) a little hairy. Perhaps all depends upon what is meant by
"intelligent and complete" or "through," or even "was reading": one
might apply to Lowry his own anecdote from "Through the Panama"
about the person who borrowed *Ulysses* and returned it the next day:
"Thanks awfully. Very good" (*HL* 34).

Of greater interest is the comment that Lowry made about himself
and Joyce: his own method, he claimed, was basically the simplification
of "what originally suggested itself in far more baffling, complex and
esoteric terms," whereas Joyce's method, he implied, was the amplifica-
tion and complication of an essentially simple insight (*SC* 1:506). That
Lowry did indeed perceive his universe in "baffling, complex and esoteric terms" there can be no doubt; but it is not my intention here to
establish precisely what those terms were, save to underline the obvious
fact that he was fascinated by (and largely believed in) such matters as
coincidence, synchronicity, the Law of Series, the occult, and other non-
material matters. I would argue, further, that his interest was eclectic
rather than disciplined, and that he did not possess any defined "system," but rather a broad general principle. Discussing Lowry's acquaintance with Charles Stansfeld-Jones, Tony Kilgallin sums up the case: "Both
men held that analogy was the key to all of Nature's secrets and the sole

fundamental principle behind all revelations. Correspondences, as Baudelaire had taught Lowry, were based on the laws of analogy fundamental to the *Corpus Hermeticum*. Put simply, every phenomenon in the natural world has its counterpart, upon which it depends for existence, in the spiritual world. The rhyming of the natural with the spiritual enables man to communicate with the heavenly mysteries, the celestial machinery" (Kilgallin 46).

More recently, Patrick McCarthy's *Forests of Symbols* has explored in depth this aspect of Lowry's thought, essentially agreeing with Matthew Corrigan that for Lowry "'truth is something already there in the universe,' needing only to be provoked 'through "correspondence" into revealing itself'" (McCarthy 57).[12] McCarthy stresses Lowry's tendency to see himself in relation to a cosmic web of symbols and circumstances, and documents the difficulty that Lowry had in separating life from art, or in seeing it "in simple and direct terms rather than as part of an elaborate series of coincidences" (McCarthy 146). He deals fully with Lowry's sense of the world as shaped and determined by the Law of Series and various doctrines of correspondence; yet he also acknowledges that one of the most striking things about *Under the Volcano* is that "its reliance on coincidences and correspondences [is] less suggestive of random occurrence than of the operations of a partly self-imposed fate" (McCarthy 45). It is this notion that I should like to pursue a little further.

The universe of *Under the Volcano* is based upon fundamental and persistent laws of analogy, spiritual and material worlds interpenetrating in such a way that every phenomenon in the latter, from the horse with number 7 on its rump to the mysterious ringing of telephones throughout the day, implies a correspondence with the former.[13] Yet, as McCarthy notes, Lowry worked seriously and ironically to treat coincidences as both "an aspect of 'reality'" *and* the "product of the Consul's overwrought imagination" (McCarthy 48). Surface and symbol seem to be united in a vision of the world in which the Infernal Machine constructed by the gods (Day 323) and the Consul's subjective reality operate according to the same laws—a fundamental principle of correspondence between macrocosm and microcosm—and yet, at the level of human reality, there is a tragic dimension.

McCarthy argues that Geoffrey's "obsessive private readings of events are a major cause of his destruction," and that his sense of himself as part of the web of coincidences and forest of symbols ultimately undermines his sense of individual identity (McCarthy 7-8). While it could be argued that Stephen Dedalus's "reading" of signatures is also a way of constructing (rather than simply having revealed to him) his destiny, the Consul's acts of interpretation have a more sinister outcome. Seduced by his own metaphors of destruction, and predisposed to read symbolic meaning into every occurrence, the Consul envisages his world as an Infernal Machine, the secular arm of a cabalistic universe, perhaps, but fails to recognize to what extent it has been self-chosen as a model of his own fate.[14]

The Consul has more or less constructed a hostile universe and a fatal destiny as a means of avoiding the horrors of reality: his inability to love and the guilt arising from his repeated failures to be a Good Samaritan. To some extent that construction is inevitable. Much of his guilt has been conditioned by events over which he has had little or no control. To use the paradigm from *War and Peace,* the more we know of causes and influences the more we will see his actions as determined, the result of long series of events going back to the distant past: "a childhood and adolescence of loneliness and vulnerability" (Day 323); the mysterious disappearance of both his mother and father; heavy drinking by the Taskersons; and an early instance of sexual inadequacy. There is thus an "explanation" of why Yvonne should have had an affair with Hugh so early in the marriage and why the Consul should have turned to alcohol, in terms of a psychology determined by a network of circumstances that go back to childhood and beyond.

When Lowry wrote to Cape that the novel was concerned principally with "the forces in man which cause him to be terrified of himself" (*SC* 1:506-7), he emphasized the drunkenness of the Consul as a symbol of the universal drunkenness of mankind, teetering toward the abyss. That drunkenness is both the cause and the product of his guilt, but it is also the product of some misdirected mysticism. Lowry suggested in the same letter that the agonies of the drunkard "find their most accurate poetic analogue in the agonies of the mystic who has abused his powers," and he referred to William James in support of this (*SC* 1:511). The passage in *The Varieties of Religious Experience* that he seems to have had in mind is from Lectures XVI and XVII, on mysticism, where James writes that "the sway of alcohol over mankind is undoubtedly due to its power to stimulate the mystical faculties of human nature," and then adds: "The drunken consciousness is one bit of the mystic consciousness, and our total opinion of it must find its place in our opinion of that larger whole" (James 297). The Consul, Yvonne tells Hugh (*UV* 118), has talked about going on with his book, but even though that project (a "great work on 'Secret Knowledge'") is quite clearly at an impasse, not even the Consul's irony ("one can always say when it never comes out that the title explains this deficiency" [*UV* 39]) can quite fend off its insidious power over his mind. The Consul has immersed himself in mystical speculation to such an extent that it largely prescribes the way in which he experiences the world. In this respect, a comment from the end of William James's chapter "Mysticism" seems particularly chilling: "In delusional insanity, paranoia, as they sometimes call it, we may have a *diabolical* mysticism, a sort of religious mysticism turned upside down. The same sense of ineffable importance in the smallest events, the same texts and words coming with new meanings, the same voices and visions and leadings and missions, the same controlling by extraneous powers; only this time the emotion is pessimistic: instead of consolations we have desolations; the meanings are dreadful; and the powers are enemies to life" (James 326).[15]

James's sense of "a sort of religious mysticism turned upside down" is expressed symbolically in the Consul's vision of himself as "teetering over the awful unbridgeable void" (*UV* 39), and that vision receives its literal ratification when at the end of the novel he is thrown down the ravine (*UV* 375). In this state of inverted mysticism, things that should have symbolized salvation to an initiate serve only to confirm his sense of death: light is shunned, lightbulbs shattered, and sunflowers stare into his room all day (*UV* 179). The natural world, which should be an emanation of the divine, instead signifies in his mind the terrors of his inevitable damnation: he sees not eagles but vultures (awaiting the ratification of death); he is haunted by pariah dogs, snakes, and scorpions— all of which correspond (he believes) "to some faction of his being" (*UV* 362); and at the end of chapter 5 he has a fearful vision of the insect world closing in. He is, in effect, condemned by a paranoid consciousness that creates terrifying visions and selects from the natural world the symbols of damnation that it seeks.[16]

For this reason, Yvonne's arrival in chapter 2, on the Day of the Dead, has for the Consul a peculiar unreality that it cannot possess for others, including Yvonne herself. And her arrival poses a problem for the reader, who is first invited to share her perspective of things, before gradually and increasingly becoming aware of the ominous implications of the tranquil scene. There is here a complexity to the narrative technique that is not immediately obvious. To adapt the words of Schopenhauer, from the beginning of this essay, the description stands in at least three different kinds of connection, and any complete "reading" of the scene requires a simultaneous sense of them all:

1. Yvonne's is the innocent eye. For her, the hurricane of butterflies is "immense and gorgeous," the volcanoes are "beautiful," the equestrian statue of Huerta forms part of the familiar zócalo, and Venus burns brightly in the lovely dawn. And she sees herself (*UV* 46) as she "knew" the Consul must see her, half jaunty, a little diffident.

2. The problem is, the Consul does not quite "see" her in this way. He has been studying the Mexican National Railways timetable, with its

express (and threatening) conditions concerning the transport of a corpse;
he has just been looking at a picture of a "scarlet" woman, right next to
the cinema advertisement for *Las Manos de Orlac*—and that film, he probably knows, projects an image of bloody hands trying to strangle the
heroine, by coincidence (?) named Yvonne (Ackerley and Clipper, *Companion*, 40); and although (or because) he has spent the previous night
howling and praying for his wife's return (*UV* 217 and 289), her "appearance" in apparent answer to that prayer on (of all days) the Day of
the Dead, when the living may communicate with the spirits and souls
of those lost to them, invests her in his mind with the unreality of an
incubus. And for the rest of the day, no matter what she may do, for him
she will possess in part those qualities of unreality.

3. For the reader, the connections are complex. Initially, and on a
first reading especially, we may assume Yvonne's perspective; but when
the trochal structure of the book forces us back to the beginning again
we "inevitably" find ourselves reading the scene the way the Consul
might—and that is not healthy. Thus, we could find a hint of "Huracán"
in the gorgeous butterflies, which might intimate in turn the myth of
Psyche and the story of a love doomed never to exist on earth. The "air
of slumbering Harlequin" might assume the beat of demonic horsemen
(Kilgallin 157), and the equestrian statue foreshadow a threatening men-
ace. The volcanoes would appear as symbols of both hopeless aspiration
and inevitable damnation; the woods as dark and Dantean; and the
"horn" of Venus would insinuate its mythical assertions of adultery. Finally, and irrevocably, Yvonne's arrival by the little red plane, that "red
demon, winged emissary of Lucifer," would confirm in our minds the
essentially daemonic nature of her apparition.[17]

The trochal structure of the book, in other words, has been designed
so as to seduce the reader into perceiving the world of the novel as a
forest of symbols. The novel itself works as an Infernal Machine, finely
balanced between an objective reality and the subjective projection of
the Consul's mind, without giving ultimate value to either position. Key
phrases and images throughout the novel are so often neither quite the
projection of a perceiving consciousness nor a statement of simple fact:
"the swimming pool ticked like a clock" (*UV* 70); the armadillo as miniature "engine of destruction" (*UV* 113); Laruelle coming forward "as it
were impelled by clockwork" (*UV* 190). And yet Lowry has protected
himself against the charges of proliferating symbols, of creating a "fan-
tastically spun-out web" of "empty abstractions" (Day 273-74) by two
simple devices (I am tempted to call them "posture-governing designs"):

1. There is a perfectly "reasonable" explanation of all the correspondences in the novel, in that chapters 2-12 can be seen, and indeed should

be seen, as mediated through and by Laruelle's controlling consciousness, so that the novel may read as *his* cinematic reconstruction of past
events. This is a compelling argument, and, indeed, one put forward by
Lowry himself, in defence of the novel's circular form: "In this sense, if
we like, we can look at the rest of the book through Laruelle's eyes, as if
it were his creation" (*SC* 1:511). Read this way, many of the larger coincidences are no longer problematic: the same film showing exactly one
year later; the aura of unreality in Yvonne's appearance; the simultaneous but interrelated deaths of the Consul and Yvonne. To be sure, one
might accept this rationalization and yet remain skeptical, saying that
this strategy simply transposes the problem of realistic ratification to
another level; to which the only reply could be that *that*, precisely, is the
point—levels of symbolic construction, each faithfully enacting at a mi-
croscopic level the wider laws of the cosmos.[18]

2. The compulsion to read the world as Geoffrey Firmin might do is
so powerful an impulse that (as we have seen, above) we are tempted to
attribute to him the symbolic readings and interpretations that we find
ourselves making, even when there is no "real" need to do so: after all,
the surface has been so compellingly designed as to conceal the "depths"
(*SC* 1:506). However, the poetry of the novel is such that it is an easy
matter to suspend disbelief and enter into an imaginative world where,
indeed, the wider drama of the macrocosm is faithfully enacted in the
microcosm. The sense of Fate engendered by this Chinese-box technique
leads to a reading of the narrative in terms of an increasing intensity of
symbolic implications and seriality, and with a growing sense of the complex correspondences between apparently unrelated things: the different bells that ring all day; the "faded blue Ford" seen by Laruelle (*UV*
13), the car "lost" by the Consul (*UV* 52), and the Cadillac for sale in the
English pages of the *Universal* (*UV* 181); or the number of Hugh's passport (*UV* 77), intended to match that on the block of lottery tickets (*UV*
329).[19] This is indeed a vision of a universe based on analogy, and, as
such, quite different from the world of *Ulysses*, where Stephen's reading
of signatures implies a dramatic and even figural sense of destiny, and
the human apprehension of significance is set against an underlying sense
of the void.

To conclude: while *Ulysses* and *Under the Volcano* are often linked as novels steeped in a world of correspondence and raised upon a foundation
of coincidence, the thrust of this essay has been to accentuate a crucial
difference between them, and to indicate how the central action of each
novel, the fates of their major characters, and the structure of the novels
themselves have been designed in terms of that difference.[20] Both novels

ask the reader to connect "an infinite number of references and cross-references which relate to one another independently of the time-sequence of the narrative" (Frank 232); but the irony implicit in Joyce's sense of such correspondence shapes itself into a figural vision (that is, one unfolding in time) of destiny, rather than a microcosmic one. Stephen's reading of the signatures of the world there all the time, "without" him (*U* 3.27), translates a simple ambiguity (does "without" mean exterior to his perceiving self, or essentially indifferent to his presence?) into the dramatic and creative problem of understanding his future, in terms of the choices he must make. In the Consul's reading of his world, however, while choice is apparently emphasized, the wider coincidence is seen by him to have an immediate personal application: his response to "Es inevitable la muerte del Papa" (*UV* 230), while similar in the mechanics of misapprehension to Bloom's "Bloo . . . . Me? No" (*U* 8.8), and sharing with Bloom's response the same intimations of sacrifice,[21] has a more tragic impact because of the way *he* chooses to read it: whereas Bloom at first is struck by coincidence and then responds with irony, the Consul first assumes irony and then attributes to that a deeper underlying significance. It might seem odd, at first glance, to suggest that *Under the Volcano*, a novel in which the surface and dramatic ironies are so obviously pervasive, at the deeper level lacks irony; but in this respect it is perhaps the antithesis of *Ulysses*. Both novels are structured upon coincidence, and both writers found in the material world the signatures they wished to read; but Joyce's ironic and ambiguous vision dramatizes the process of Stephen's meeting with Bloom and the implications of that meeting in a way that is essentially different from the Consul's tryst with a destiny that (he believes, and the structure of the novel affirms) is already written for him.

Notes

1. Jung 431. The epigraph that opens this essay is from Arthur Schopenhauer"s "On the Apparent Design in the Fate of the Individual," in *Parerga und Paralipomena*, vol. 1, ed. R. von Koeber (Berlin, 1891); as cited and translated in Jung's essay on synchronicity (Jung 428).

2. Schopenhauer explains such apparent design: "All this, of course, is something that surpasses all our powers of comprehension and can be conceived as possible only by virtue of the most marvellous *harmonia praestablia*" (Schopenhauer 1:220).

3. Kammerer 93; as cited and translated in Koestler 85-86.

4. I have drawn upon my earlier article "'After Lowry's Lights': Coincidence in *Ulysses* and *Under the Volcano*" for part of the previous argument and for some of the following details. That article is not readily available (Patrick McCarthy's *Forests of Symbols* and his contribution to the present volume are the only studies I know to have cited it); and I have extended its simpler principles into a more complex argument here.

5. An instructive example of such inevitability is recorded in *Private Eye* (Nov. 2, 1973, p. 7), concerning the decision of Courage Breweries to label each brew with a letter plus number plus letter: "Informed sources tell us that the batch codes used by Courage's unfortunately came up with the legend *K 9 P* for this week's brew—all the kegs being duly so labelled. It seems that, fearing the laughter of cellarmen throughout Courage's Bristol-based West of England Empire, a yard full of draymen—fully laden with the fizzy stuff—were held up while agitated representatives of the management replaced all the offending labels with the hastily emended one reproduced below: *K 8A P.*" A classic literary example of the same phenomenon is the Frog Song in Beckett's *Watt,* and the suggestion of a serial universe thereby implied (Beckett 137-38).

6. For the reader, but not for Bloom, there is a rather neat irony at the thought of Tommy Boardman's wetting his own new *tan* shoes (*U* 13.77), and perhaps a further satisfaction in linking that to Bloom's wishful thinking: "Big blaze. Might be his house" (*U* 15.171).

7. The phrase "mechanism of events" is used by Borges in "The South," p. 156, to invoke exactly this kind of discrepancy between actual and perceived reality.

8. Bloom at this point may not appreciate that Zoe's surname is Higgins, but the coincidence of that name with his mother's (*U* 17.536) should not be lost on the reader.

9. For a detailed consideration of such changes, see Steinberg 73-82.

10. Whatever editorial principles are invoked, I remain unconvinced that Gabler's "D.B." Murphy should replace the Random House "W.B.," with its magnificently pseudoangelic echo of Yeats and Blake.

11. This suggestion has in fact been made by Richard Ellmann in *The Consciousness of Joyce,* 90-95, but in a rather strange pseudopolitical context, so that its implications have not been fully developed.

12. McCarthy is citing Matthew Corrigan, "Malcolm Lowry: The Phenomenology of Failure," *Boundary* 2 3 (1975): 431.

13. For the general cabalistic significance of the horse, see Lévi 98: "Jehovah is He who dominates Nature like a magnificent horse and makes it go where He wills; but CHAVAJOH—otherwise, the demon—is an unbridled horse which overthrows its rider and precipitates him into the abyss." For comments on the esoteric significance of telephone calls throughout *Under the Volcano,* see various entries in Ackerley and Clipper's *Companion,* where cabalistic correspondences are indexed in some detail.

14. I have treated other aspects of this self-destructive tendency elsewhere; see, for example, "The Consul's Book," where I consider in detail the effect of

his esoteric reading, his desire to sense analogies between Mexico and India (the subject of his Great Work), and his sense of himself as a sacrificial heart for the Gods of Mexico. The matter is also considered by Patrick McCarthy (McCarthy 99-100).

15. I should like to thank Simon Dickie for bringing this passage to my attention, and for suggesting some of the implications that follow. The relevance of the James passage is also noted by Day (335).

16. To those who argue that the cabalistic qualities of the novel are largely incidental on the grounds that the main lines of the action were clearly defined in the 1940 text, I reply that an essential difference between that version and the final one is precisely the difference between a (very poor) narrative and a (brilliant) prose-poem, and that Lowry needed the Infernal Machine and the notion of the Consul as a black magician to bring his fuzzy text into poetical focus. But that may be an issue too big to be debated here.

17. For a more detailed reading of these images (yet one lacking this sense of dramatic perspective), see the commentary in Ackerley and Clipper's *Companion*, 76-82.

18. Thus Frater Achad, in his *Anatomy of the Body of God*, which Lowry had consulted, insists that "the *Great Work* for Man consists in the adjustment of the Soul, or Intellectual Sphere, so that it becomes a perfect resemblance and correspondence to the Material and Natural Order of the Universe" (2) and presents diagrams of macrocosmic structures that (rather like computer-generated fractals) are made up of identical and infinitely regressing microcosms, which in turn are made up of identical and infinitely regressing microcosms. . . .

19. Of course, in the published novel it does not. Or rather, the connection is not explicit. But in one earlier draft (UBC 28:5, p. F) Lowry wrote: "the block of ten lottery tickets, the number of which—Yvonne distinguished—was 21312"; while on the menu itself, in the Lowry archives, another note is written: "number should be number of Hugh's passport"—presumably, to intimate something of his likely fate. I have included this as a striking example of the way that Lowry would blur the margins between fact and fiction to further his design: in reality, the number on the lottery tickets is a non-palindromic "12261," which may have been why he dropped the idea.

20. In my original proposal for this essay I anticipated a discussion of Samuel Beckett's *Watt* as well, but exigencies of time and space have made this impossible. I had intended to use Joyce's sense of coincidence as a bridge between the phenomenal world and the significance that might be attributed to it as a point of departure: firstly, for Lowry's vision of the world as a forest of symbols with analogy as its fundamental law; and then for Beckett's radically different vision of an absurdist universe, in which the very attempt of the human agent to read significance into phenomena is doomed. It is difficult to imagine two novels as different from one another as *Under the Volcano* and *Watt*, and yet I was (and am) intrigued by some strange similarities, which receive, of course, a fundamentally different intonation: the Frog Song as image of a serial universe; Watt's arrival by tram (compare the Consul's express) on his journey to disintegration; and the extent to which that disintegration is the outcome of a self-inflicted

reading of the world in which macro- and microcosm (the Big and Little Worlds) do not coincide. Like and yet so much unlike the Consul (and perhaps Stephen Dedalus, with his faith in epiphany), Watt's "ancient error" is to suppose that an awareness of pattern necessarily entails a like apprehension of meaning.

21. The apparent coincidence between my example here and the similar discussion in Pat McCarthy's essay in this volume would be truly coincidental were it not for the mundane explanation that Pat kindly sent me a copy of his essay before mine was written.

Works Cited

Achad, Frater [Charles Stansfeld-Jones]. *The Anatomy of the Body of God*. Chicago: Collegium ad Spiritum Sanctum, 1925.

Ackerley, Chris. "'After Lowry's Lights': Coincidence in *Ulysses* and *Under the Volcano*." In *The Interpretative Power: Essays on Literature in Honour of Margaret Dalziel*, edited by C.A. Gibson. Dunedin, New Zealand: Univ. of Otago Press, 1980.

———. "The Consul's Book." *Malcolm Lowry Review* nos. 23 and 24 (Fall 1988 and Spring 1989): 78-92.

Ackerley, Chris, and Lawrence J. Clipper. *A Companion to "Under the Volcano."* Vancouver: Univ. of British Columbia Press, 1984. Cited as *Companion*.

Beckett, Samuel. *Watt*. New York: Grove Press, 1959.

Borges, Jorge Luis. "The South." In *Fictions*, translated and edited by Anthony Kerrigan. London: Calder and Boyars, 1965.

Bowker, Gordon. *Pursued by Furies: A Life of Malcolm Lowry*. London: HarperCollins, 1993.

Budgen, Frank. *James Joyce and the Making of "Ulysses."* 1934. Reprint, with additional material, London: Oxford Univ. Press, 1972.

Costa, Richard Hauer. "*Ulysses*, Lowry's *Volcano*, and the *Voyage* Between: A Study of an Unacknowledged Literary Kinship." *University of Toronto Quarterly* 36.4 (July 1967): 335-52.

Day, Douglas. *Malcolm Lowry: A Biography*. New York: Oxford Univ. Press, 1973.

Dunne, J.W. *An Experiment with Time*. 1927. 5th ed., London: Faber and Faber, 1939.

Ellmann, Richard. *The Consciousness of Joyce*. London: Faber and Faber, 1977.

Frank, Joseph. "Spatial Form in Modern Literature." *Sewanee Review* 53.2 (Spring 1945): 221-40; 53.3 (Summer 1945): 433-56; and 53.4 (Autumn 1945): 643-53.

Goldberg, S.L. *The Classical Temper: A Study of James Joyce's "Ulysses."* London: Chatto and Windus, 1961.

James, William. *The Varieties of Religious Experience: A Study in Human Nature*. New York: Mentor Books, 1958.

Jung, C.G. "Synchronicity: An Acausal Connecting Principle." In *The Collected Works of C.G. Jung*, vol. 8, *The Structure and Dynamics of the Psyche*, translated by F.R.C. Hull. London: Routledge and Kegan Paul, 1960.

Kammerer, Paul. *Das Gesetz der Serie: Eine Lehre von den Weiderholungen im Lebens- und im Weltgeshehen*. Stuttgart und Berlin: Deutsche Verlags-Anhalt, 1919.

Kilgallin, Tony. *Lowry.* Erin, Ontario: Press Porcepic, 1973.

Koestler, Arthur. *The Roots of Coincidence.* New York: Random House, 1972.

Larbaud, Valery. "James Joyce" (*Nouvelle revue française* 18 [April 1922]); translated as "The *Ulysses* of James Joyce" (*Criterion* 1.1 [Oct. 1922]); and reprinted in *James Joyce: The Critical Heritage,* vol. 1, edited by Robert H. Deming. London: Routledge and Kegan Paul, 1970.

Lévi, Éliphas. *Transcendental Magic: Its Doctrine and Ritual* (1855-56), translated by A.E. Waite. 1896; reprint, London: Rider and Co., 1968. (Note, incidentally, that both dates have the same figures.)

Litz, A. Walton. *The Art of James Joyce: Method and Design in "Ulysses" and "Finnegans Wake."* London: Oxford Univ. Press, 1961.

Lorenz, Clarissa M. *Lorelei Two: My Life with Conrad Aiken.* Athens: Univ. of Georgia Press, 1983.

McCarthy, Patrick A. *Forests of Symbols: World, Text, and Self in Malcolm Lowry's Fiction.* Athens: Univ. of Georgia Press, 1994.

Nabokov, Vladimir. *Strong Opinions.* London: Weidenfeld and Nicolson, 1973.

Ouspensky, P.D. *Tertium Organum: The Third Canon of Thought. A Key to the Enigmas of the World,* translated by Nicholas Bessaraboff and Claude Bragdon. 2d ed. London: Kegan Paul, Trench, Trubner and Co., 1928.

Schopenhauer, Arthur. *Parerga and Paralipomena: Short Philosophical Essays,* 2 vols., translated by E.F.J. Payne. Oxford: Clarendon Press, 1974.

Senn, Fritz. "Book of Many Turns." *James Joyce Quarterly* 10.1 (Fall 1972): 29-46.

Steinberg, Erwin R. *The Stream of Consciousness and Beyond in "Ulysses."* Pittsburgh: Univ. of Pittsburgh Press, 1973.

Tindall, William York. *A Reader's Guide to James Joyce.* London: Thames and Hudson, 1959.

four

Ulysses and Under the Volcano: The Difficulty of Loving

Richard K. Cross

It is clear that the soul of each [lover] has some . . . longing which it cannot express, but can only surmise and obscurely hint at. Suppose Hephaestus with his tools were to visit them as they lie together, and stand over them and ask: " . . . Is the object of your desire to be always together as much as possible, and never be separated from one another day or night? If that is what you want, I am ready to melt and weld you together, so that, instead of two, you shall be one flesh; as long as you live you shall live a common life, and when you die, you shall suffer a common death, and be still one, not two, even in the next world."
—Aristophanes, in Plato, *The Symposium*

In the last resort we must begin to love in order not to fall ill.
—Freud, "On Narcissism: An Introduction"

In his masterful historical survey *The Nature of Love,* Irving Singer observes that Western attempts to understand love tend to fall into two categories. On one side are the idealizers, who try to account for affective relations chiefly in terms of mental or spiritual needs and gifts. It is this, the idealist tradition, "that Plato codifies for the first time, that Christianity amalgamates with Judaic thought, that courtly love humanizes, and that romanticism redefines in the nineteenth century" (*The Nature of Love,* 2:3). The stress in much, if not most, idealist thinking is on transcending the bounds between lovers—as in the celebrated passage from Plato above—in what amounts to a merging of identities. On the other side of the issue are the critics of idealism, such as Freud, who oppose the notion of fused identity, questioning whether such a union is attainable or even desirable. These critics, whom Singer refers to as realists, typically focus on the psychological distinctness of human beings, grounded in each person's bodily existence, a separateness that passion or affection can palliate but never abolish. Although Singer's concern is primarily with sexual love, the categories of idealism and realism, with the inflection he gives them, have a bearing on parental love of a child, filial love of a parent, and related kinds of affective ties as well.

Reading *Ulysses* and *Under the Volcano* as instances of a dialectic between these two approaches to love—with particular attention to Joyce's and Lowry's attempts to negotiate the respective claims of spirit and flesh—offers one as direct a route into the heart of the two novels as he is likely to find. That the books hinge on the issue of love, broadly construed, can scarcely be doubted. "What is that word known to all men?" asks Stephen Dedalus at the end of "Proteus" (*U* 3.435). The situation in which Stephen poses his question—alone and lonely on Sandymount strand, wishing for someone to touch him—indicates that, as a member of the class "all men," he understands well enough what the word is. Hans Walter Gabler, in the most controversial single emendation in his edition of *Ulysses,* recovers a passage from a manuscript version of "Scylla and Charybdis" that makes Stephen's knowledge explicit: "Do you know what you are talking about? Love, yes. Word known to all men. *Amor vero aliquid alicui bonum vult unde et ea quae concupiscimus*" (*U* 9.429). How is it, then, that later, in "Circe," we find him beseeching his mother's ghost: "Tell me the word, mother, if you know now. The word known to all men" (*U* 15.4191)? Has the foray into nighttown caused him to forget what he had discerned six episodes earlier, assuming that Joyce did, finally, mean Stephen to say what Gabler's emendation has him say? Why the mystification? The answer, textual questions aside,[1] is that Stephen both knows and does not know. As a student of Aquinas—the Latin in the "love passage" splices together phrases from adjacent sentences in the *Summa contra gentiles*—he can acknowledge *amor* intellectually as the linchpin of human existence; in terms of practice, however, he has much to learn—as what twenty-two-year-old does not?—about giving and receiving love.

Fortunately Stephen is on the verge of meeting one who, while hardly the perfect master, is nonetheless a good deal further along the way than he is. "But it's no use," declares Bloom. "Force, hatred, history, all that. That's not life for men and women, insult and hatred. And everybody knows that it's the very opposite of that that is really life." Pressed to clarify his utterance, he puts it in a word: "Love . . . the opposite of hatred" (*U* 12.1481-85). This formulation is no more likely to satisfy Stephen, with his scholastic penchant for "dagger definitions" (*U* 9.84), than it does Bloom's immediate audience, the hangers-on in Barney Kiernan's pub. Whatever his notional shortcomings, however, Bloom compares favorably as an exemplar of love in several of its varieties with the other Dubliners we encounter in *Ulysses.*

No se puede vivir sin amar, reads the inscription on Jacques Laruelle's tower. That phrase, taken from the sixteenth-century Spanish poet and mystic Fray Luis de León's *De los nombres de Cristo,* translates as "one cannot live without loving." The accent falls, to borrow C.S. Lewis's distinction, on gift-love rather than need-love. Like the "word known to all men" in Joyce's novel, *no se puede vivir sin amar* recurs at strategic points in the *Volcano.* In the opening chapter Jacques, in conversation with Dr. Vigil, speaks of the maxim as having been inscribed by "that estúpido . . . on my house" (*UV* 6), while in chapter 7 Geoffrey Firmin registers, or half-registers, the inscription in the following manner: "A panel of rough stone, covered with large letters painted in gold leaf, had been slightly set into the wall to give a semblance of bas-relief. These gold letters though very thick were merged together most confusingly. The Consul had noticed visitors to the town staring up at them for half an hour at a time. Sometimes M. Laruelle would come out to explain that they really spelt something, that they formed that phrase of Frey [*sic*] Luis de León's the Consul did not at this moment allow himself to recall" (*UV* 195). Like Stephen, the Consul knows and does not know. Chris Ackerley and Lawrence Clipper's inference (12, 273) that Geoffrey himself has painted the words on Jacques's *zacuali* as a reminder of the latter's adultery with Yvonne seems tenuous. For one thing, the Consul's hand is not steady enough to have accomplished the task; one suspects that the confused merging of the letters has at least as much to do with his drunken perception of them as with their actual appearance. For another, Jacques would hardly place himself in the role of tourist guide if he regarded the inscription as the equivalent of a scarlet letter. And, finally, the maxim bears more on the Consul's own transgressions than it does on anyone else's, which is why he refuses to bring it fully to mind on this occasion, although the words do surface further on in the chapter (*UV* 209).

While Geoffrey may not be the *estúpido* who painted the inscription, he is, plainly enough, the *pelado,* "the pilferer of meaningless muddled ideas" (*UV* 374), who has failed to heed it. He passes that judgment on himself as he lies agonizing outside the Farolito in Parián. The verdict is not, however, necessarily final. Six months earlier, sitting inside this same cantina, he has written in a letter to Yvonne, a letter that remains unposted and that he knows even as he writes it will never be sent: "Love is the only thing which gives meaning to our poor ways on earth: not precisely a discovery, I am afraid" (*UV* 40). Taken in isolation the Consul's insight sounds banal; in context it is heartrending—sufficiently so that he keeps trying to banish it from his consciousness. The narrative rounds the circle when Geoffrey, in the all-but-last moment of his life, imagines "friendly voices around him, Jacques' and Vigil's. . . . 'No se puede vivir sin amar,' they would say, which would explain everything" (*UV* 375). He is, in effect, anticipating the dialogue between his two friends that will take place exactly a year later, the one we have overheard in the first chapter. Word known to all men, *no se puede vivir sin amar*: there is no disputing the pivotal importance of love in the two novels.

Idealist and realist accounts of love have in common a tendency, as Irving Singer points out, to begin with the harsh actualities of isolation, loneliness, and vulnerability. Both strains of thought are evident in Joyce's treatment of Stephen's bereavement, the "pain, that was not yet the pain of love, fret[ting] his heart" (*U* 1.102) as he ruminates on his mother's memory. His suffering stems in part from a thwarting of need-love, a feeling of forlornness at his mother's absence from, or merely spectral presence in, his life. Musing on his pupil Cyril Sargent, whose suscepti- bilities remind Stephen of himself in his Clongowes days, he reflects: "Someone had loved him, borne him in her arms and in her heart. But for her the race of the world would have trampled him underfoot, a squashed boneless snail. She had loved his weak watery blood drained from her own. Was that then real? The only true thing in life?" From which point Stephen's meditation on maternal tenderness and solici- tude glides seamlessly into thoughts of his own mother: " . . . the trem- bling skeleton of a twig burnt in the fire, an odour of rosewood and wetted ashes. She had saved him from being trampled underfoot and had gone, scarcely having been. A poor soul gone to heaven" (*U* 2.140- 47). What we are seeing here is the beginning of a shift away from needi- ness toward gift-love. Stephen's mother has borne and sustained him. How has he repaid the boon? "Silent with pity and awe" at the prospect of her death, he has sung for her Yeats's "Who Goes with Fergus?" with its haunting evocation of "love's bitter mystery" (*U* 1.253). Aside from that he has offered her but scant return.

Stephen feels especially guilty about having refused the request to pray at his mother's deathbed. For him it is a matter of integrity; he has too much respect for the religion he is determined not to serve to make sacrilegious use of its forms. To the materialist Buck Mulligan, his towermate's defiance is absurd: "It's all a mockery and beastly. . . . Humour her till it's over" (*U* 1.210-12). The question is whether, in this instance at least, Stephen's *non serviam* has not entailed unpardonable self-centeredness. Indeed he cannot but wonder whether filial piety might not still demand prayers in his mother's behalf. "Where now?" he asks. Gone to heaven? What assurance can there be of that? Images of burnt twig and wetted ashes torment him. For in spite of his hostility toward the institutional church, he remains a believer in many of its doctrines, including that of the soul and its persistence beyond physical death.[2]

Thumbing through the used books on a huckster's cart, Stephen comes across a manual on "how to win a woman's love. For me this," he recognizes (U 10.847). The young man must lay his mother's ghost, must cease brooding on his role in her death and offer her the truer homage of establishing a family of his own. At the close of "Circe" Bloom hears him murmuring snatches of "Who Goes with Fergus?" and makes an appo-site mental turn: "Face reminds me of his poor mother. . . . Ferguscn, I think I caught. A girl. Some girl. Best thing could happen him" (U 15.4949-51). Stephen still has much work to do in resolving the attachment to his mother, but at least he has some sense of the line he must take if he is to convert the pain "not yet the pain of love" into genuine tenderness and get on with his life.

The death of Geoffrey Firmin's mother while he was still a child, in Kashmir, and the subsequent mystery concerning his father, who one day "had walked up into the Himalayas and vanished" (UV 19), have created a chasm in the protagonist's emotional life.[3] It is an abyss that love alone can fill, and yet the catastrophes that have cost him his par-ents render him so fearful of love that he cannot, for long, accept it when it comes. The Consul's recurrent fantasy of scaling Popocatepetl gener-ally figures as a purgatorial feat, but the peak is also a reminder of his childhood in India and his wish to climb it a veiled recapitulation of his abandonment, with an eye toward either reunion with the father or steel-ing himself to the loss. Popocatepetl is, one should bear in mind, a vol-cano—hollow at its core, but having the potential to fill that void to furious overflowing. In the end Geoffrey imagines the "noise of foisting lava in his ears" (UV 375), and indeed all of the things that have been churning in the depths vent themselves in the final chapter.

His mother's death appears to be the most decisive factor bearing on the Consul's difficulties in love. Everywhere he goes her image rises to meet him. Talking with the kindly cantina proprietress Señora Gregorio, he thinks for a moment he is "looking at his own mother. . . . he wanted to embrace Señora Gregorio, to cry like a child, to hide his face on her bosom" (UV 229). In the Farolito the aspect of a legless beggar changes to Señora Gregorio's and then "in turn to his mother's face, upon which appeared an expression of infinite pity and supplication" (UV 342). Even after his copulation with the prostitute María, "the final stupid unprophylactic rejection" (UV 348) that completes his degradation, Geoffrey hears a voice reassuring him: "My poor little child, you do not feel any of these things really, only lost, only homeless" (UV 354). This is the residue of an unconditional love, longed for and at one time, it seems, actually enjoyed. "Mother's love is bliss, is peace," observes Erich Fromm; "it need not be acquired, it need not be deserved. . . . If it is there, it is like a blessing; if it is not there it is as if all the beauty had gone out of life" (33). And it is this love, of which he has been so early and cruelly deprived, that the Consul continues to seek in one or another form.

The principal surrogate for Geoffrey's mother is, of course, his wife. He has offered prayers to that most compassionate of maternal figures, the Virgin "for those who have nobody with," pleading that Yvonne be returned to him. And yet rather than rejoice when she does come back, he remembers

> all over again as for the first time, how he had suffered, suffered, suffered without her; indeed such desolation, such a desperate sense of abandonment, bereavement, as during this last year without Yvonne, he had never known in his life, unless it was when his mother died. But this present emotion he had never experienced with his mother: this urgent desire to hurt, to provoke, at a time when forgiveness alone could save the day, this, rather, had commenced with his stepmother, so that she would have to cry:—"I can't eat, Geoffrey, the food sticks in my throat!" [UV 197-98]

Geoffrey's unconscious motives appear to be threefold: in the first place, he visits punishment upon the two surrogates on whom he depends most, his stepmother and Yvonne, exacting retribution for what he has experienced as his mother's abandonment of him; secondly, he fears, like Stephen Dedalus, that he is in some obscure manner responsible for his mother's death and therefore unworthy of any substitute for her affection; and thirdly, anticipating that he will lose those he cares about most deeply and unable to tolerate the sense of vulnerability that accompanies this foreboding, he preemptively destroys the relationships that promise him fullest sustenance. "Far too soon," he reflects, his marriage to Yvonne "had begun to seem too much of a triumph, it had been too good, too horribly unimaginable to lose, impossible finally to bear" (UV 201).

If the Consul has fashioned his wife in his mother's image and allowed their marriage to rehearse the disasters of his childhood, then Yvonne is the perfect collaborator, mirroring his key moves. Her mother too died while she was very young, leaving her in the custody of her father, an impractical dreamer and former army officer who imagines that he has been cashiered and uses that as an excuse for drinking. Yvonne's father ends his career, such as it has been, as American consul to Iquique, Chile. Little wonder, then, that she sees in the face of her husband "that brooding expression of her father's" (UV 259). (Yvonne and Geoffrey are, plainly, in the hands of a firm believer in correspondences.[4]) The Consul's relation to his wife seems almost wholly a matter of need. He wishes to be "loved for [his] reckless and irresponsible appearance" (*UV* 129), to be accepted and cherished, that is, without conditions, in the way he supposes his mother has loved him. Yvonne's relation to him, on the other hand, appears to entail substantial gift-love but is, at bottom, the sort of codependency (see MacGregor) into which she has been all too thoroughly initiated while ministering to her father.

The choice of a mate based on ties, for the most part unconscious, to one's actual parents is evident in the *Volcano* in a way that it is not in *Ulysses*. It seems strange to say, but just as the realist Freud may be our best guide to the fundamental affinity between the cabalistic Geoffrey and the star-gazing starlet Yvonne, so the idealist Jung can help us to understand the primary bond between the commonsensical Leopold and the earthy Molly. "Every man carries within him the eternal image of woman," remarks Jung, "not the image of this or that particular woman, . . . [but] an imprint or 'archetype' of all the ancestral experiences of the female, a deposit, as it were, of all the impressions ever made by woman. . . . The same is true of the woman: she too has an inborn image of man. Actually, we know from experience that it would be more accurate to describe it as an image of *men*, whereas in the case of the man it is rather the image of *woman*" (173).

Molly remembers that "the first night ever [she and Leopold] met . . . we stood staring at one another for about 10 minutes as if we met somewhere I suppose on account of my being jewess looking after my mother" (*U* 18.1182-85).[5] She may well be right about the resonance her dark complexion has for him, but the novel establishes no significant connection between Molly and Bloom's mother, Ellen, who appears only fleetingly in his thoughts. Molly's experience of being transfixed at her initial meeting with Bloom and her sense of their having unaccountable prior knowledge of one another are unmistakable marks of an encounter between, in Jung's terms, anima and animus.[6] Sixteen years after the fact she is still excited by the recollection of "his mad crazy letters my Precious one everything connected with your glorious Body everything underlined that comes from it is a thing of beauty and of joy for ever something he got out of some nonsensical book that he had me always at myself 4 and 5 times a day sometimes" (*U* 18.1176-79). Bloom, "kinetic poet" (*U* 17.410), has his own tender remembrance of having sent Molly, on February 14, 1888, an acrostic ("P-O-L-D-Y") valentine that concludes:

> *Dearer far than song or wine.*
> *You are mine. The world is mine.*
> [*U* 17.415-16]

"There's destiny in it, falling in love" (*U* 13.973), acknowledges Bloom.[7] The decisive memory of passion for both Leopold and Molly is the radiant day in that same year when, among the rhododendrons on Howth Head, they became engaged. Here is the way he recalls the occasion:

> Pillowed on my coat she had her hair, earwigs in the heather scrub my hand under her nape, you'll toss me all. O wonder! Coolsoft with ointments her hand touched me, caressed: her eyes upon me did not turn away. Ravished over her I lay, full lips full open, kissed her mouth. Yum. Softly she gave me in my mouth the seedcake warm and chewed. Mawkish pulp her mouth had mumbled sweetsour of her spittle. Joy: I ate it: joy. Young life, her lips that gave me pouting. Soft warm sticky gumjelly lips. Flowers her eyes were, take me, willing eyes. . . . Hot I tongued her. She kissed me. I was kissed. All yielding she tossed my hair. Kissed, she kissed me. [*U* 8.903-16]

The passage occurs in "Lestrygonians," shortly after Bloom's gorge has risen at the sight and sound of the luncheon crowd in the Burton restaurant. Would that gift of prechewed seedcake have occasioned anything akin to joy had it come from someone he did not love? Placed in apposition to the seedcake incident, Bloom's phrase about everything that comes from Molly's body being "a thing of beauty and of joy" no longer seems nonsensical; his words may or may not be of intertextual origin, as she supposes, but there is no reason to regard them as any less heartfelt than the Poldy valentine.

Whatever the ontological status of lovers might seem to a detached observer, it feels to the couple themselves as though they had, in Robert Nozick's words, "united to form and constitute a new entity in the world, what might be called a *we*" (70). As the recollected exchange of lingual kisses indicates, Leopold and Molly have breached one another's boundaries in ways that make their identities, for better or worse, inextricable. That she feels this to be the case as surely as he does is clear from the closing pages of *Ulysses;* her mind moves from thoughts of nature and divinity to that same courtship memory, which forms the tonic chord of her soliloquy and thus of the entire novel:

> the sun shines for you he said the day we were lying among the rhododendrons on Howth head . . . the day I got him to propose to me yes first I gave him the bit of seedcake out of my mouth and it was leapyear like now yes 16 years ago my God after that long kiss I near lost my breath yes he said I was a flower of the mountain yes so we are flowers all a womans body yes that was one true thing he said in his life and the sun shines for you today yes that was why I liked him because I saw he understood or felt what a woman is and I knew I could always get round him and I gave him all the

pleasure I could leading him on till he asked me to say yes and I wouldnt answer first only looked out over the sea and the sky I was thinking of so many things he didnt know of . . . Gibraltar as a girl where I was a Flower of the mountain yes . . . and how he kissed me under the Moorish wall and I thought well as well him as another and then I asked him with my eyes to ask again yes . . . and his heart was going like mad and yes I said yes I will Yes. [U 18.1571-1609]

However much or little general truth resides in Jung's observation about each woman's having an image of *men* rather than *man* amid her hoard of archetypes, it is germane to Molly's case. The antecedents of her pronouns are characteristically vague, but the context makes it clear that Bloom is not the one doing the kissing under the Moorish wall—there *are* no Moorish walls on Howth Head, nor anywhere else in Ireland— but rather her first beau, Mulvey. Molly conflates Mulvey, Bloom, and the other men in her life into a single composite image.[8] "As well him as another" appears to betoken indifference to Bloom's singularity, and indeed it makes no great difference to Molly which man acknowledges her "a flower of the mountain." But the one with whom she is going to spend her life must be, at a minimum, capable of that recognition. And who better than a Bloom to appreciate such blossoming? It is not a job for Blazes Boylan, an "ignoramus that doesnt know poetry from a cabbage" (U 18.1370-71), or any of his ilk. Her husband is no hero to her, but she does understand that Bloom is "not one of your common or garden" (U 10.581-82) variety, as Lenehan has put it, that he stands well above the ordinary cut of Dubliner. Indeed she is prepared to take his part against such folk: "Theyre not going to get my husband again into their clutches if I can help it making fun of him . . . because he has sense enough not to squander every penny piece he earns down their gullets and looks after his wife and family" (U 18.1275-79). All is far from well with the Blooms' marriage, but for Leopold and Molly alike what has transpired on Howth Head remains crucial, both as a benchmark against which the measure of present discontents can be taken and as a source of solace in difficult times: at one stage in their lives, at least, they were romantic lovers, and the memory has not dimmed.[9]

Memories of their early days together remain vivid for the Firmins as well, but far from serving as a repository of strength, instead these recollections are a source of torment. "Most of us fall in love well advanced in our development," observes Robert Solomon, "when the self is full-formed. . . . The development of love is consequently defined by a *dialectic*, often tender but sometimes ontologically vicious, in which each lover struggles for control over shared and reciprocal self-images, resists

them, revises them, rejects them" (513). In the unposted letter to his wife
or, more accurately, ex-wife—he has just received news of their divorce—
the Consul laments:

> oh, Yvonne, I am so haunted continuously by . . . the sweet beginnings of our
> marriage. Do you remember the Strauss song we used to sing? Once a year
> the dead live for one day. Oh come to me again as once in May. The Generalife
> Gardens and the Alhambra Gardens. And shadows of our fate at our meet-
> ing in Spain. The Hollywood bar in Granada. Why Hollywood? And the
> nunnery there: why Los Angeles? And in Malaga, the Pensión México. And
> yet nothing can ever take the place of the unity we once knew and which
> Christ alone knows must still exist somewhere. . . . do we not owe it to
> ourselves, to that self we created, apart from us, to try again? [*UV* 39-40]

That "self" their passion has constituted seems to have a life of its own
and, at the same time, to crave their continuing solicitude: "It was as
though their love were wandering over some desolate cactus plain, far
from here, lost, stumbling and falling, attacked by wild beasts, calling
for help" (*UV* 49). The image brings to mind nothing so much as an
abandoned child.

Yvonne conceives of the frayed bond between them in similar terms.
In one of the letters written after her departure from Quauhnahuac—
letters that Geoffrey has mislaid and that are returned to him in the hour
before his death—she inquires plaintively: "Surely you must have
thought a great deal of *us,* of what we built together, of how mindlessly
we destroyed the structure and the beauty but yet could not destroy the
memory of that beauty. It has been this which has haunted me day and
night. . . . My heart has the taste of ashes, and my throat is tight and
weary with weeping. What is a lost soul? It is one that has turned from
its true path and is groping in the darkness of remembered ways—"
(*UV* 345-46). What has she been reading, the Consul wonders, the correspondence of Héloïse and Abélard?[10] As with Molly's doubts about the
originality of Bloom's florid phrases, Geoffrey's question really concerns
the authenticity of the sentiment being expressed. "Yvonne had certainly
been reading *something*" (*UV* 346), he concludes. Whether the intensity
of her love for the Consul is all she claims it to be is, of course, debatable.
The instances of adultery with his brother, Hugh, and his oldest friend,
Jacques Laruelle, to cite only the most salient defects, cast shadows. Still,
it is evident that Geoffrey's and Yvonne's souls *are* profoundly entwined
with each other, much as Catherine's and Heathcliff's are in *Wuthering
Heights.* If Yvonne were truly inclined to literary borrowing, the words
she could most readily appropriate are Catherine's concerning her relation to her beloved: "He's always, always in my mind—not as a plea-

sure, any more than I am always a pleasure to myself—but as my own being" (Brontë 74).

Exhausting to sustain and impossible to relinquish, Geoffrey and Yvonne's love tends at times to migrate outward from the tumult of their lives and look for sanctuary in the hills. To Geoffrey's mind the volcanoes Popocatepetl and Ixtaccihuatl, which bear the names of a native prince and princess, constitute an "image of the perfect marriage" (*UV* 93). The beauty of the Indian couple's legend consists in their faithfulness unto death and beyond; its horror resides in their being able to consummate their passion only in a version of *Liebestod*. At moments an analogous "mountain peace" seems to fall between the Consul and Yvonne; unfortunately "it was false, it was a lie" (*UV* 64). For Yvonne a photo of La Despedida, a glacial rock in the Sierra Madre rent by forest fires, becomes an emblem of Aristophanic disjunction: "Oh, but why— by some fanciful geologic thaumaturgy, couldn't the pieces be welded together again! She longed to heal the cleft rock. She was one of the rocks and she yearned to save the other, that both might be saved. By a superlapidary effort she moved herself nearer it, poured out her pleas, her passionate tears, told all her forgiveness: the other rock stood unmoved. 'That's all very well,' it said, 'but it happens to be your fault, and as for myself, I propose to disintegrate as I please!'" (*UV* 55). Lowry's mastery of tone in this passage is superb. As Yvonne's fervent whimsy tips into bathos, it is undercut still further by the Consul's truculent irony.[11] One would be hard pressed to find a clearer instance of Robert Solomon's dialectical struggle over the control of images. Which half of the couple is more to blame for the failure of their love seems immaterial, for the fault is "geologic," inherent in the very grain of their being-in-the-world, and hence irreparable.

"Satisfying sexual intercourse in marriage takes place only for a few years," declares Freud in his essay "'Civilized' Sexual Morality and Modern Nervous Illness": "Fear of the consequences of sexual intercourse first brings the married couple's physical affection to an end; and then, as a remoter result, it usually puts a stop as well to the mental sympathy between them, which should have been a successor to their original passionate love" (9:194). Those consequences that arouse anxiety are, obviously enough, the physical risk to the woman of pregnancy and childbirth, the possibility of having an unhealthy baby or of losing the child altogether, the practical implications of bringing a new being into the world who will have to be protected, fed, and educated, and the psychological adaptations required of what had been at the outset a community of just two.

The Blooms' sexual failure, their nearly eleven-year abstinence from full coition, centers not on any initial reluctance on the part of either

Leopold or Molly to having children, which both of them regard as the proper issue of married life. Concerning the love between men and women and its natural consequence, Bloom reflects: "As God made them he matched them. . . . Twice nought makes one" (*U* 13.976-77).[12] His natural piety with regard to generation is apparent in the solicitude for Mina Purefoy that takes him to the Holles Street lying-in hospital, where she is in her third day of labor. There he aligns himself, in the face of the medical students' derision, with Stephen Dedalus's defense of nascent life. "For, sirs," declares Stephen, "our lust is brief. We are means to those small creatures within us and nature has other ends than we" (*U* 14.227-28). Lust may be brief, but love is, or should be, long, with children constituting "an incarnation in the world of the valuable extended self" created by the parents' affection (Nozick 85).[13]

Plainly Bloom sees in his daughter, Milly, an outgrowth of his wife's nature: "Molly. Milly. Same thing watered down. Her tomboy oaths. O jumping Jupiter! Ye gods and little fishes! Still, she's a dear girl. Soon be a woman" (*U* 6.87-89). He worries about her being on her own, working in a photography studio in Mullingar. At fifteen Milly already evinces many of her mother's charms, and her father is concerned about the uses to which they are being put. He ponders paying her a surprise visit, but reconsiders: "She mightn't like me to come that way without letting her know. Must be careful about women. Catch them once with their pants down. Never forgive you after" (*U* 6.482-84). Depending on one's point of view, Bloom is either wonderfully mature in reining in his misgivings and coming to terms with Milly's growing independence or he has been all too thoroughly initiated by Molly into the perils of crossing the female will. In any case, his affection for his daughter seems genuine, if not especially deep.

One of Bloom's most tender—and, at the same time, sensual—recollections centers on the moment of his son's conception: "Must have been that morning in Raymond terrace [Molly] was at the window watching the two dogs at it by the wall of the cease to do evil. . . . She had that cream gown on with the rip she never stitched. Give us a touch, Poldy. God, I'm dying for it. How life begins" (*U* 6.77-81). Unfortunately the memory is also shot through with melancholy and regret, for their son, Rudy, has died in infancy. In "Hades," witnessing a child's coffin flash past, Bloom muses: "A dwarf's face, mauve and wrinkled like little Rudy's was. . . . Our. Little. Beggar. Baby. Meant nothing. Mistake of nature. If it's healthy it's from the mother. If not from the man" (*U* 6.326-29). Don Gifford and Robert J. Seidman claim that Bloom's sense of responsibility for Rudy's death stems from an "ancient Jewish belief that the health of a child is a reflection on the virility of the male" (111). Whatever the source of the belief, Molly appears to subscribe to it—without, however, holding her husband specifically accountable for their son's frailty. After ruminating on her assignation with Boylan and on Mina Purefoy's parturition, she goes on to think: "Supposing I risked having another not off him though still if he was married Im sure hed have a fine strong child but I dont know Poldy has more spunk in him" (*U* 18.166-68). It is evident that she would like to have another baby, that she is acutely conscious of the biological hazard entailed and wonders which possible father would minimize it, and that the balance tilts in her husband's favor. Her recollection a few lines earlier (18.154) of the disappointing amount of "spunk" Boylan has ejaculated on her belly that afternoon indicates that the term refers primarily to semen, although a comparison of the two men's pluck and vitality is almost surely implied as well. Bloom too considers whether he and Molly might try again: "Last of my race. . . . No son. Rudy. Too late now. Or if not? If not? If still? . . . Soon I am old" (*U* 11.1066-69).[14] The truth is that Rudy's death has left them both very much afraid of offering fortune any additional hostages (see Hall 588) and that there is little likelihood of their resuming full genital intimacy—"I knew well Id never have another," recalls Molly; "we were never the same since" (*U* 18.1449-50)—although they can still enjoy moments of mental sympathy such as their correspondent memories of Howth Head.

There is an infant's funeral in the *Volcano* as well. As the Firmins head homeward from the Hotel Bella Vista in chapter 2, a cortège comes "sailing out of nowhere, . . . the tiny lace-covered coffin followed by the band: two saxophones, bass guitar, a fiddle, playing of all things 'La Cucaracha,' the women behind, very solemn" (*UV* 56-57). The spectacle is especially poignant for Yvonne, who has lost a child, aged six months, by her first husband—a child "strangely named Geoffrey too" (*UV* 72), or perhaps not so strangely in a novel ruled by coincidences. In one of her letters, recovered in the Farolito, she asks the Consul: "Why did we postpone it? Is it too late? I want your children, soon, at once, I want them. I want your life filling and stirring me. I want your happiness beneath my heart" (*UV* 346). Unfortunately it seems that the Firmins' love can speak in such tones, the idiom of fusion, only when they are at a distance from one another, only in letters. When they are face to face, their hearts contract. As his response to the youthful panhandlers at the Quauhnahuac fair demonstrates, Geoffrey is at moments susceptible to the charm of children: "Yvonne and he should have had children, would have had children, could have had children, should have . . ." (*UV* 223). That string of subjunctives, tailing off into an ellipsis, indicates just how remote the possibility has been. In the quarrel that takes place in the

Salón Ofélia, just prior to their final parting, the Consul plumbs the depths of his capacity for cruelty: "What have you ever done for anyone but yourself," he charges Yvonne. "Where are the children I might have wanted? You may suppose I might have wanted them. Drowned. To the accompaniment of the rattling of a thousand douche bags" (*UV* 313). How should she have *supposed* that he *might* have wanted children? Has he ever said so when it would have made a difference? Yvonne might, in any case, have had second thoughts about the parenting talents of someone as self-absorbed as Geoffrey, someone in need of a mother himself.

The Consul's one attempt, in chapter 3, to make love to the wife who has come back to him after a year's separation fails. There are a number of possible explanations for his impotence, but perhaps all of them come down to what one might call his Manichaeism, a worldview that, as Denis de Rougement puts it, "holds the fact of being alive in the body to be the absolute woe, the woe embracing all other woes; [while] death it holds to be the *ultimate* good, whereby the sin of birth is redeemed" (69). If one of the leitmotifs of *Ulysses* is the wish to be touched, then the contrapuntal motif in the *Volcano* is Geoffrey's recoil from the corporeal and, more particularly, from the sexual. He describes Jacques Laruelle's penis as "that hideously elongated cucumiform bundle of blue nerves and gills," and he reduces, synecdochically, Yvonne's lovers as a class to "ninneyhammers with gills like codfish and veins like racehorses" (*UV* 207, 313). And he looks in no more kindly fashion upon his own "crucified evil organ" (*UV* 349). Incapable of coitus with his wife, he is one who "only develops full potency when he is with a debased sexual object" (Freud, "On the Universal Tendency to Debasement in the Sphere of Love," 11:185). The specific roots of Geoffrey's puritanism would appear to be his Wesleyan schooling and the scant affection he received early in life. Whatever the source, it is clear that his attitude not only prevents him from enjoying intercourse but makes the experience of it downright distressing. As he penetrates the harlot María, he thinks, "Out of this suffering something must be born, and what would be born was his own death" (*UV* 349). It is that birth into death—out of the world of embodied selves and into another, more lustrous, one—that he ultimately craves. "Where is love?" he asks in one of his prayers to the Virgin. "Give me back my purity, the knowledge of the Mysteries, that I have betrayed and lost. . . . Let [Yvonne and me] be happy again somewhere, if it's only together, if it's only out of this terrible world" (*UV* 289).

One of the fundamental differences between Joyce's and Lowry's protagonists resides precisely in their attitudes toward death. For Geoffrey Firmin mortality holds no particular terror—none, at any rate, worse than those that are already his daily fare. For some time he has

been courting the finale that awaits him in the Farolito, with whose essence his soul has become so deeply invested that, given the prospect of
drinking there, he is "gripped by thoughts like those of the mariner who,
sighting the faint beacon of Start Point after a long voyage, knows that
soon he will embrace his wife. . . . Could one be faithful to Yvonne and
the Farolito both?" (*UV* 201). Clearly one cannot.[15] Geoffrey has become
the bridegroom of hell. The reader must grasp the fact that this was not
always so, that the Consul as we see him on November 2, 1938, has suffered a long descent. Nothing indicates the extent of his fall more acutely
than the persistent affection and loyalty of those he has wounded, not
just Yvonne but Hugh and Jacques as well. Toward his younger half-
brother he has acted, when the two of them were orphaned, as a father,
and indeed Hugh—who now seeks to reverse their roles and come to
the aid of "this man of abnormal strength and constitution and obscure
ambition, whom Hugh would never know, could never deliver nor make
agreement to God for, but in his way loved" (*UV* 184)—refers to him as
"Papa" (*UV* 117). During their adolescent years Jacques has stood in
awe of Geoffrey, and in chapter 1 he continues to testify, after his friend's
death, to his stature: "He was an extremely brave man, no less than a
hero in fact, who had won, for conspicuous gallantry in the service of his
country during the last war, a coveted medal. Nor with all his faults was
he at bottom a vicious man. Without knowing quite why M. Laruelle felt
he might have actually proved a great force for good" (*UV* 31).

Hugh's and Jacques's liaisons with Yvonne seem less betrayals of
the Consul than oblique attempts to connect with a man they love but
whose character remains an enigma to them, and the same is true for
her: "Through Jacques she had been mysteriously able to reach, in a sense
to avail herself of, what she had never known, the Consul's innocence"
(*UV* 264). Nor is it only figures who have become involved with Geoffrey
in better times who remain true to him. Señora Gregorio, the old fiddler
who whispers the word "compañero" in his ear outside the Farolito, the
Tarascan woman with the chicken and the dominoes, and the kindly Dr.
Vigil are all latter-day friends who respond to those vestiges of charisma
the Consul retains till the very end.[16]

Death holds no allure for Bloom, the down-to-earth naturalist, but
rather it spurs him on to make the most of this world: "Plenty to see and
hear and feel yet," he muses among the tombstones in Glasnevin cemetery. "Feel live warm beings near you. Let them sleep in their maggoty
beds. They are not going to get me this innings. Warm beds: warm
fullblooded life" (*U* 6.1003-5). It is no accident that many of his pithiest
meditations on love, especially the love that binds one generation to
another, occur in "Hades." That is the episode in which Stephen crosses

his path for the first time on June 16, 1904. "Your son and heir" (*U* 6.43),
remarks Bloom, pointing Stephen out to Simon Dedalus. "Full of his
son," he thinks regarding the latter. "He is right. Something to hand on"
(*U* 6.74-75). More than anything else, it is the absence of a son and heir
that draws Bloom to Stephen, a response that reflects not so much the
older man's own sense of lack as the fact that he truly does have qualities worth handing on.

The Stephen that Bloom encounters at the maternity hospital and
pursues into nighttown is not, after his drinking bout with the medical
students, competent to handle his own affairs. "What am I following
him for?" asks Bloom. "Still, he's the best of that lot. If I hadn't heard
about Mrs Beaufoy Purefoy I wouldn't have gone and wouldn't have
met. Kismet" (*U* 15.639-41). Clearly he regards the meeting with Stephen
as more than a chance matter, as the good karma accrued, perhaps,
through his concern for Mina Purefoy (whose name he confuses, in typical middle-aged fashion, with that of Philip Beaufoy, author of the prize
story he has read that morning). He is able to look beyond Stephen's
present condition and intuit the worth of the young man's gifts, intellectual and other. There is no doubt that Bloom's ministrations in Bella
Cohen's brothel and during the subsequent contretemps with the British soldiers and the Dublin watch serve Stephen well. The decision to
take him back to 7 Eccles Street—Stephen, having relinquished the key
to the Martello and resolved not to return there, is in effect homeless—
appears to proceed from the same paternal impulse. As Bloom lights the
stove preparatory to making cocoa for his guest, Stephen does in fact
associate him with other nurturing figures—parents, teachers, his aunt,
his godmother—"who, kneeling on one knee or on two, had kindled
fires for him" (*U* 17.135-36).

And yet Bloom's taking the young man home with him is not so
altogether charitable an act as it first seems, for in the back of his mind is
the possibility that Stephen might displace Blazes Boylan in Molly's affec-
tions or that a permanent bond might eventuate between Stephen and
Milly, a "reconciliatory union between a schoolfellow and a jew's daughter,"
or, for that matter, both: "Because the way to daughter led through mother,
the way to mother through daughter" (*U* 17.942-44). While it is a father's
good right to imagine a young man he sees as "far and away the pick of
the bunch" (*U* 16.1477-78) as a future son-in-law, Bloom's readiness to
lay down this same young friend for his wife (cf. *U* 14.361) is, to say the
least, a dubious matter. Stephen himself has asked, in connection with
Shakespeare's *Pericles*, "Will any man love the daughter if he has not
loved the mother?" (*U* 9.423-24), but presumably without intending an
element of fleshly desire so far as the mother was concerned. There is

nothing to suggest that he is being anything more than polite when, in "Eumaeus," he calls the picture of Molly that Bloom shows him "handsome" (*U* 16.1479)—hardly the word a young man would use with regard to a woman he found erotically appealing. Apart from the offer of a bed for the night, which Stephen declines, and some tentative proposals for future meetings, Bloom does nothing to press his project. He may be, outwardly, a complaisant husband, but if he is a pander he is so only in mind. And even there his envisioning a romantic tie between Stephen and Molly—she is only too receptive to the idea, imagining herself the young poet's muse—is a roundabout way of bridging the gulf that has opened between himself and his wife since their son's death, and in that respect it is comparable to Hugh's and Jacques's affairs with Yvonne.

> *Nel mezzo del cammin di nostra vita*
> *mi ritrovai per una selva oscura . . .*

Stephen Dedalus quotes the first verse of the *Inferno* verbatim (*U* 9.831), while Geoffrey and Hugh Firmin offer fractured versions of the opening lines. In the middle of their life journeys, Leopold and Molly, Geoffrey and Yvonne, Stephen, Hugh, and Jacques find themselves in a dark wood through which love alone can light the way. They discern well enough what it is—word known to all men, *no se puede vivir sin amar*—that undergirds the meaning of their lives, indeed of the common life. And yet, flawed as the protagonists are, drawn onward by blemished Beatrices and piloted by not very effectual Virgils, they encounter excruciating— and in the case of Lowry's hero, insurmountable—difficulties in their attempts to realize its promise. It is no "heavengrot" (*U* 17.1139) they traverse but a world that, broken, can well break hearts. Although the elements of that world are not, or at least not obviously, *legato con amore in un volume* (*Paradiso* 33.86), as they are in Dante, the authors of *Ulysses* and *Under the Volcano* must have glimpsed such a realm, for—the signs are unmistakable—Joyce and Lowry have bound the leaves of their books together with love, "the word that shall not pass away" (*U* 14.293-94).

Notes

1. Much as such issues exercise Joyce scholars, it is hard to disagree with Jean Kimball's contention that "the 'love passage,' however we see it, is not likely to change significantly our conflicting notions of what the text of Joyce's *Ulysses* says, let alone what it means" ("Love in the Kidd Era," 376). Which is

not to say that it makes no difference at all whether or not the passage appears in "Scylla and Charybdis." In fact Kimball makes a strong case for its inclusion. See also Kimball's earlier article "Love and Death in *Ulysses*," especially pp. 143-47, and Gordon 241-43, 246. The scholar who has done the most to establish the centrality of love in Joyce's life and art is, of course, Richard Ellmann. For his identification, *avant* Gabler, of love as the "word known to all men," see *Ulysses on the Liffey*, 147.

2. Discussing the soul with Bloom, who is given to positivism, Stephen declares: "They tell me on the best authority it is a simple substance and there-fore incorruptible. It would be immortal, I understand, but for the possibility of its annihilation by its First Cause Who, from all I can hear, is quite capable of adding that to the number of His other practical jokes" (*U* 16.756-59). That which he mocks, Stephen still in one way or another serves.

3. The mystery of the Consul's father, who "had simply, yet scandalously, disappeared" (*UV* 19), finds a parallel in *Ulysses* in the dishonor Bloom suffers in the eyes of his fellow Dubliners as the son of a Hungarian Jew who has com-mitted suicide. The circumstances are, of course, quite different. Rudolph Virag takes aconite after his wife's death because he cannot endure the loneliness; as an adult—rather than a vulnerable child as Geoffrey had been—Leopold, while he is sad, has no great difficulty in accepting his father's act.

4. For a suggestive analysis of the nature and function of correspondences in the *Volcano*, see the chapter on the Law of Series in McCarthy (44-66).

5. Contrary to Stephen's belief in *amor matris* as the bedrock of human expe-rience, the story of Molly's ties to her mother, Lunita Laredo, is among the most problematic features of Joyce's narrative (see Quick).

6. "There are certain types of women who seem made by nature to attract anima projections," declares Jung. "A woman of this kind is both old and young, mother and daughter, of more than doubtful chastity, childlike, and yet endowed with a naive cunning that is extremely disarming to men. . . . The animus must be a master not so much of fine ideas as of fine words. . . . He must also belong to the 'misunderstood' class, or be in some way at odds with his environment, so that the idea of self-sacrifice can insinuate itself. He must be a rather ques-tionable hero, a man with possibilities" (174-75).

7. Bloom's homage to kismet is all the more telling in that it occurs at the point in "Nausicaa" where he acknowledges the chance character of his en-counter with Gerty MacDowell and the unlikelihood of its being repeated.

8. Joseph Boone argues, plausibly, that by "interchanging fantasies about men for her private erotic gain, Molly becomes, within the realm of her imagi-nation, an acting subject, not merely a passive object whose existence is entirely dependent on male approval" (217). See Unkeless (especially pp. 164-65) for a thoughtful discussion of Joyce's mythologizing and demythologizing of Molly, particularly in the closing pages of her monologue.

9. Irving Singer observes that "there can be a feeling that just in staying together, standing by each other despite everything that impinges on them, the couple are jointly validating their romance and still experiencing the vestiges of it" (*The Pursuit of Love*, 161).

10. One can indeed imagine elements in Yvonne's letters, or for that matter in Geoffrey's own, deriving from the Héloïse/Abélard correspondence. Consider the following passage from one of Héloïse's missives: "Oh! think of me; do not forget me; remember my love, my fidelity, my constancy; love me as your mistress, cherish me as your child, your sister, your wife. Consider that I still love you, and yet strive to avoid loving you. What a word, what a design is this! I shake with horror, and my heart revolts against what I say" (Solomon and Higgins 53).

Joyce rings a comic variation on the question of originality when Martha Clifford, with whom Bloom is conducting an epistolary flirtation, sends a letter full of lapses (e.g., "my patience are exhausted"). "Wonder did she wrote it herself" (U 5.254, 268-69), he speculates.

11. "'Superlapidary' is plainly substituted for 'superhuman' here," notes Victor Sage, "and the bathetic effect inevitably satirises the self-dramatising quality of Yvonne's fantasy. But who speaks?" (42). The idiom in the passage is surely not her own. Lowry, as stylistic thaumaturge, has transmuted her thoughts in a manner that at once heightens Yvonne's emotion and calls it into question.

12. Walking along Sandymount strand earlier in the day, Stephen has employed the same formula with reference to parturition: "A misbirth with a trailing navelcord, hushed in ruddy wool. . . . Aleph, alpha: nought, nought, one" (U 3.36-39). (This is "Kinch" Dedalus attempting to place an imaginary long-distance call to our first parents in "Edenville.")

13. Cf. Schopenhauer's claim in The World as Will and Idea that "the growing inclination of two lovers is really already the will to live of the new individual which they can and desire to produce. . . . They feel the longing for an actual union and fusing together into a single being, in order to live on only as this; and this longing receives its fulfillment in the child which is produced by them, as that in which the qualities transmitted by them both, fused and united in one being, live on" (Solomon and Higgins 125).

14. See Henke 113 on the relation between Bloom's attitudes toward his dead father and son and his own generative capabilities.

15. "Yvonne and the cantina, love and alcohol, are so entangled," observes Sue Vice, "that he cannot have one without the other; and since it is Yvonne who objects to having a rival, it seems that she must be renounced. . . . Drink has the limitlessness of desire, the only end-point of both being death—which drink at once desires and conveniently effects" (95).

16. On the importance of the minor characters in establishing the reader's sympathy for Geoffrey, see Bareham 52-54 and Binns 32.

Works Cited

Abélard, Peter, and Héloïse. Letters. In The Philosophy of (Erotic) Love, edited by Robert C. Solomon and Kathleen M. Higgins. Lawrence: Univ. Press of Kansas, 1991.

Ackerley, Chris, and Lawrence J. Clipper. A Companion to "Under the Volcano." Vancouver: Univ. of British Columbia Press, 1984.

Bareham, Tony. *Malcolm Lowry.* New York: St. Martin's, 1989.

Binns, Ronald. *Malcolm Lowry.* London: Methuen, 1984.

Boone, Joseph A. "Staging Sexuality: Repression, Representation, and 'Interior' States in *Ulysses.*" In *Joyce: The Return of the Repressed,* edited by Susan Stanford Friedman. Ithaca: Cornell Univ. Press, 1993.

Brontë, Emily. *Wuthering Heights,* edited by William M. Sale Jr. and Richard J. Dunn. New York: Norton, 1993.

Dante Alighieri. *The Divine Comedy,* translated by Charles Singleton. Bollingen Series LXXX. 6 vols. Princeton: Princeton Univ. Press, 1970-75.

Ellmann, Richard. *Ulysses on the Liffey.* New York: Oxford Univ. Press, 1972.

Freud, Sigmund. *The Standard Edition of the Complete Psychological Works of Sigmund Freud,* edited by James Strachey et al. 24 vols. London: Hogarth, 1953-74.

Fromm, Erich. *The Art of Loving.* New York: Harper, 1956.

Gifford, Don, and Robert J. Seidman. *"Ulysses" Annotated.* 2d ed. Berkeley and Los Angeles: Univ. of California Press, 1988.

Gordon, John. "Love in Bloom, by Stephen Dedalus." *James Joyce Quarterly* 27 (1990): 241-55.

Hall, Gail. "'Plots and Plans': Molly Bloom's Fiction." *Massachusetts Review* 31 (1990): 582-98.

Henke, Suzette A. *James Joyce and the Politics of Desire.* London: Routledge, 1990.

Jung, Carl Gustav. "Marriage as a Psychological Relationship." In *The Portable Jung,* edited by Joseph Campbell, translated by R.F.C. Hull. New York: Viking, 1971.

Kimball, Jean. "Love and Death in *Ulysses:* 'Word known to all men.'" *James Joyce Quarterly* 24 (1987): 143-60.

———. "Love in the Kidd Era: An Afterword." *James Joyce Quarterly* 29 (1992): 369-77.

Lewis, C.S. *The Four Loves.* New York: Harcourt, 1960.

MacGregor, Catherine. "Conspiring with the Addict: Yvonne's Co-Dependency in *Under the Volcano.*" *Mosaic* 24 (1991): 145-62.

McCarthy, Patrick A. *Forests of Symbols: World, Text, and Self in Malcolm Lowry's Fiction.* Athens: Univ. of Georgia Press, 1994.

Nozick, Robert. *The Examined Life: Philosophical Meditations.* New York: Simon and Schuster, 1989.

Plato. *The Symposium,* translated by Walter Hamilton. Harmondsworth, England: Penguin, 1951.

Quick, Jonathan. "Molly Bloom's Mother." *ELH* 57 (1990): 223-40.

Rougement, Denis de. *Love in the Western World.* Rev. ed., translated by Montgomery Belgion. New York: Pantheon, 1956.

Sage, Victor. "The Art of Sinking in Prose: Charles Jackson, Joyce and *Under the Volcano.*" In *Malcolm Lowry Eighty Years On,* edited by Sue Vice. New York: St. Martin's, 1989.

Singer, Irving. *The Nature of Love.* 3 vols. Chicago and London: Univ. of Chicago Press, 1984-87.

————. *The Pursuit of Love*. Baltimore: Johns Hopkins Univ. Press, 1994.

Solomon, Robert C. "The Virtue of (Erotic) Love." In *The Philosophy of (Erotic) Love*, edited by Robert C. Solomon and Kathleen M. Higgins. Lawrence: Univ. Press of Kansas, 1991.

————, and Kathleen M. Higgins, eds. *The Philosophy of (Erotic) Love*. Lawrence: Univ. Press of Kansas, 1991.

Unkeless, Elaine. "The Conventional Molly Bloom." In *Women in Joyce*, edited by Suzette Henke and Elaine Unkeless. Urbana: Univ. of Illinois Press, 1982.

Vice, Sue. "Fear of Perfection, Love of Death and the Bottle." In *Malcolm Lowry Eighty Years On*, edited by Sue Vice. New York: St. Martin's, 1989.

five

Nationalism at the Bar: Anti-Semitism in *Ulysses* and *Under the Volcano*

Brian W. Shaffer

> The barbarian is . . . not only at our gates; he is always within the walls of our civilization, inside our minds and our hearts. In times of storm and stress within any society, his appeal is very strong. He offers immediate satisfaction of the simple instincts, love, hatred, and anger. He offers to help us to forget our own unhappiness by making other people still more unhappy. He shows us how we may forget our sense of frustration and the intolerable burden of responsibility in blind obedience. . . . He gives us the simple satisfaction of violence and destruction, the destruction of society. . . .
> —Leonard Woolf, *Barbarians Within and Without* (1939)

Readers of Joyce and Lowry have for years explored structural, stylistic, linguistic, and even thematic links between the two writers' works, and especially between *Ulysses* and *Under the Volcano*, citing Lowry's use of Joyce's allusive method, interior monologue narration, and "spatial form." Interestingly, one significant and neglected point of intersection between *Ulysses* and *Under the Volcano* is that both novels represent and worry, anticipate or reflect, blatant acts or sentiments of anti-Semitism. More specifically, both novels critique anti-Semitic behavior as a phenomenon inextricably bound up with bogus nationalism and heavy drinking; indeed, both novels tellingly situate major anti-Semitic incidents in drinking establishments in the context of nationalist rhetoric and the perceived threat of foreign infiltration (the "Cyclops" episode of *Ulysses* and chapter 12 of *Under the Volcano*).

Although anti-Semitism is a recurrent presence in modern fiction—we encounter it in *The Sun Also Rises*, *Women in Love*, and *The Great Gatsby*, to name only a few famous examples—no other celebrated novel of the period treats this connection and worries this problem in the same way or to the same degree. E.M. Forster's *A Passage to India* is an exception in this respect, but the novel raises the subject of anti-Semitism only briefly, when Ronny Heaslop grasps absurdly at this variety of fool's gold to explain England's political difficulties in India: "Incident after incident, all due to propaganda, but we can't lay our hands on the connecting thread. The longer one lives here, the more certain one gets that everything hangs together. My personal opinion is, it's the Jews" (345).

What follows is not an influence study, even if it is perhaps not merely coincidental that the protagonists of both fictions encounter anti-Semitic hostility within bars (Barney Kiernan's and the Farolito) in which nationalist sentiment is being espoused. Rather, I am interested in exploring the representation of anti-Semitism in two novels whose publications were separated by twenty-five years (1922, 1947)—and, more importantly, separated by the second world war and by the major anti-Semitic event of that period, the attempted genocide of European Jewry—in order to illuminate each novel's critique of anti-Semitism. Indeed, both *Ulysses* and *Under the Volcano* suggest that twentieth-century anti-Semitism arises from and comports with nationalism, narcissism, intoxication, and alienation. Moreover, both texts exemplify Theodor Adorno's claim that "charging the Jews with all existing evils seems to penetrate the darkness of reality like a searchlight and to allow for quick and all-compromising orientation"; such anti-Semitism is a "device for effortless 'orientation' in a cold, alienated, and largely ununderstandable world."[1]

Max Horkheimer and Theodor Adorno's *Dialectic of Enlightenment* (1944) and Theodor Adorno's contribution to *The Authoritarian Personality* (1950) are particularly useful in approaching *Ulysses'* and *Under the Volcano's* representation and critique of anti-Semitism. In their chapter "Elements of Anti-Semitism" in the earlier text, the authors relate and correlate nationalism, anti-Semitism, narcissism, and intoxication in ways that illuminate Leopold Bloom's and Geoffrey Firmin's experiences of anti-Semitism and group violence. Indeed, for all of their great and obvious differences, "Elements of Anti-Semitism," *Ulysses,* and *Under the Volcano* all depict the "civilized" West (and particularly early-twentieth-century Europe) as paralyzed by modes of thinking that reveal anti-Semitism to be the product not of a *mythological* but of a *rational* mode of understanding—yet a mode of understanding in which stereotype replaces individual judgment and blindness replaces genuine reflection (Horkheimer and Adorno 201). In *The Authoritarian Personality* Adorno continues his project; he examines "the relation of antiminority prejudice to broader ideological and characterological patterns" (605) and argues for a connection between "anti-Semitism" and "anti-democratic feeling" (653).[2]

The raison d'être of the aphoristic and polemical *Dialectic of Enlightenment* is to explain a key paradox of this century: that the myth-laden phenomenon of Nazism could flourish in a nation presumed to be the bastion of Enlightenment-rational ideas. Instead, as its authors note, "the fully enlightened earth radiates disaster triumphant" (Horkheimer and Adorno 3). For Horkheimer and Adorno this paradox is the fault and culmination of the rational tradition in Western thinking dating from antiquity. They argue that reason has always been split between "abstract idealism" and "crass materialism," instead of being holistically conceived and exercised. Consequently, "ideals, values, [and] ethics," as C. Fred Alford succinctly articulates Horkheimer and Adorno's position, "are removed to the abstract realm of the intellect and the spirit, where, like religion . . . they are applauded in the abstract." "However," Alford continues, "precisely because they come to be seen as an expression of our higher selves, they are split off from everyday life, which is then given over to a crass materialism that tolerates no opposition to the merely given" (105). For Horkheimer and Adorno, the human need defined by Freud to construct civilization in order to dominate nature necessitates this dependence on material over idealistic reason. Hence, for all practical purposes, "reason" becomes synonymous with "instrumental reason"—the reason behind science, technology, and industrialism— whose goal is to dominate nature. Yet this "manipulation" spreads from the natural to the human realm: Enlightenment rationality, as the existence of anti-Semitism suggests, ends in the domination of people—"enlightenment" proves to be "as totalitarian as any system," and "progress" proves to be "regression" (Horkheimer and Adorno 24, xv). In an argument reminiscent of Walter Benjamin's, Horkheimer and Adorno here explicitly link "terror and civilization," barbarism for them being little more than "the other face of culture" (Horkheimer and Adorno 111-12).[3]

Resonances of anti-Semitism appear in virtually every episode of *Ulysses*—from Haines's comment in "Telemachus" that England's "national problem" is that it has fallen "into the hands of German jews" (*U* 1.667-68), to the final lines of "Nestor," in which Mr. Deasy jokes to Stephen that Ireland "has the honour of being the only country which never persecuted the jews" because "she never let them in" (*U* 2.437-38, 442), to the middle of "Hades," in which Bloom experiences anti-Jewish sentiment while driving in a carriage to Paddy Dignam's funeral, to name only the earliest instances.[4] Nowhere, however, is it more concentrated and potent than in "Cyclops," the episode, as James H. Maddox observes, "which most persistently regards Bloom as a social being . . . forced into a hostile confrontation, not with citizens but with the Citizen, who is in grotesque form the spokesman for the Community" (Maddox 85).

Dialectic of Enlightenment's treatment of the connection between group blindness, unreflectiveness, paranoia, and anti-Semitism holds particular relevance for my discussion of "Cyclops." Horkheimer and Adorno explain that "anti-Semitic behavior is generated in situations where blinded men robbed of their subjectivity are set loose as subjects" (Horkheimer and Adorno 171). "The morbid aspect of anti-Semitism," they write, "is not projective behavior as such, but the absence from it of reflection. When the subject is no longer able to return to the object what he has received from it, he becomes poorer rather than richer. He loses the reflection in both directions: since he no longer reflects the object, he ceases to reflect upon himself, and loses the ability to differentiate" (Horkheimer and Adorno 189-90). What better way than this to characterize Bloom's experience with the Fenian Citizen in "Cyclops"? Surrounded in Barney Kiernan's pub by talk of "Shylock" (*U* 12.765), the "perverted jew," a defrauder of "widows and orphans" (*U* 12.1635, 1622), the "wolf in sheep's clothing" (*U* 12.1666), and "that bloody jewman" (*U* 12.1811), Bloom is viewed by the crowd as stereotypically both "clever and stupid," as lagging "behind advanced civilization" and yet "too far ahead of it" (Horkheimer and Adorno 186). Against Bloom's "both / and" orientation (his "moderation" and his "but on the other hand"), "the public eye" in Barney Kiernan's is depicted as possessing an orientation that is "either / or." Indeed, it is because this anti-Semitic voice is a collective one that it can maintain its favorite myths ("I'm told those jewies does have a sort of a queer odour coming off them" [*U* 12.452-53]), despite all evidence to the contrary.[5] For Horkheimer and Adorno, anti-Semites gather together to celebrate the moment when authority permits what is normally outlawed; their pathological hatred of Jews is incurable precisely because there can be no convincing argument against their materially false judgments.[6] Like other paranoiacs, anti-Semites perceive the world around them only to the extent that it corresponds to their "blind purposes" (Horkheimer and Adorno 184, 193, 190). For this reason the "compulsively projecting self can project only its own unhappiness—from the very basis of which it is cut off by reason of its lack of reflective thought" (Horkheimer and Adorno 192).

Of course, the real basis of the anti-Semitic feeling directed against Bloom is that he cannot be both Jewish and Irish. "The nationalist brand of anti-Semitism," Horkheimer and Adorno write, "ignores religious considerations and asserts that the purity of the race and the nation is at stake" (Horkheimer and Adorno 176). Indeed, for the Citizen as for the I-Narrator (a "collector of bad and doubtful debts"), the will to national purity is taken to its logical—and narcissistic—conclusions. Whether these patriots speak of "Irish games" (*U* 12.858), the "Irish language"

(*U* 12.679), or "Irish industries" (*U* 12.1577), there is the sense that legitimate Otherness is unthinkable, much less acceptable, that "everyone is either a friend or an enemy; there are no half measures" (Horkheimer and Adorno 202). In "Cyclops" this historical revisionism clearly takes on narcissistic dimensions: "There's no-one as blind as the fellow that won't see, if you know what that means. Where are our missing twenty millions of Irish should be here today instead of four, our lost tribes? And our potteries and textiles, the finest in the whole world! And our wool that was sold in Rome in the time of Juvenal . . . ?" (*U* 12.1239-43). Clearly, Horkheimer and Adorno's understanding of the function of anti-Semitism in Nazi Germany reveals something of what Joyce is suggesting in "Cyclops." In both cases "illness is socialized" and the "intoxication of joint ecstasy" culminates in "horror or fright" for the victims (Horkheimer and Adorno 197). In both instances members of the crowd engage in "false projection" such that "all words become part of the delusive system, of the attempt to possess through the mind everything for which experience is inadequate, to force meaning upon the world which makes [them] meaningless" (Horkheimer and Adorno 195).[7] At the conclusion of "Cyclops" the violence attempted by the Citizen against Bloom is depicted in proliferating verbiage as a humorous parody of biblical legend—"And they beheld Him even Him, ben Bloom Elijah, amid clouds of angels ascend to the glory of the brightness at an angle of fortyfive degrees" (*U* 12.1915-17)—even if the "terror" of genuine communal "blindness" and "ecstasy" is readily apparent between the lines.

Phillip Herring argues that the Citizen is a bigot and a "petty Irish chauvinist who cares little whom he strikes with the boulders he hurls" (3), and Joyce comments that his Citizen "unburdens his soul about the Saxo-Angles in the best Fenian style" (*LJJ* 1:126). Beyond these insights, however, *Dialectic of Enlightenment* helps reveal Joyce's representation of the mechanism by which Jews (or any other marginal group) are used to hold together a civilization otherwise on the brink of collapse.[8]

Horkheimer and Adorno's observation that "the blind murderer has always seen his victim as a persecutor against whom he must defend himself" has roots in Freud's *Civilization and Its Discontents*. There, Freud argues that, far from gentle, people are instinctually aggressive. "As a result, their neighbour is for them not only a potential helper or sexual object, but also someone who tempts them to satisfy their aggressiveness on him . . . to humiliate him, to cause him pain" (58). In "Cyclops" it is Bloom who becomes the dangerous neighbor, the "threatening other" against whom the community's aggression is directed. It is he who is associated with Ireland's European neighbors, likewise enemies of "the fair hills of Eire" (*U* 12.1264), making the paradox of external enemy and internal victim complete: "The friends we love are by our side," the Citizen warns Bloom, "and the foes we hate before us" (*U* 12.523-24). Insisting that "foreign wars" are the cause of Ireland's economic problems, that foreigners come "over here to Ireland filling the country with bugs," and that we want "no more strangers in our house" (*U* 12.138, 12.1141-42, 1150-51), the Citizen, as Bloom correctly notes, perpetuates both "national hatred among nations" and "persecution" within Ireland (*U* 12.1417-18). As Freud argues, and as the Citizen exemplifies, the "civilized commandment" to "love thy neighbour as thyself" is "really justified by the fact that nothing else runs so strongly counter to the original nature of man" (59):

> —Well, says John Wyse. Isn't that what we're told. Love your neighbour.
> —That chap? says the citizen [of Bloom]. Beggar my neighbour is his motto. [*U* 12.1490-91]

Clearly, the Citizen here projects his own "civilized" aggressiveness onto Bloom, providing this Fenian with the two "threats" necessary to continue under present contradictory circumstances: an inferior group within and a barbarous one without the glorious yet besieged homeland.[9]

If Joyce uses his parodic and satiric powers to emphasize the distorted and distorting subject-object relations that make anti-Semitism seem rational, Lowry uses his feel for the tragic and the pathetic to emphasize anti-Semitism's power as a scapegoating tool for the purposes of theft, murder, and the consolidation of power. And just as *Ulysses* represents anti-Semitic sentiment at numerous points even if it only centers upon it at one, *Under the Volcano* depicts anti-Semitic elements in Hugh Firmin's past even if it is most fully dealt with in Geoffrey Firmin's present. In the instance of the Consul's half-brother, Hugh is said to have "left behind" his anti-Semitism (*UV* 162); his present "passion for helping the Jews" has "some basis in a dishonorable action" of his past (*UV* 151). Likened, in his earlier anti-Semitic incarnation, to "another frustrated artist, Adolf Hitler," Hugh is guilty of plagiarizing two songs he claims to have composed, but he blames Jews in general, and his publisher, "the Jewish firm of Lazarus Bolowski and Sons" (*UV* 156), in particular, for inadequately publicizing and distributing his "two numbers." In essence, Hugh charges not only Bolowski but all Jews with being, in the words of *Dialectic of Enlightenment*, "materialists and hucksters" (Horkheimer and Adorno 173) who are "not only [guilty] for individual maneuvers and machinations but in the broader sense" for "the economic injustice[s] of the whole class" (174). Horkheimer and Adorno's point that "only those who suffer from a delusion of persecution accept

the persecution to which domination must necessarily lead, inasmuch
as they are allowed to persecute others" (198), is borne out in Hugh's
imagined persecution of Jews for the imagined persecution he receives
from them:

> Yet his life once more began to bear a certain resemblance to Adolf Hitler's.
> . . . A form of private anti-Semitism became part of his life. He sweated
> racial hatred in the night. If it still sometimes struck him that in the stokehold
> he had fallen down the spout of the capitalist system that feeling was now
> inseparable from his loathing of the Jews. It was somehow the fault of the
> poor old Jews, not merely Bolowski, but all Jews, that he'd found himself
> down the stokehold in the first place on a wild goose chase. It was even
> due to the Jews that such economic excrescences as the British Mercantile
> Marine existed. In his day dreams he became the instigator of enormous
> pogroms—all-inclusive, and hence, bloodless. And daily he moved nearer
> his design. [*UV* 171][10]

Rather than acting on his "day dreams," however, the largely ineffectual
Hugh strikes back by seducing Bolowski's wife (*UV* 172). Bolowski
counters by suing Hugh (both for plagiarism and as a "co-respondent"
in his divorce suit), but then abruptly drops "the whole thing" (*UV* 172-
73). The Jewish Bolowski in effect turns the other cheek, prompting Hugh
to abandon his anti-Semitic pursuits for his former philo-Semitism—
which began in public school, where, despite "a certain amount of anti-
Semitism" in the air, Hugh chose "Jews as his particular friends" (*UV*
156): "And once again one's best friends were often Jews, often the same
Jews who had been at school with one. . . . only a Jew, with his rich
endowment of premature suffering, could understand one's own suffering, one's isolation, essentially, one's poor music" (*UV* 177). At no point
in Lowry's novel is the connection between narcissism and anti-Semitism
treated more fascinatingly or directly than here.[11]

Of most significance in *Under the Volcano*'s treatment of anti-Semitism,
however, is Geoffrey's encounter in the Farolito with what Hilda Thomas calls "the political reality of fascism" (88); yet this event is closely
related to Hugh's anti-Semitic past in a number of ways. It is certainly
no coincidence, for example, that Hugh's rebelliousness is traceable to
the "Headmaster of his former prep school, and Scoutmaster, Dr. Gotelby.
. . . Goat old boy!" (*UV* 171), in that "goats" are linked in the novel both
with tragedy in general and with Geoffrey's personal tragedy in particular. As Lowry himself notes in a letter, "The goat means tragedy (tragedy—goat song) but goat [also suggests] *cabrón*—cuckold (the horns)"
(*SC* 2:208).[12] Moreover, "goat" in this latter context is also to be linked
with "scapegoat,"[13] for the Consul is a scapegoat of his Nazi-German-

connected Unión Militar murderers. Specifically, he is a scapegoat of the "antisemitic campaign" sponsored by the "german legation" in Mexico City (*UV* 94)[14] in that his "Jewishness" provides the toughs in the cantina with an excuse to steal from and murder him.[15] Yet as *Dialectic of Enlightenment*, *The Authoritarian Personality*, and *Under the Volcano* reveal, the Consul's scapegoating as a Jew is all the more poignant precisely because he is *not* Jewish (indeed, there is not a Jew to be found anywhere in the novel). This in turn suggests that what is at issue is not the objective nature of Jews (or any other pariah group) so much as their usefulness as scapegoats—as excuses to murder, steal, promote violence, and consolidate power. As Horkheimer and Adorno note in this connection, "Anti-Semitism has as much chance in areas where there are no Jews as it does, say, in Hollywood" (Horkheimer and Adorno 201). Adorno subsequently puts it even more directly: "Anti-Semitic prejudice has little to do with the qualities of those against whom it is directed"; it "is not so much dependent upon the nature of the object as upon the subject's own psychological wants and needs" (Adorno 607, 609).

Horkheimer and Adorno's point that "the portrait of the Jews that the nationalists offer to the world is in fact their own self-portrait"—that "they long for total possession and unlimited power, at any price" (Horkheimer and Adorno 168-69)—is germane to Geoffrey's victimization in the Farolito. Indeed, the "incriminating" telegram discovered in Geoffrey's jacket pocket by the Mexican fascists ("It say you are Juden" [*UV* 369])—which points to recent "antisemitic propaganda" against alleged Jewish influence, power, and corruption (*UV* 94)—more accurately refers to the Mexican killers than to anyone else in the novel. It apparently matters little that in the Farolito the implied "fantasies of Jewish crimes," such as "international conspiracy" and the "poisoning of the nation" (Horkheimer and Adorno 186), hold no water, in that those "to whom the cry for the blood of the Jews has become second nature do not know the reason" for their hatred any more than those "who are called upon to spill that blood" (Horkheimer and Adorno 171). Not only is Geoffrey not Jewish, but his murderers do not even seem to understand or believe in what they are saying. Rather, they seem "aware deep down that ultimately" all they can get out of their anti-Semitic violence is "the pleasure of seeing others robbed of all" they possess (Horkheimer and Adorno 170).

This helps to explain the Consul's brutal murder at the hands of the Mexican fascists in the Farolito. Described as "no friend[s] of Mexican people" (*UV* 367)—as "diablos" and "murderers" who "kill ten old men," who "kill twenty viejos" (*UV* 368)—the assembled "semi-fascist *brutos*" (*SC* 1:527) are depicted finally as less interested in any recognizable ideology than in the money they can steal and the violence they can commit. After calling Geoffrey a "Jew," a "pelado," and a "cabrón" almost interchangeably (*UV* 372-73), the "Chief of Rostrums" then threatens, "I blow you wide open from your knees up, you Jew chingao" (*UV* 373), suggesting that he uses Geoffrey more as an *excuse* for violence and theft than as the "legitimate" symbol of all that this thug genuinely abhors.

Horkheimer and Adorno's point that "the content of the Fascist program is so meaningless that, as a substitute for something better, it can only be upheld by the desperate efforts of the deluded," that "its horror lies in the fact that the lie is obvious but persists" (Horkheimer and Adorno 208), squarely addresses the Consul's experience at the novel's end. Anti-Semitism for this reason "acquires its impenetrable, meaningless character"; Jews are randomly lumped together with communists (Horkheimer and Adorno 206, 201) or any other "threatening" group that comes to mind. Within minutes, for example, Geoffrey is accused of being "Trotsky. . . . You are Juden?" (*UV* 358), of being a "Bolsheviki prick" (*UV* 357), of being "Al Capón . . . a Jew chingao" (*UV* 371) (Capone is about as Jewish as the Consul), and of being an "antichrista prik. . . . And Juden" (*UV* 370) (a convenient misreading of "anarchista" on Hugh's telegram). All of this linguistic confusion belies a key intellectual confusion: these anti-Semites simply do not understand their own assumed ideology. Instead, they merely fantasize that the Jews "are everywhere"— that they possess a "dangerous, mysterious ubiquity" (Adorno 614)— and scapegoat them on that basis.

Having considered Joyce's and Lowry's convergent representations and divergent critiques of anti-Semitism, I would like, by way of conclusion, to suggest a point of common ground between the two on the latter score. Both authors view nationalist anti-Semitism to be dangerous not only due to its antidemocratic character but also due to the specious patriotic ideology that underwrites it—an ideology that maintains that there is a pure race or nation that needs protecting against a foreign (in this case, Jewish) influence. As Joyce puts it of this specious ideology in "Ireland, Island of Saints and Sages," an essay from which he clearly borrowed material when writing "Cyclops" (see *CW* 167),

> Our civilization is a vast fabric, in which the most diverse elements are mingled. . . . In such a fabric, it is useless to look for a thread that may have remained pure and virgin without having undergone the influence of a neighboring thread. What race, or what language . . . can boast of being pure today? And no race has less right to utter such a boast than the race now living in Ireland. Nationality (if it really is not a convenient fiction like

so many others . . .) must find its reason for being rooted in something that surpasses and transcends and informs changing things like blood and the human word. [CW 165-66]

Hence, for Joyce in this essay, "to exclude from the present nation all who are descended from foreign families would be impossible, and to deny the name of patriot to all those who are not of Irish stock would be to deny it to almost all the heroes of the modern movement" for Irish independence (CW 161-62). Lowry certainly would have appreciated Joyce's notion that national and cultural purity (like racial, linguistic, or genetic purity) is a chimera. Indeed, in a letter, Lowry reproduced an excerpt from a magazine with which we can only assume he was sympathetic. The excerpt argues that "a community's virtue is the capacity of its institutions and traditions to evoke the spiritual greatness of its members"; and it goes on to distinguish between the failed community, which will "in the long run perish, because it will come to consist of men and women who pass through life without ever becoming what they were intended to be," and the "community worth preserving and dying for," the community "which fires men with the desire to live nobly, to love, to create beauty" (SC 2:220). Clearly, for both Joyce and Lowry, the nationalist brand of anti-Semitism that rears its ugly head in both *Ulysses* and *Under the Volcano* is lethal—not only for its "foreign" victims, but for the "patriotic" victimizers themselves.

Notes

1. See Adorno 619 and 608.
2. That both of these critical texts in large measure owe their theoretical orientations to Freud's *Civilization and Its Discontents* provides another point of connection between them. See *Civilization and Its Discontents*, pp. 61-62, for Freud's discussion of the connection between narcissism and anti-Semitism.
3. Specifically, Benjamin writes: "There is no cultural document that is not at the same time a record of barbarism" (359). For two other perspectives on the origin and development of modern European anti-Semitism, see Arendt 3-120 and Sartre. Interestingly, many of Sartre's insights about anti-Semitism coincide with Adorno's.
4. For more on anti-Semitism in *Ulysses*, see Cheyette 207-34, Nadel 57-69, and Manganiello 52-56.
5. Adorno's observation nicely characterizes Joyce's Citizen: "The statement that the Jews are all alike not only dispenses with all disturbing factors but also, by its sweep, gives to the judge the grandiose air of a person who sees

the whole without allowing himself to be deflected by petty details—an intellectual leader" (Adorno 621).

6. In *The Authoritarian Personality*, Adorno puts all of this in terms of "stereotypy"—a "device for looking at things comfortably." However, since stereotypy "feeds on deep-lying unconscious sources, the distortions which occur are not to be corrected merely by taking a *real* look. Rather, experience itself is predetermined by stereotypy" (617).

7. In *The Authoritarian Personality*, Adorno writes in this connection: "Since the [anti-Semitic] cliché regularly makes the outgroup bad and the ingroup good, the anti-Semitic pattern of orientation offers emotional, narcissistic gratifications which tend to break down the barriers of rational self-criticism" (619).

8. See, for example, the epigraph that introduces this essay.

9. For more on the *Ulysses–Dialectic of Enlightenment* connection, see Knapp 141-43. And see Cixous 241-63 for another reading of Joyce's politics in "Cyclops."

10. In *The Authoritarian Personality*, Adorno argues that persecution mania typically accompanies anti-Semitism: "While the paranoid is beset by an overall hatred, he nevertheless tends to 'pick' his enemy. . . . he falls, as it were, negatively in love" (611).

11. As Hilda Thomas correctly observes, "The temptations of anti-Semitism and narcissism" in *Under the Volcano* "are not unconnected" (86).

12. As Ackerley and Clipper point out, the appearance of a hostile billy goat in chapter 4 "is a materialization of the Consul, who has already called himself a cabrón" (151).

13. At one point Hugh utters a Freudian slip, revealing that he associates goats and scapegoats with the Consul. He calls goats "the lowest form of animal life," and then remarks of journalists (with whom he has confused goats), "There's no punishment on earth fit for them. Only the Malebolge" (*UV* 99-100)—anticipating Geoffrey's violent end ("Somebody threw a dead dog after him down the ravine" [375]). In this connection, it is perhaps no coincidence that *Under the Volcano* closes with an image of Geoffrey's personal holocaust depicted in the image of mass warfare and the Holocaust of European Jewry: "The world itself was bursting, bursting into black spouts of villages catapulted into space, with himself falling through it all, through the inconceivable pandemonium of a million tanks, through the blazing of ten million burning bodies, falling" (*UV* 375).

14. This is made clear to the extent that the Mexican murderers in the Farolito are associated with the shady Weber, "one of these American semi-fascist blokes" (*UV* 97), who remains "in the bar, though at a distance, . . . staring at [Geoffrey] with a remote speculation" (370).

15. Hugh's role in the Consul's victimization is clear, however indirect it may be: Geoffrey is accused of being Jewish, as Hilda Thomas observes, "at least partly because he is wearing the jacket in which Hugh has left the politically incriminating telegram" announcing the anti-Semitic campaign (88).

Works Cited

Ackerley, Chris, and Lawrence J. Clipper. *A Companion to "Under the Volcano."* Vancouver: Univ. of British Columbia Press, 1984.

Adorno, T.W., et al. *The Authoritarian Personality.* New York: Harper and Brothers, 1950.

Alford, C. Fred. *Narcissism: Socrates, the Frankfurt School, and Psychoanalytic Theory.* New Haven: Yale Univ. Press, 1988.

Arendt, Hannah. *The Origins of Totalitarianism.* New York: Harcourt Brace Jovanovich, 1973.

Benjamin, Walter. *One-Way Streets and Other Writings.* London: New Left Books, 1979.

Cheyette, Bryan. *Constructions of 'the Jew' in English Literature and Society: Racial Representations (1875-1945).* Cambridge: Cambridge Univ. Press, 1993.

Cixous, Hélène. *The Exile of James Joyce.* New York: David Lewis, 1972.

Forster, E.M. *A Passage to India.* New York: Harcourt Brace Jovanovich, 1924.

Freud, Sigmund. *Civilization and Its Discontents,* translated and edited by James Strachey. New York: Norton, 1961.

Herring, Phillip. "Joyce's Politics." In *New Light on Joyce from the Dublin Symposium,* edited by Fritz Senn. Bloomington: Indiana Univ. Press, 1972.

Horkheimer, Max, and Theodor W. Adorno. *Dialectic of Enlightenment.* New York: Continuum, 1987.

Knapp, James F. *Literary Modernism and the Transformation of Work.* Evanston, Ill.: Northwestern Univ. Press, 1988.

Maddox, James H. *Joyce's "Ulysses" and the Assault upon Character.* New Brunswick, N.J.: Rutgers Univ. Press, 1978.

Manganiello, Dominic. *Joyce's Politics.* London: Routledge & Kegan Paul, 1980.

Nadel, Ira B. *Joyce and the Jews: Culture and Texts.* Iowa City: Univ. of Iowa Press, 1989.

Sartre, Jean-Paul. *Anti-Semite and Jew.* New York: Schocken Books, 1965.

Shaffer, Brian W. *The Blinding Torch: Modern British Fiction and the Discourse of Civilization.* Amherst: Univ. of Massachusetts Press, 1993.

Thomas, Hilda. "Praxis as Prophylaxis: A Political Reading of *Under the Volcano.*" In *Swinging the Maelstrom: New Perspectives on Malcolm Lowry,* edited by Sherrill Grace. Montreal and Kingston: McGill-Queen's Univ. Press, 1992.

Woolf, Leonard. *Barbarians Within and Without.* New York: Harcourt Brace, 1939.

six

The Construction of Femininity in *Ulysses* and *Under the Volcano:* A Bakhtinian Analysis of the Late Draft Versions

Sue Vice

This is an examination of points of comparison between the works of James Joyce and Malcolm Lowry in terms of their prepublication revisions to their central female characters: Yvonne in *Under the Volcano* and Molly Bloom in *Ulysses*. Did Lowry and Joyce have methods of revision in common? Are these women characters affected by such revisions in similar ways? Do they become "freer" and more dialogized, in Mikhail Bakhtin's terms, or is there a negative connection between their linguistic gender and the authors' masculinity, the wielding of a blue pen[1] over a textual body? And finally, how do such prepublication revisions affect the textual construction of femininity that we read in the published form? Can a case be made for such authorial transvestism actually putting into question accepted gender roles, voices, and behavior patterns?

To start with *Under the Volcano:* in Yvonne's case an evolving drama occurs in the five full drafts that Lowry produced over ten years. It could be seen as Oedipal: the drunken Consul's daughter becomes the alcoholic Consul's wife; Hugh, the daughter's boyfriend, becomes the Consul's half-brother and possibly the adulterous lover of Yvonne; and Laruelle looms increasingly larger, first as a hoverer over the Consul's daughter, then as another possible lover of his wife. However, what Yvonne's metamorphosis from daughter to wife also shows is, first, how Lowry's writing practice involved progressively casting off the conventional intrusive narrator and allowing the characters to speak for themselves, so that, as Bakhtin would say, "we have a plurality of consciousnesses, with equal rights, each with its own world" (Bakhtin 104); and

96

second, how Yvonne becomes increasingly similar to her ex-husband, as the daughter's outspokenness is replaced with a wifely version of his melancholia.

The published version of Yvonne has been critically treated in a manner similar to Molly Bloom: she is both disapproved of *and* the eternal feminine.[3] Richard Cross calls her "a rather frigid Gretchen" to Geoffrey's Faust (Cross 40), while Ron Binns speaks of her "ruthless sexuality" (Binns 57). It is as if Yvonne's previous incarnations in draft cannot be forgotten, and are used as evidence of her ill-faith. Binns remarks, "Until a very late stage in the writing of the novel, chapter 11 was to have ended with Hugh and Yvonne making love under the trees, Yvonne's impressions of rising towards the stars expressive not of death, but of orgasm" (Binns 36). Yet this observation seems somewhat unfair in view of the lengths to which Lowry went to alter Yvonne's rebelliousness and wifely role, and to excise any unwarranted feeling for Hugh, even anger, in the final galleys. Binns thus treats the drafts as if they were the text's unconscious, its repository of "true" meaning.

Nevertheless, this inability to forget the textual past is testimony to the fact that traces of the old meanings can still be detected. The reader who, like Binns, has a total recall of the drafts becomes like the obsessively jealous person described by Freud, who pays such pathologically close attention to the loved one's unconscious that he or she sees evidence of betrayal that may really be there, but on such a small scale that anyone else would have ignored it (Freud, "Some Neurotic Mechanisms," 18:223-32). This reader then becomes a kind of double for the Consul, who is a pathologically jealous reader of his ex-wife's unconscious—an unconscious that does in fact consist of traces of the earlier versions of the text. The tremors of sexual guilt Yvonne feels in relation to Laruelle and, particularly, Hugh are as much due to the fact that in the earlier versions of the novel she did indeed have a reason for guilt as to the fact that she still has something on her conscience in the published version; except that in the final version we simply cannot tell what is the case.

In the final draft version Yvonne's death, for instance, does still sound a bit like that other, less terminal kind of death. Indeterminacy, for which Jonathan Quick praises Joyce in his article on Molly Bloom's mother, has replaced overt and overinsistent statement of the following kind from draft four of *Under the Volcano*: "She knew that the horse would kill her. Her bowels were bayoneted with an agony of fear. . . . Then the horse came down" (UBC Templeton 1:5, 17).[2]

Lowry's method is similar to Joyce's in being what James Van Dyck Card has called "accretive" (Card 12): in the final version the writing is not a seamless whole, as it may appear, but a complex bundle of layers.

(This is particularly significant in the case of Molly's monologue, which gives the impression of free-flowing naturalness and yet is in fact quite the opposite.) Elaborate tinkering, the incorporation of large extra units of material, the addition of whole series of details late in the process— the horses in *Under the Volcano,* Gibraltar in *Ulysses*—characterize this accretion. However, to say that this is so conceals a difference of kind between the two works: Lowry's revisions are synchronic in that at this late stage they affect the characters' present and the whole text horizontally; Joyce's are diachronic: he tunnels out a history behind one of the characters and thus adds a vertical strand of femininity to his text.

In the case of Yvonne, various other changes accompany the transformation from daughter to wife. In draft, as the daughter of Priscilla— the wife who has left the Consul to go off to Los Angeles—Yvonne is angry and outspoken. She weeps, defends her mother, and comments in the following manner on well-loved episodes in *Under the Volcano.* To the memorable opening scene of the morning after and the Consul's remark, "A corpse will be transported by express!" (*UV* 43; see also *UV* [1940] 68), Yvonne responds, "Cockeyed, in your dress clothes, at seven o'clock in the morning, howling about a corpse—" (*UV* [1940] 70-71). Of the Consul's failure to recall W.J. Turner's volcano poem, she says, "How can *you* hope to remember anything accurately, drink absolutely *rots* your memory, any doctor will tell you" (*UV* [1940] 164). This is quite different from the self-accusation and reticence of the published Yvonne; coming upon the Consul discussing the corpse, she does not rebuke him but feels *herself* to be "repellent" (*UV* 48).

As she turns into a wife, Yvonne's desire, as well as her anger, gets crossed out—literally, in the second draft: "She stumbled and Hugh picked her up and lifted her over a fallen log. Was it her imagination, her own longing, or had he held her tightly to him for a moment before he set her down?" (UBC Templeton 1:3, 11). The second sentence is deleted by Lowry. It suits the indeterminate, less realist nature of the published text that Yvonne moves toward the unexpressed and inexpressible. Instead of "real" events, adultery and betrayal, these things become part of the Consul's consciousness. (It is interesting to speculate why the infidelity of a wife is so useful in *Under the Volcano* and *Ulysses* in demonstrating indeterminacy; it is as if that is the one thing husbands and readers really expect to know the truth about. Perhaps this is the ultimate in dialogism: everything takes place within people's field of vision, so that no fact of the matter can be objectively determined, to the possible chagrin of the patriarchal world.)

Intermediate in the various versions between angry daughter and silent wife is a married Yvonne who really is adulterous. It is as if the

Consul's fantasy of betrayal is written out to see what it would look like, and it does not look very good: "Hugh! Say nothing can separate us!" (UBC Templeton 1:4, 7-8), and so on. Here, the plot catches up with the Consul's internal state and gives him reasons to be paranoid before moving on to its final indeterminacy and making those reasons less certain.

Shards of phrases remain in the published version, often half-erased, or transposed, and the altered context at a particular moment also alters the sense of the words, in perfect illustration of Bakhtin's theory of how meaning is constructed. Words are never original, contexts always are: "The meaning of a word is determined entirely by its context. In fact, there are as many meanings of a word as there are contexts of its usage" (Volosinov 79). A particularly striking example of this process is the genesis of a passage in the published *Under the Volcano* where the Consul wishes Yvonne would come and rescue him "as a daughter . . . as he had seen the Indian children lead their fathers" (*UV* 360). It is one thing to wish this of an undutiful daughter, which Yvonne once was; quite another to wish it of your wife, which she is here. Lowry treats his own work as he does the writing of others, extracting and grafting into a coherent surface. (A similar family shift occurs in Joyce's last changes to "Penelope," where Molly's memories of motherhood usually alter to refer to Milly, rather than Rudy: "what I went through with Rudy nobody would believe" becomes, in the corrections to the Rosenbach manuscript, "what I went through with Milly nobody would believe cutting her teeth too" [Card 92] and "I had a great breast of milk with Rudy" turns into "I had a great breast of milk with Milly enough for two" [Card 109]).[4]

The changes in familial relations occur as the Consul imagines them and he converts Yvonne into his faithless wife, Priscilla. He drunkenly calls his daughter the wrong name and then realizes that the logical extension of this transformation is that he has been cuckolded by Yvonne's boyfriend, Hugh, the man who is also his own prospective son-in-law— and who becomes instead, in published form, his half-brother: "Secretly he had always longed to appear to good advantage before Yvonne, to show her what a bargain her mother had lost—no—he grew flushed at the thought—Yvonne *was* her mother, his own Priscilla, Hugh a rival, a Laruelle to be dispatched" (*UV* [1940] 300-301). Laruelle at this point has nothing to do with Yvonne; it is as if the Consul has apprehended this betrayal as a possibility that goes on to be fulfilled, and so connects his wife, logically enough, with Hugh: "In the silence, rancorous chaotic thoughts sprang up at him. Vronsky and Anna, they babbled: Priscilla and Hugh" (*UV* [1940] 311). The quadrangle of *Under the Volcano*, which is to be condensed out of these separate elements, is prefigured here in draft for the first time.

The Consul's errors become equivalent to and precursors of Lowry's corrections. Yvonne's two personae in *Under the Volcano*, the one who has come back on the Day of the Dead and the one in the past before she left Geoffrey, have their roots in what were originally two different women. "Yvonne had called the country too divine when they first came" (UBC 26:3, 155; see also *UV* [1940] 77) is echoed in "Priscilla had also called the country too divine" (*UV* [1940] 149), with the result that, instead of Yvonne's being divided up into a loving, if hot-tempered, present daughter and an absent ex-wife, the two are brought together here as the same person separated by time.

The total effect of the various changes over ten years' rewriting is, in Yvonne's case, that she becomes more silent, more unhappy, more passive, and less angry; she ends up deriving identity solely from her loved one and his plight, codependent on alcohol. On another level, she and the rest of the text become "better"; she herself is less like a soap-operatic cipher, and the context grows richer, with more implication, less description. (This is less clearly true of Joyce's rewritings in *Ulysses*, which are more homogenous than Lowry's; by accident, the latter's radically alter the structure and genre of his novel.[5]) Yvonne consequently appears to correspond to all five of the melancholic traits Freud notes in his essay "Mourning and Melancholia": one, "a profoundly painful dejection"; two, "abrogation of interest in the outside world"; three, "loss of the capacity for love"; four, "inhibition of all activity"; and five, "a fall in self-esteem" (Freud 14:254-58).[6]

According to Freud, melancholics act as if someone has died without realizing that the loss is really an internal one. Freud's essay has been used by analysts treating alcoholics; the assumption is that the ego-loss leading to melancholia is the result of internalizing a lost or disappointing object. This is a process that alcoholics keep repeating through constant introjection of the object by drinking it. The problem with describing Yvonne as melancholic in this Freudian sense is that Freud was concerned with *male* victims of melancholia. Luce Irigaray suggests that this must be so by definition—according to Freud's own descriptions of female sexuality, melancholia is central to women's very being and therefore not a special, pathological state. Passivity, lack of interest in sex or the outside world, loss of the capacity to love: these are traits of Yvonne as a woman, and of the Consul as an alcoholic. Lowry's draft revisions thus make Yvonne into a figure similar to her husband: a melancholic, suffering from a "sourceless sorrow." In Yvonne's case, this sorrow may be regret at the place of femininity in a man's world and a male text.

In the case of Molly in *Ulysses,* there are several distinct areas of
signification added to the Rosenbach manuscript;[7] the corrections and
additions that make up the published version come from Rosenbach's
own versos, from additions to the additions, typescript additions, five
generations of galleys, and one of page proofs. The eighth sentence of
"Penelope," equivalent to the last seven pages of the Gabler edition,
appears separately, handwritten, Card guesses, while the typist was at
work on the rest of the manuscript (Card 31).[8] Joyce was composing
"Penelope"—and "Ithaca"—while working on the first sets of page proofs
of the rest of the text in the summer of 1921 (Rabaté 252). The areas of
added signification are: references to Molly's Gibraltar background, to
her vanished mother, Lunita Laredo, and to increased awareness of and
interest in sexual difference, including references to people's clothing
and hair; a move from the spoken to the written, especially in the case of
numbers and punctuation; and many of the overt examples of affirmation: at least thirty instances of "yes" appear post-Rosenbach. (Molly
also, of course, says "no" with some frequency.)

These areas are all linked; it is as if Joyce, in making these final revisions to "Penelope," were seeding the text with an unconscious, giving
it what Julia Kristeva has called a "semiotic disposition" (*Desire,* 87). All
the same, I do not mean by this remark that Molly's voice is an example
of *écriture feminine.* As Derek Attridge has rightly pointed out, any ho-
mogeneous flow in "Penelope" is the effect of printing and reading, not
the thinking of a womanly mind. Analogously, what looks like Joyce's
buying into rather foolish stereotypes of femininity is actually his "self-
conscious anatomy of feminine as well as masculine roles" (Devlin 77);
what one looks to for "authenticity" in either form or content is by no
means straightforward. This fact is signaled by the last-minute changes
to the Rosenbach manuscript that involve increased awareness of or-
thography. For instance, "and the oysters 2/6 a dozen" becomes "per
doz"; "will he take a first class for me" turns into "1st class" (Card 88,
101). These small telling touches emphasize both that what we are dealing with is a printed text, where such distinctions between numbers as
words or as figures are possible, and not a privileged insight into a female mind; and also that Molly has a typographically aware memory: as
Devlin says of the new costume Molly imagines herself wearing to greet
Stephen—"a peachblossom dressing jacket like the one long ago in
Walpoles only 8/6 or 18/6" (*U* 18.1497-98)—this is garb "scripted by
contemporary advertising . . . as the prices and unmistakable ad lingo . . .
make clear" (Devlin 79).

The addition of the orthographical is most clear in a case that never
made its way into the pre-Gabler published versions of *Ulysses* (it ap-

pears in the Gabler edition: U 18.730). The following phrase was marked to be inserted: "your sad bereavement symphathy I always make that mistake and new/phew with 2 double yous in" (Card 116)—with the offending letters, "h" in "sympathy" and "w" in "nephew," to be printed with a slash through them. As Card points out, the typesetters ignored, or could not reproduce, Joyce's instruction "w reproduisez ainsi" (Card 158), so that although the relevant letters are "crossed out" in the Rosenbach manuscript and the typescript that followed, they are not in the galleys, which makes nonsense of Molly's "I always make that mistake." (It is interesting to note that any typesetter of poststructuralist texts, particularly those of Derrida or Lacan, must today have the facility to reproduce letters and words thus "under erasure"; Joyce was clearly ahead of his time in this matter too.)

Moreover, the formally textual and the mimetically human intersect effectively yet paradoxically; the changes that Joyce makes for Molly to seem more "rounded" can only be ones that increase the text's writtenness and its distance from matters of human character. In *Under the Volcano*, too, additions make the novel more textually scrupulous and self-conscious, and as a consequence the characters they constitute become more "rounded"-seeming; this is a curious example of an increase in writtenness making the text paradoxically appear more transparent and *less* written.

All these areas of addition to "Penelope" are linked by their textuality. The semiotic realm they impart to the text is constructed out of a Bakhtinian polyphony of voices from various sources. To start with Gibraltar: several critics have pointed out that we get a tourist's-eye view through Molly, and they suggest that Joyce could find no realist account of the everyday on the isthmus. What Molly recalls as a time of flower-laden, and remarkably boring, leisure took place in a poor, humid, unhealthy British garrison. However, determining the textual process of construction and revision not only explains but actually constitutes this fictional oddity. The way in which Molly (and Yvonne) is put together as text fits very well with, and is indeed indistinguishable from, what we might call her "temperament"—circling around associatively from one subject to another, intermittently returning to certain central themes, moving widely in time and space. If Joyce is accretive, then so (and therefore) is Molly. As Phillip Herring puts it, "Molly's memory of Alameda concerts as occasions for flirtations is indebted to the *Gibraltar Directories* and the 1878 edition of Ford" (Herring 503). Expressed in this way, rather than ascribing her memories to a Gibraltar childhood, it is clear that Molly is a textual entity, since her memories are *literally* constructed out of the shards of other texts—which not she but Joyce alone has read. Presumably we are supposed to recognize that Molly is made out of the "stylized" (Bakhtin 189-90) and artificial language of tourist pamphlets, just as Yvonne in *Under the Volcano* is in her own chapter rendered not by the narrator but by the discourse of a movie magazine (*UV* ch. 9).[9]

Jonathan Quick suggests that Molly has been listening to her father's censored and colorful version of the past, rather than that Joyce has been reading the wrong books. Herring concludes that Gibraltar is a "dash of colour not meant to be examined closely" (Herring 516). Yet close examination is in fact essential to determine that Molly's memories are a giant case of what Bakhtin calls "active double-voiced words," specifically here what he terms "hidden dialogicality" (Morson and Emerson 156): that is, words that recall their origins and react to "the unspoken words of another person" (Bakhtin 197). In this instance, the silent other voice is that of "Major" Tweedy, who, Quick claims, would have known of the seamier side of life in Gibraltar that Molly never mentions—smuggling, prostitution, the ghettoizing of different groups of people—which is conspicuous by its absence. Tweedy deliberately, and Molly unconsciously, are covering up a secret concerning Molly's mother, whose very name, Quick suggests, is a "pseudo-Iberian transmogrification of Lily Langtry" (Quick 225), a figure whom Kimberly J. Devlin suggests Molly herself identifies with (Devlin 75). Quick connects Lunita with Bella Cohen, and proposes that Molly may be the child of a prostitute; whether or not we are meant to divine this, what *does* seem clear is that the whole area surrounding Molly's mother is as indeterminate as Molly's lovers. It has been pointed out that if her mother were really Jewish, surprisingly little awareness of that culture or of Gibraltarian prejudice exists in Molly's thoughts; however, a different effect is achieved by this ambiguity. Children take on their mother's faith in Jewish law, because one is at least usually certain who one's mother is, even if the father is not known; but in Molly's case, uncertainty about Jewishness—she pretends to read the Hebrew on gravestones (*U* 18.837)—represents the even more surprising uncertainty about her own mother.

The references to the mother Molly never had are added by Joyce at the same time as those to Gibraltar. Molly's memories of her youth concern a lost, idealized material realm: a Gibraltar that never existed and a beautiful, exotic Jewish mother she may also never have had. Tweedy's voice can even be heard in Molly's comparison of her own looks to her mother's—since she does not remember Lunita, we must be hearing Tweedy's words as ventriloquized by Molly: "Ive my mothers eyes and figure anyhow" (*U* 18.890-91). The question put by Suzette Henke is therefore answered: "How, one might wonder, does Molly know that she has Lunita's 'eyes and figure'? . . . This is one of the titillating gaps in Joyce's text" (Henke 250).

Like Stephen (a point made by Shari Benstock in *Textualizing the Feminine*), Molly cannot properly take up her place in the symbolic order without first recognizing and then rejecting her mother—losing her is not enough. Yet it is also as if Molly is always already motherless, simply an exaggerated version of what is true of all subjects in the symbolic realm. Luce Irigaray argues that maternity within patriarchy curtails both the mother, who can only overwhelm or abandon, and the daughter, who is in exile. Molly is both a geographical and (therefore) a psychic exile. Women's apparently privileged relation to loss of the mother and castration (she turns into her own mother, far from losing her; she may be lacking but she is not castrated, and therefore has not lost the phallus either) means that women's relation to signification is problematic, as use of language requires desire and therefore loss. As Mary Ann Doane puts it in *Femmes Fatales*, "Prohibition, the law of limitation, cannot touch the little girl. . . . She can only mime representation" (171-72). Devlin points out that while Molly, and all women, may "masquerade" because that is how femininity operates under patriarchy, Molly also indulges in the more subversive practice of "mimicry": she ironically appropriates "culturally determined images" that, under the sign of masquerade, are assumed and internalized "passively and unconsciously" (Devlin 72). By "doing" ideology, Molly undoes it.

The additions Joyce makes to "Penelope" concerning sexual difference help confirm Kristeva's observation in *Powers of Horror* that the "archaic maternal abject" is present in Joyce's work (22-23). Now Molly's identity as a mother as well as a daughter is relevant. The huge and therefore unspeakable debt of life owed to all mothers surfaces on occasions when, according to Kristeva, the subject feels bodily disgust at one of three things: food, waste, or sexual difference. The latter category is exemplified by, for example, menstruation; menstrual blood is surrounded by all kinds of cultural taboos to keep the social body clean. As Kristeva says, "Menstrual blood . . . stands for the danger issuing from within identity (social or sexual); it threatens the relationship between the sexes" (*Powers*, 71)—its presence is a reminder of motherhood, and of the repressed maternal debt. It is essential to patriarchy to maintain sexual difference, in the home and workplace, but menstruation is a feature of that difference that strays too close for comfort to the lost maternal body.

Molly's abject maternity is affirmed by her menstruating at the chapter's end, and this event seems to be prepared for by the increasing emphasis on sexual difference that was added by Joyce to the Rosenbach manuscript, in terms both of culturally coded difference—"only of course the woman hides it," "a woman is so sensitive"—and of a more psychoanalytically inflected difference—the girl in Gibraltar "didn't make much secret of what she hadn't"; "grey matter they have it all in their tail" (Card 87, 93, 104, 115). The kind of fear that Molly's toying with gender difference can induce is summarized by Barbara Creed in an article on the 1982 Ridley Scott film *Alien,* which Creed says presents as horrifying the "archaic mother, the reproductive/generative mother" (Creed 73). This is a concept Joyce seems almost to have anticipated in his remark to Harriet Weaver, that he meant in "Penelope" to portray the earth, "which is prehuman and presumably posthuman" (*LJJ* 1:180).

The late additions Joyce made to "Penelope" that relate to sexual difference fall into two categories. First, there are the additions that accentuate Molly's consciousness of heterosexual norms, through memories of flirtation, thoughts about men's relations with women, and calling other women "bitches" and "sparrowfarts" (Card 40, 123). Second, there are those that threaten to collapse the signifiers of gender difference. For example, there are several additions concerning mustaches, most of which do not belong to men—Molly thinks fellatio may explain women's facial hair (Card 143). However, Molly may simply be recognizing the necessity for women under patriarchy to masquerade—either as extremely feminine or cross-dressed as men.[10] Hair, which is grafted onto Rosenbach, is recognized by Molly as an index of femininity; as Devlin observes, "In Molly's thoughts, identity is inextricably linked to signifiers in a variety of forms" (Devlin 72), and when that hair is false, as in the case of Mrs. Rubio, Molly knows it, through her refusal to "see the cultural as natural" (Devlin 81).

Elizabeth Grosz points out the phallic power of a feminized, hairless woman: "The narcissistic woman strives to make her body into the phallus. . . . She paints/shaves/plucks/dyes/diets/exercises her body" (Grosz 121). Ironically enough, emphasizing one's own gender identity in an extreme way moves one closer to the other gender. Molly's pride in her own femininity coupled with interest in transgressing gender boundaries suggests this action; the mustachioed woman, according to this logic, is most "feminine," unlike her phallic, shaved female counterpart.

Finally, we must examine Molly's habit of being affirmative. Joyce misquoted Goethe in respect to her—"I am the flesh which affirms" (*LJJ* 1:170)—which rather sinisterly sounds like Freud's pronouncement on Dora, that there is no word in the unconscious for "no." Dora may have thought she was rejecting Herr K. when he tried to kiss her by the lake— in fact she was simply repressing an affirmation that is normal in an inexperienced young woman of fourteen caught in a lonely spot by a middle-aged family friend (see Toril Moi's essay on Dora). Women are

signifieds without a signifying system of their own; their voices may be
disregarded, as is shown in the scene in Ridley Scott's film *Thelma and
Louise,* where the rapist, Harlan, is killed. He will not listen to Thelma's
"no," so Louise shoots him. However, Molly's fondness for saying "yes"
and "no" does not necessarily correspond to positive and negative frames
of mind. As Card points out, the things Molly dislikes outnumber those
she likes (the former include "people who come at all hours answer the
door you think its the vegetables" [*U* 18.333-34]); but, as he adds, it is far
from clear that "what she is against is 'negative.' If hating women with
knives is negative, what are we in favor of?" (Card 72—a revealing choice
of example). Maternity is one route of access to signification for women,
toward a voice that could be heard to say other things than "yes," as
Kristeva has suggested: "For the mother . . . the Other is not (only) an
arbitrary sign, a necessary absence: it is the child," and if "to love (her
child) is, for a woman, the same thing as to write" (quoted in Suleiman
367[11]), then maternity and signification are united in one plenitudinous
stroke; as Molly says of men: "I wouldnt give a snap of my two fingers
for all their learning why dont they go and create something" (*U* 18.1564-
65). Devlin sees the irony of a male author's masculine-imitating female
character saying such a thing as a positive feature of "Penelope": "Putting on 'womanliness' that repeatedly puts on 'manliness' allowed Joyce
to articulate one of his canniest critiques of the ideology that produces
the oppressive categories themselves" (Devlin 89). The assumption of a
feminine voice may indeed be more likely to happen if women do not
have to imitate men in order to speak, and if men do not have sole charge
of describing women's thoughts.

Notes

I am indebted to Richard Brown, Neil Corcoran, John Haffenden, Erica
Sheen, and Andrew Treip for bibliographical suggestions and helpful discussions related to this paper.

1. Sue Murphy notes that Joyce used thirteen different media in the annota-
tions to the proofs of *Ulysses,* and she lists their different colors. They range
from very dark brown ink to a purple pencil/crayon used only once (Murphy
260-61). Lowry's typescripts are usually annotated in graphite pencil.

2. The William Templeton Papers, which I quote from here together with
the more complete draft versions of *Under the Volcano,* are miscellaneous but
crucial transitional collections of typed chapter variants and handwritten notes
in the University of British Columbia Library Special Collections Division. See
Victor Doyen's discussion of dating the individual drafts.

3. See Bonnie Kime Scott's survey of the critical reception of Molly Bloom as alternating between earth mother and "shilling whore" (Scott 156-83).

4. By contrast, the references to Rudy himself are changed in Rosenbach to implicit hints: "when was that 93 the canal was frozen yes it was a few months after" is added (Card 109), as is "when I was knitting that woollen thing" (Card 89).

5. Michael Worton makes a similar point about Tournier's rewritings, which he claims are the product of "a desire not to write better but differently" (Worton 11).

6. See also my "Mourning, Melancholia, and Femininity in *Under the Volcano.*"

7. This is the second copy of the holograph manuscript of the whole of *Ulysses,* which Joyce sent to John Quinn. It is now known as the Rosenbach manuscript after the man who bought it from Quinn in 1924, A.S.W. Rosenbach. The later episodes of *Ulysses,* such as "Penelope," are particularly well represented in this manuscript.

8. See Arnold and the special issue of *Studies in the Novel* (Summer 1990) devoted to the controversy over the Gabler edition of *Ulysses.*

9. See also Head on internalized use of romantic fiction discourse in Joyce's "Eveline."

10. "Masquerade" suggests both dressing up as what (gender) you are not, and the very construction of gender itself, which also depends on the successful deployment of certain signifiers. The term was first used by Joan Riviere in her article "Womanliness as a Masquerade," in which Riviere discusses a case study of a female academic who glamorized herself excessively to compensate for her "unwomanly" intellectual prowess. See also Devlin for an excellent discussion of Molly and masquerade.

11. Susan Rubin Suleiman (366-67) quotes from Kristeva's article "Un nouveau type d'intellectuel: Le dissident," *Tel Quel* 74 (Winter 1977). One might of course question the biological basis for this assertion.

Works Cited

Arnold, Bruce. *The Scandal of "Ulysses."* London: Sinclair-Stevenson, 1991.
Attridge, Derek. "Molly's Flow: The Writing of 'Penelope' and the Question of Women's Language." *Modern Fiction Studies* 35 (Autumn 1989): 543-65.
Bakhtin, Mikhail. *Problems of Dostoevsky's Poetics.* Minneapolis: Univ. of Minnesota Press, 1984.
Benstock, Shari, and Robert Con Davis, eds. *Textualizing the Feminine.* Norman: Univ. of Oklahoma Press, 1991.
Binns, Ronald. *Malcolm Lowry.* London: Methuen, 1984.
Card, James Van Dyck. *An Anatomy of Penelope.* London: Associated University Presses, 1984.
Creed, Barbara. "Horror and the Monstrous Feminine: An Imaginary Abjection." In *Fantasy and the Cinema,* edited by James Donald. London: BFI Publishing, 1989.
Cross, Richard K. *Malcolm Lowry: A Preface to His Fiction.* Chicago: Univ. of Chicago Press, 1980.

Devlin, Kimberly J. "Pretending in 'Penelope': Masquerade, Mimicry, and Molly Bloom." *Novel* 25 (Fall 1991): 71-89.

Doane, Mary Ann. "Woman's Stake: Filming the Female Body." In Doane's *Femmes Fatales: Feminism, Film Theory, Psychoanalysis*, pp. 165-77. London: Routledge, 1991.

Doyen, Victor. "Fighting the Albatross of Self: A Genetic Study of the Literary Work of Malcolm Lowry." Ph.D. diss., University of Louvain, 1973.

Freud, Sigmund. *The Standard Edition of the Complete Psychological Works of Sigmund Freud*, edited by James Strachey et al. 24 vols. London: Hogarth, 1953-74.

Grosz, Elizabeth. *Jacques Lacan: A Feminist Introduction*. London: Routledge, 1990.

Head, Dominic. *The Modernist Short Story*. Cambridge: Cambridge Univ. Press, 1992.

Henke, Suzette A. *James Joyce and the Politics of Desire*. London: Routledge, 1990.

Herring, Phillip F. "Toward an Historical Molly Bloom." *ELH* 45 (1978): 501-21.

Irigaray, Luce. *Speculum of the Other Woman*. Ithaca: Cornell Univ. Press, 1985.

Kristeva, Julia. *Desire in Language*, edited by Léon S. Roudiez. Oxford: Blackwell, 1984.

———. *Powers of Horror*. New York: Columbia Univ. Press, 1982.

Moi, Toril. "Representation of Patriarchy: Sexuality and Epistemology in Freud's *Dora*." *Feminist Review* 9 (1981): 60-73.

Morson, Gary Saul, and Caryl Emerson. *Mikhail Bakhtin: Creation of a Prosaics*. Stanford: Stanford Univ. Press, 1990.

Murphy, Sue. "Conservation Treatment for the Final Page Proofs of James Joyce's *Ulysses*." *Joyce Studies Annual* (1991): 257-64.

Quick, Jonathan. "Molly Bloom's Mother." *ELH* 57 (1990): 223-40.

Rabaté, Jean-Michel. "'Thank Maurice': A Note about Maurice Darantière." *Joyce Studies Annual* (1991): 244-51.

Riviere, Joan. "Womanliness as a Masquerade." In *Psychoanalysis and Female Sexuality*, edited by Hendrik M. Ruitenbeck, pp. 209-20. New Haven: College and University Press, 1966.

Scott, Bonnie Kime. *Joyce and Feminism*. Bloomington: Indiana Univ. Press, 1984.

Suleiman, Susan Rubin. "Writing and Motherhood." In *The (M)other Tongue*, edited by S. Garner et al. Ithaca: Cornell Univ. Press, 1985.

Vice, Sue. "Mourning, Melancholia, and Femininity in *Under the Volcano*." In *Beyond the Pleasure Dome: Writing and Addiction from the Romantics*, edited by Sue Vice, Matthew Campbell, and Tim Armstrong. Sheffield: Sheffield Academic Press, 1994.

Volosinov, V.N. *Marxism and the Philosophy of Language*. Cambridge: Harvard Univ. Press, 1986.

Worton, Michael. "Michel Tournier and the Masterful Art of Rewriting." *PN Review* 41 (1984): 10-15.

seven
A Portrait of the Artist as a Young Man and Ultramarine: Two Exercises in Identification

Suzanne Kim

The reasons for reading Joyce's *Portrait of the Artist as a Young Man* and Lowry's *Ultramarine* together as twin works are obvious on various levels. Both books, describing (or fictionally rearranging) the lives of the writers as young men, can be considered autobiographical, calling into existence real worlds with names of actual places, people, and environments of personal interest to their authors. *Ultramarine*, the story of Dana Hilliot, recalls a first sea-voyage from Liverpool to the Eastern Seas, which Lowry made as an ordinary seaman in 1927, before he registered at St. Catharine's College in Cambridge, England, when he was eighteen— that is, when he was approximately the same age as his hero. Joyce, too, with the story of Stephen Dedalus, his alter ego, presents his readers with the details of his own youth, since the *Portrait* narrates his life up to 1902, when he departed for the Continent, covering thus his early childhood at home, his schooldays in the Class of Elements at Clongowes Wood, his education at Belvedere College in Dublin, and his later academic days at University College, Dublin.

Moreover, both works were conceived as novels of formation and show the importance of youthful experience playing a major role in the process of the development of the identity of each protagonist as person and as artist; they are bildungsromane in the manner of Goethe's *Dichtung und Wahrheit*. Both narratives deal with the creative process of writing as praxis—although more obliquely so in Lowry's case. Furthermore, both books were published more or less at the beginning of their authors' careers. *Ultramarine* was in fact Lowry's first work of any length when Jonathan Cape published it in 1933 in London. Lowry, fresh from the university, was then only twenty-four. In a way, he had been recognized as a writer somewhat earlier, in his schooldays at the Leys and at St. Catharine's, where he had produced poems, sports reports, and short stories from 1925 to 1931. To him, the publication of *Ultramarine* meant public recognition: in fact, despite its many detractors, it was received as a more than promising first book, given its maturity of content and the literary craftsmanship of its form. For Joyce, of course, the *Portrait* published in 1916 was not exactly a first fictional production, since *Dubliners* had come out in 1914; it was moreover a rewriting of *Stephen Hero*, which appeared in print only posthumously.

Most importantly, on a still deeper level, both novels finally testify to the impact of self-identificatory processes upon their very style and manner. The parallels I shall address will nearly always start with Lowry; although Lowry came later, I reached a better understanding of what Joyce was doing by seeing him in the mirror of what Lowry does, irrespective of any attempt at defining any kind of hierarchy in their art.

Lowry's *Ultramarine* and Joyce's *Portrait* both function through two patterns that stand out on an immediate level. One is the pattern of the initiatory journey, highly metaphoric in essence and dealing in symbols en masse. The other is the pattern of the structuration and / or individuation of the subject, which analytically makes use of notions like father-mother-brother figures and figures of authority, as well as such working concepts as alienation and integration, frustration and symptom, inferiority complex and projection, guilt and self-punishment, identification with models and sublimation, blockage and reaction.

In both books the journey pattern is used as overall fictional design. In *Ultramarine* it binds together the whole structure. The voyage outward and the start of the return journey are seen as initiation into manhood—as well as structuring the parts: the constant shifting of Dana's eye from sky to sea, from the topsail to the decks or depths of the ship, provides as many intrusions into radically different worlds. In *Portrait*, "the walk is itself one of the novel's most effective rhetorical devices, allowing for conversations, flashbacks, meditations" (Deane xiv).

Again, on the last pages of *Ultramarine*—as in the first three sections of *Portrait*, which seem to have been redrafted after Joyce's reading of Freud and Jones[1]—the analytical trend is quite obvious if not openly admitted as "crude jargon" (*Ult* 185) in Dana's last letter. On the strictly narrative level of both books, the identificatory processes are presented through the same type of incidents that show how an individual person draws on his environment for the formation of the self, and also how the self can be posited only through a series of tests—that is, action and reaction—that pit him against the reality of the world and of others. But in their reaction toward the real in a Lacanian sense, though similar subjective structures such as repetition-compulsion and obsessional neurosis can be observed, Dana and Stephen finally find their proper individuation in a clear vision of the self with widely different results as persons and writers. Dana Hilliot, negating the present, will constantly lock himself into the past in imaginary identifications, whereas Stephen Dedalus, rejecting the past he has used, will re-create a present through words in a mental alchemy. The former declares "I have changed" (*Ult* 184) when, in fact, there is stasis and the only change is more consciousness of what he has been until then. The latter will proclaim himself begetter of a self created by his Irish social, political, and religious contexts.

In the case of Dana Hilliot, the young toff breaking away from youth, family, and love, the problem of identification is stated in terms of how to establish himself in a new world of adult males. Dana's practical problems may be summed up as: (1) how to get recognized by the crew as one of them, particularly by Andy, the cook, as a son; by Norman, the galley boy, as a friend; and by Nikolai, the fireman, as a brother; and (2) how to justify himself to Janet, the girl he has left behind. Proofs and justification of what he says or pretends will have to be given. Action must be taken and tests passed. Consequently the plot will be constructed in six well-defined—neatly separated according to chapter—episodes devoted to Dana's actions.

First, to be accepted by Andy and the crew he wants to project himself as a hero; he wants to win his entrance into the circle of the real seamen by some highly heroic salvatory deed. In chapter 1, the occasion soon arises: a carrier pigeon is dying on the topmast and has to be retrieved. Who is going to get it down? Dana immediately seizes the opportunity, but only in his mind and speech. He misses it in fact: Norman is the quicker in execution and will win the day and . . . the bird. Then, in chapter 2, in order to belong to the "men" of the crew, Dana must show that he is a man. He is asked to prove Janet's existence through a letter of hers. Unfortunately, there is no mail, so Dana fails. As an alternate test, he is told to go ashore on a night's drift. He goes, but alone, and comes back to the ship, where, in lieu of a Jane, he confronts the homosexual demands of the quartermaster—which horrify him. Dana's laughter on leaving the man has nothing to do with a healthy Meredithian comic laughter; it only denotes how deeply he smarts under the derision of his ephebe's aspect.[2] In chapter 3, he gets two letters: one from his mother, the other from Janet. Yet he does not show either: he keeps them to himself, ashamed of a doting mother and fearful of losing Janet's letter. Boastingly he goes ashore and tries to make friends with an older sailor from another ship. Yet Dana cannot identify with him as man and sailor: the process works the other way round. The older man identifies the youthful imago of his self that Dana offers him. And so, Dana makes him read his mother's letter. They drink and visit brothels but shyness, a fear of sexual disease, and scruples about faithfulness prevent Dana from acting there again. Worst of all, after Dana again attempts to prove his virility to the crew, Andy (the father substitute) takes his place as a lover.[3]

In chapter 4, the next morning, he decides to kill Andy as rival father-figure. He is determined to face him in the manner of any Homeric hero, by insulting him about his weak chin. He does so, but revenge is deflated: since Andy has lost his chin in heroic war action, Dana's gesture falls flat. In chapter 5, Dana decides to ask Andy to forgive him, but the real again intervenes and he cannot find him alone. Following suit, a new occasion for manly conduct crops up: Norman's pigeon is drowning. Yet once more, Dana is prevented from acting by Andy himself (the ship needs all hands). Dana has to obey orders, so the pigeon drowns and Norman, infuriated, accuses them all of cowardice. As a result, Dana falls back in with the rest of the crew; he becomes one of them and he is accepted—but on the wrong side as one sharing a common guilt. Now Dana can make it up with Andy, who calls him *son* and invites him to the messroom for a *manly* drink. All seems well, but an ominous note is sounded by the sea.

In chapter 6, the homebound ship takes her course back. Dana writes an answer to Janet, yet a new stasis intervenes: the letter will remain unforwarded, thus canceling his new power for decision. In fact, he mentally decides to postpone his life with Janet and to sail until he comes to a place where he can find more universal expansion of the self by doing social work—one more salvatory proposition. Worse: choosing not to write any more for the present, he castrates himself as a writer and even as a mature man by delegating Janet or "any woman" to write in his place because he does not feel ready: "I don't know a damn thing yet" (*Ult* 186). The book suddenly ends with a new order: Dana is sent to work as a fireman down in the ship's very entrails, where he joins Nikolai, the third target in his desire. On an analytical level, therefore, Dana's self-identificatory process shows a system of blockage developing a repetitive model without end. The ultimate end of *his* quest (finding the right place on board the ship, i.e., in the world) only comes in now, when the novel and/or Dana reach chapter 6. Dana now dives into his subconscious, into the mental layers where he has concealed all the repressed, and thus starts a new quest.

The whole novel as a fabric achieves thereby a deadly circularity. On Dana's arriving in the firemen's hell, the old rites leading to identifi-

cation, seen on the initial page, can start all over again—only now the
passage is toward a descent into the fire of a hell for which he does not
seem any better adapted and which is only symbolic of another deep
sinking into the abyss of "under under the volcano" to which he will be
"cribbed, cabined, confined" like Macbeth in his guilt. Each chapter, with
its overall tone of frustration, is highly dramatized in a most repetitive
way: the narrative is constantly punctuated by noises and sounds made
by the sea, by the ship, and by the sailors appropriately chiming in to
warn ominously of forthcoming catastrophe. The same kind of device is
used in *Macbeth*, but here there is no mere copying of Shakespeare, for
the symbolic meaning ascribed to numbers is deftly played upon as early
as in chapter 1, where the chiming of six bells is omitted, though a string
of references otherwise running from one bell to eight bells is scattered
throughout the chapter. According to esoteric lore, the number 6 as inscribed in Solomon's seal would mean the macrocosm, or universal man,
whereas the number 5 would be the figure of microcosm, or ordinary
man.[4] Dana will never hear six bells or the call to transcendence of past
and present times into the a-temporality of myth. As early as the first
chapter, the omitted or lost number foretells the negative result of Dana's
quest for maturity and unity of self.

The entire plot has been worked out as a system of foreshadowings
that constitute as many clues to the elucidation of Dana's plight. Hints
are dropped, puns are proffered, letters are lost or reappear out of the
blue, are read or not, are sent or not, really written or just mentally pro-
nounced, negating the very possibility of the act of writing and privileging memories over facts, memory over reality, past over present. To come
to a realistic definition of himself in the present, Dana must take his
bearings through the polyphony or cacophony of many voices that, in
turn, represent sundry worlds for him to recognize and to get recognized by. The voices of the sailors' world on board or on land—crude,
dirty, practical, raucous from wind and drink, heard in snatches of conversation or yarns, recorded in a realistic tone, mimetic of the reality and
essence of the sailors and their lives—represent to him the state of virility and maturity he hankers after, so he believes that by being recognized by them he would at the same time justify himself to Janet. Further,
the somewhat contradictory voices of the sky and the sea still mean to
him two opposed states of a desired self, a self full of order, harmony,
and beauty, but also of tediousness, isolation, and ill omens—even if the
deromanticizing of the sea, which also belongs to the hard core of a working reality and bitter suffering, is felt as necessary for a progress to maturity. Because they represent only a potential unified state of the ideal
self, the voices here will range from the irrational to the highly emo-

tional, from the realistic to the most sadly sentimental, from the highly cultural to the mystically poetic, contrasting with the cacophony of the man-made world of the ship. Its deck filled with restive animals and its engine room resonant with harsh disharmony represent, in fact, the real condition of Dana's body, mind, heart, and soul, a state of chaos and disunion that he finally ascribes to "the principles of life" (*Ult* 169).

Dana's voice encompasses them all, mainly because he is the writer in search of the self, and this self tries to integrate the two former worlds while keeping his personal accents culturally and socially different from the seamen's. The complexity of his search explains why each chapter is composed of a series of scenes in which the crew's dialogues, like ground noises, alternate with Dana's soliloquies and become as many bits of subconversation or mental ejaculation. The overall effect gives an impression not of reality but of linguistic metonymy—the best sample of it being the one-word title of the book. "Ultramarine," an emblematic metaphor for places, situation, and quest, is a mimetic rendering of Dana's inner and outer worlds, as well as of the "philosophy of composition" of the book, the pseudoharmony of the prefix "ultra" affixed to a grammatically undefined word suggesting only an intermediary condition of floating between word and world.[5]

Now, what of Joyce? What about the *Portrait* as fiction describing an identificatory process? How has the book been organized? What mechanisms are at work in the narrative? Contrary to *Ultramarine*, Joyce's book as an object does not at first sight appear to have been structured in blocks called chapters. The *Portrait* appears as one continuum of five so-called paragraphs or sections forming units that each include up to five subsections separated by diacritic signs, the total effect being that the composition mimics the continual flow of life and time; further, the text represents the very medium in which the artist's sensibility will be structured.

The sections are artistically interrelated by the description of the outward world or references to former incidents in each. Unlike those in *Ultramarine*, the descriptions from chapter to chapter are less like an operatic setting. They are well integrated into the process that might be described as the making of Stephen; they are realistic, yet always functional in relation to Joyce's aim.

In the *Portrait* again a series of ordeals and revelations integrate various factual landmarks in the unfolding narrative. The identification theme again is constantly set in a process of walking or running, traversing bridges, ambulating along the mazelike web of the Dublin streets, or proceeding to half-lit chambers, the places for Stephen's ordeals, reached along dark and cold corridors. Again and again Stephen will walk over playgrounds and quadrangles or go to chapel either alone or with friends.

This palpable background linked with the identificatory process does not just provide a social or cultural setting, it becomes one of the powerful forces at work *in* the process. Joyce provides meaning through impressionistic and expressionistic suffusion that is less obviously overt than Lowry's; yet Joyce, like Lowry, creates a compelling ambiance that is an active agent in the making of Stephen: see the careful expressionist description of effects of light vs. darkness, the grey color of Dublin's streets, rain or light, the slow coming up or falling away of day and night. What emerges, in effect, is an interplay between the symbolic and the realistic, or representative. Joyce's characterization, too, is a combination of allegorical and realistic treatments. The school fellows are used to both purposes: they are alive and real enough, yet grouped by threes, and often if not always they are endowed with the function of awakeners. Three swimmers will reveal to Dedalus his real mythical name (*P* 167-69).

Unlike Dana, Stephen "achieves creative relation to the world by means of separation" (Brivic 8). First the process of individuation is effected through a course of conflictual situations. This Stephen does in the first three sections, which Joyce rewrote in Freudian terms. Stephen has to separate as an individual from parental ties and from the objective world by estranging himself from the coziness of the maternal haven and liberating the self from the father's authority; that he does so is due, in a way, both to his prize money and to his ironic perspective. (Whether the process leaves the effects of fear or not is hardly the problem here.) Stephen symbolically succeeds in effectuating the patricidal dream of the dying marshal, just as he frees himself from confusion with— though not from the threat of—reality by framing the world in words or songs, that is, in rhythm and time. In this long progress toward identification, *Portrait*, unlike *Ultramarine*, is never pent up in a kind of *huis clos* but travels in time and space from world to world,[6] from each of which Stephen will have to free himself until the last "non serviam" is fully stated in words.

Strangely enough, as soon as the second subsection starts, Joyce's method of development again resembles Lowry's, but it ends with the opposite result. As with Dana, Stephen is faced with the problem of action, though without the imaginary fantasies of action Dana is inclined to. Stephen will not wait and talk till he misses the opportunity; he will be both a battered and a battering hero, unlike Dana, who remains a romantic hero more acted upon than acting, a ship adrift on a sea of uncertainties, an unconscious daredevil and a conscious fabulator playing with fire instead of turning into a Daedalus reconstructing world and work through words.

Just as Lowry does in *Ultramarine*, Joyce in the *Portrait* makes use of reduplicated meetings: Dana's two pigeon episodes find their counterparts in Stephen's two private meetings with the higher authorities at school. But in the *Portrait* the meetings end differently because Stephen chooses to act and react, thus involving himself in an open process that permits him to overcome and progress. In the first encounter, the wronged schoolboy wins the day by a mature conduct acknowledged by the rector himself, who calls him "my little man" (*P* 56). As a result, he will gain some self-confidence and fuller articulation as the conscience and voice of a community. When he eventually reappears outside, he is greeted as a hero by the others, and for the first time he is able to enjoy his isolation as freedom and a new sense of accordance with (not immersion in) the universe (*P* 59). Only later will the boy fully realize his victory, when it is refracted within the family circle through his father's words reporting the rector's view of the incident as a fine joke between the authorities and his own (as father's) view of the incident as a proud feat of rebellion. The fact that no comment should ensue from either Stephen the young man or Joyce, the older writer, only shows how far Stephen has grown.[7]

The second private interview takes place much later, near the end of his studies, when Stephen is asked to give an answer about his priestly vocation. Yet here the pattern is not strictly repetitive, for in between Stephen has struggled with the religious fathers to liberate the self from the Church discourse. He has had to experience the chapel itself as a battlefield. Stephen realizes from the implacable logic of Jesuit rhetoric how real his sin is and, after much hesitation and a great sense of guilt for his carnal appetites, sets out to confess. Why has Jesuit rhetoric such impact on the boy who is going to be an artist? Because here the process is not one of projection, as it would have been with Dana; it is a matter of the power of the word to raise an image or feeling. Stephen does not identify with the sinners, whether Lucifer, Adam, or Eve, but he feels their plight: their sins are *his*, so their punishment is *his*, hell is *his* hell, and their tortures are *his* torture. A lay incarnation of the thing through the spoken word: such is the new experience of the artist. Yet he discovers that action and volition are not enough for a relief from guilt and tries to mortify his senses. The idea is to regress to point zero in order to progress again. But strengthening his control over each sense through mortification only serves to interiorize his problem, separating body and soul so that he cannot accept his sexual life as a unifying experience. Yet the artist, by now used to Jesuit oratory, has grown in the art of handling words with logic.

Thus when the second interview takes place, Stephen, rising to the occasion, proves to be a match for his opponent. The Jesuit director has enough psychological insight to understand the situation and puts Stephen on a level with himself, though he frightens Stephen by drawing a picture of priesthood as incarnating the power of the Word, and of the strange power given to words to become incarnate. Stephen as a creator of reality through words cannot endure such tyranny and is ready to break loose. At the same time, his own imagination will betray him in a subtle way, trapping him into musings started both by the actuality of the real and by the strength of his desires. Fantasies spring up of himself as a Jesuit in flesh and blood and also of his name objectively spelt as "the Reverend Stephen Dedalus, S.J." These words in turn flash upon his mind a picture of his face as expressing death and cunning. Not imagined reality, but reality in flesh and blood irrupts to negate the glorious aura of the phantasms with a squad of Christian Brothers. The game again is between words and symbolized reality and the real. Stephen, proceeding on his symbolic and real progress toward the sea, is steeped in an emotional state that takes him into a realm of harmony, a musically sonorous impregnation taking him to a mental state bordering the unconscious, from which his real name will emerge not through pictures but voices, real enough voices.

The experience is again one of words made flesh. Coming across his friends taking a swim, he is derided by them as they proclaim his name. He is Stephanos, the crowned one; he is the Daedalus, the unique living specimen in flesh and blood of a mythic entity; he is Bous Stephanomenos, the Ox manifested as the crowned one; he is Bous Stephaneforos, the Ox bearing the crown. Again an ideal representation is incarnated in a *living* myth, the realization of which is so violently aggressive that he perceives a physical cleaving of the brain equated with a real birth of the self (*P* 169) and so breaks away from his comrades toward a final vision with which he feels both at one and separate. The vision is composed of Stephen as subject and the girl both as art object and as physical reality. Beauty, love, femininity, and Ireland are incorporated in this Irish girl wading in a tidal pool on the strand. At this point in the narrative, the portrait of the artist is not yet completed, for his severance from Ireland and her cultural and historical past has yet to be perfected.

The last section takes up in action and in words Stephen's last definition and his mission as an artist. Its four subsections round up every one in turn of the situations of the self encountered throughout the novel. Now the time scheme is stretched at will as in any fictional world. The situations vary from a polyphonic discussion to a more sober dialogue for two voices down to the isolated voice of the poet in the creative act.

The moods vary from the elegiac to realistic mimesis, back into the disquisitive and the logical, interspersed with the most brilliantly striking epigrams and formulas or even the lousiest puns. The narrative technique itself varies from the objective dialogue to the minute probing into consciousness, from lush mystic communions of the self with nature to cultural reminiscences, from flashbacks into the past to foreshadowing of the future, from small sections of dazzling intensity to long-drawn rhetoric, from day musing to night dreaming. One cannot speak of many voices here, as in *Ultramarine*. I would rather define such a text as a kaleidoscopic vision of the self perfectly wrought as one and the same center of consciousness, that of a man-and-artist. Stephen now is able to pass on to the praxis of writing a poem in letters on the page of a master's discourse as incarnated in a poet (or Stephen) aggrandized to the stature of a myth (that of Icarus).[8]

The title of the novel both heralds the contents of the volume and defines the aloofness with which Joyce will speak of his treatment of biographical material. This aloofness explains why the first-person pronoun appears only at the very end of the book, once the poet has metamorphosed the biographical self into a mythic entity capable of undertaking the formidable tasks Joyce assigned to the self as a man and poet. He can now use the first person in the truth of his being *and* under the various technical masks. In *Ultramarine,* the first-person singular strikes the chord as early as chapter 3, which is totally devoted to it, before the narrative swings back to a technical third-person pronoun. In fact, there is no difference in Lowry's narrative between the first and the third person, but the predominance of the third-person narrative in all the chapters except one evinces the painstaking endeavor of the artist to keep the self at a distance from his material, and the increasing mixing of both by the end of the work smacks of a wish to articulate a center of consciousness in a narrative. The symptomatic aspect of Lowry's text calls for analytical interpretation of the structuration of a subject as falling back upon the past and his inability to differentiate the ego from the real, which points to a permanent privileging of the imaginary as to self-identificatory processes with Dana, alias Lowry. Dana's desire is to identify with Andy (*Ult* 185), and he realizes only later that his posture meant hero worship: he comes to understand that he was only interested in Andy's position as ruler on the deck and becomes a rival as a lover. Andy, by explaining to Dana that love to him only meant a hygienic act, loses all glamor and forfeits his father-position in Dana's eyes. But there is still left the friendship of the Norwegian sailor extant at least as telegraphic messages, and of Nikolai, the new embodiment of Dana's ultimate quest of the self on a deeper yet no less delusive level.

Both *Portrait* and *Ultramarine* finally deal with an attempt at defining what an artist is and how he can be seen. Here again, the self-identificatory processes deeply influence the writing process, as one can postulate that Dana is Lowry's alter ego as Stephen is Joyce's. An objection can be made here that it is hardly fair to compare one book (Joyce's) that *means* to show an artist's development with another book (Lowry's) that deals so excruciatingly in self-production. But Lowry also strives to define what an artist, more particularly a fiction writer, is and does. He too started as a very conscious artist with a highly cultural background (he wrote *Ultramarine* under no lesser guidance than Conrad Aiken's, the champion poet of man's consciousness). For both Lowry and Joyce the ethical problem revolves around the concept of truth as a governing posture both in art and in life.

The problem of fabulating one's life in art is treated seriously in *Ultramarine*. In chapter 3, which constitutes one of the reflexive breaks in the narrative, Dana, the would-be artist, explains to the blunt Norwegian sailor that he is far from overstepping the boundaries of truth when he pretends in the face of the whole world that he *is* Hamlet and that *he* has written the play. And right he is indeed: he does identify himself retrospectively as a living prototype to Hamlet's character pursued by guilt. As such, he can hardly lie when he pretends that he came first before Shakespeare in the production of Hamlet. Reading comes before writing, as Derrida would say. The second point developed about fabulating goes even further when Dana puts in a claim for the right of fabulating without damaging truth. The most amusing part of the claim lies in the uncertainties about Dana's parents' authority: at the beginning of the novel he declares that he is under the authority of a tutor whom every reader takes for a legal guardian, but later on, having to "forge" a doomed family, he invents a doomed father and mother. Finally, when he has changed (or so he thinks), he announces: "Let us come to a sober view. Let us take father home from his madhouse and mother back to her pills." And he explains that his fabulation did not start from an act of insincerity of the self toward the self or toward general truth, but from an act of misreading the signs of the letters, so he proclaims (not without *mauvaise foi*, from which he will readily absolve any writer) his personal innocence against the linguistic sin of his readers.

Another point in the matter of comparing Dana's action with Stephen's is that he also produces a work of art, composing various stories in the manner of dreams. Dana imagines crowning the many reminiscences of the sailors' ultimate confabulation, in which they gradually pile up real memories and dreams, with his own supposed dream about the ship, which is no less than a fable about triumphing over one's fear of being devoured. In the fable every single soul on board, except one, is devoured by the animals the ship is transporting. One can imagine which is the exception: the man absolutely necessary for telling again and again a made-up dream as fable in order to bring about laughter by representing the world as topsy-turvy. The overall technique here is the following: packing up things and items alongside each other and accumulating materials. Once more, the narrative stands as a metaphor for the structuration of both Dana and *Ultramarine*. Art and life coalesce, reality dissolves into the self as metaphor of the self.[9] Lowry's attitude to past and environment is essentially a predatory one, mostly developed in Dana's position on board as an eavesdropping voyeur.

Now, Joyce's position is different. He lets the self be immersed in the past, *his* past, in history, *his* country's, in a culture that is *his* and his country's and the Jesuits' even if he resents the pressures of history, politics, and religion. Only when the appropriation is completed does he reject country, Church, and past culture. But if he does so, it is only to project them the better and mend them the better through the artist's mind and consciousness. Joyce's attitude toward the past as material for writing results, as I shall suggest, in a different handling of verbal tenses.

Dana, constantly leaping mentally into his past with Janet and with his mother, regresses and escapes into the past, rendering it vividly as present mostly in phantasms raised by what he sees or what he hears. The self pitted against the real is at stake here.[10] Dana and Lowry tend to produce a striking lack of differentiation between the actual and the imagined, wish fulfillment and the real, the remembered and the directly observed, the reported and the directly heard. Their unusual use of verbal tenses blending past and present with future contributes to a lush blurring of time. See how in one and the same day's musing (*Ult* 72-74) Dana/Lowry starts with a future verbal tense, meaning present fantasy and past relationship to Janet, goes on with a mixture of preterits and present tenses referring to past and present situations in the narrative, the present tense being mainly tinted with bodily or emotional realities, and finishes off in the preterit, as might a press report, with an obituary notice of Dana's own death as an old man, a projection into the future of the afterbook. This is also very conspicuous in Dana's privileging the modal would-form, implying that action is expressed as wish, not as reality. Such mental activities as fantasies and daymusings or nightmares play interference with the factual story. Their role is to displace time and space and to people Dana's solitude with mental action (*Ult* 143). For Dana again, the possibility of writing stands between the modal forms "could" and "can" when he comes to drowning in the narratively actual yarns of the seamen (*Ult* 198-99). And the story he concocts results in a dream told in the preterit like any tale, yet it represents mental facts. Such a structuring process is also very conspicuous in Dana's privileging the modal would-form when he wants to imply that action is expressed as wish or as possibility (not as reality). The modal form marking reported speech is also the means of expressing future action when Dana decides to kill Andy as a revenge or when he means an action not to be real, though it represents real phantasms. Dana, representing action as fantasy, will never kill Andy—not even symbolically, as Stephen does his father. Once Dana reaches positive action, he shifts from "could" to "can" (*Ult* 198). At this point in the narrative, he imagines the story about animals devouring the crew with the exception of the writer. Dana, as a writer, has possibly come to real existence. At the same time, Dana doubts his very existence as acting man (*Ult* 143). Then he uses the present verbal tense to negate the actual narrative present, denying the real to project the self into the future: "I am not on a ship. I wish I were, since I don't know what it's like. I wish I were. I wish I were—what? A pair of ragged clauses scuttling between two dark parentheses? Possibly I am. Anyhow I am not a seaman" (*Ult* 143). Dana is oppressed by his guilt for having left Janet behind and would like to undo what he cannot: "If he could only unlive the past two months" (*Ult* 142).

In *Portrait*, Joyce has a no less complex system of changes in verbal tenses, but their issues are more technical as to enunciatory problems. Stephen most of the time swings from the preterit, the usual narrative verbal tense, to the pluperfect to mark the anteriority of action in the time of memory. Deane (xvi) cites Stephen's words to show how Joyce solves the problem of the presence of a narrator. Joyce, who envisages the word as active, rarely sunders action from actual realization, even when he aims at depicting how the mind works. Delirium is the chosen medium to express in the narrative the epic impact of an actual present of national mourning upon the artist's soul and its development: the little boy on his sickbed mixes up present shouts and wailing at Parnell's death and distorts space and time in a delirium taking place in the present of the narrative. Joyce creates a compelling image working on the boy's evolution, thus removing his realistic material one step further into a mental process that becomes another sifter for the impact of history on Stephen. Where Lowry uses a delirious style, he does it to depict an increasing disorganization of the mind under the effect of drink or under emotional stress, as when Dana discovers in the sky or the ship machinery images of the self. In the two cases, the impact of the past on the mental building up and subject's structuration is radically different. For Dana, the past inhibits development, while Stephen, as a structuring subject, may be said to use the past for further poetic development.

When Stephen comes to express his future, he clearly uses the modal will-form in the full sense of the real verb: "I will not serve" (*P* 239). Stephen states his future position and mission as an act of volition, a free decision to which he will keep true, so that the book ends on a positive imperative-form asking for the help of his patron saint and mythic father. When Dana comes to visualize his future, the future verbal tense is used but in a special way, with the accents of a positive rendering of the biblical repressive "Thou shalt not," so that his mission is more like an imposition of the self upon the self. Is it sprung from volition or from self-punishment? Here, Dana seems to confuse volition with action, wish with wish fulfillment. And when at the very end of *Ultramarine* Dana looks at the passing *Oxenstjerna*, a metaphor for his failing to establish concrete links with Janet and the real as real, he falls back into his former inhibition, regretting that their suffering gets lost with the passing of the ship out of their mutual remembrance, and also that it should get doubly lost because it will never be related to Janet, since Dana never intends to send the letter. Then Dana's sea-voyage will go on forever until, with the foundering of the ship already envisaged in the second chapter, life and art and love founder in definitive paralysis.

This is as much as to say that both written texts function as written machines operating in radically opposite ways. Lowry's textual production relies on the apparition—not just appearance—of objects that will trigger it off. The reader should then pinpoint the ambulation within the text of material objects such as the carrier pigeon, letters, ships, harbors, or the sea, together with aural objects such as noises or sea shanties.[1] They function in Lowry's text not as universal symbols but as metaphors of the self, or, better, they operate as signs on a wall to be deciphered by both the character and his reader. Lowry's use of the symbol is a degrading of more or less stable signification into a less stable system governed by the self. With him literature or fiction writing enters into what has been called the "literature of signs," signs working in a world best depicted by Nathalie Sarraute as a "doubting era" or *l'ère du soupçon*. In other terms, one could also speak of Lowry's text production as a repetitive re-citation of the self. This can very well be perceived in the status of the cultural quotations in Lowryan texts: the text is founded on a number of archetypes the repetitive re-citation of which can help with the mending of the writer's severing from words, identity, real life. Having a firm grasp on words that have already proved true with other writers is fundamental for Lowry, who thinks *that* is what he does when he recites or when he plays with the signifieds of separate words. Yet he remains shy, he does not go beyond punning, and puns serve him as concealers of the signified in an esoteric way or (less seriously) as a hoax, a practical trick played upon the reader. See again how he plays on the two meanings of the word "tutor" for narrating purposes only, or as cash drawn upon quotations.

Now when we compare Joyce's textual practice, we clearly see that it relies upon the Word established as overall problematic. The keywords circulating within the texts constitute as many incarnations of the Word made Flesh in the letter. Watch therefore for the apparition—not the appearance once more—of such words as "see," or consider how the word "ivory" runs through the text both as multiple signifiers and signifieds from the sensuous to sensual translations of Eileen's nails to the metaphoric chant of the Virgin's litany through to its final use as "ivory/ivy" in Stephen's first attempt at writing poetry. Again what follow are some fundamental, even essential comparisons, bearing at the same time a metaphoric meaning. I suggest the following sequences: wave/ tide/ trickling stream/ overwhelming fluidity/ to fluidity itself as an image of the flowing of the consciousness being transferred to the flexibility of the sentence structure in the manner of Rousseau's *Fifth Reverie*. Or the following one: bous/ bird/ hawk/ lynx/ labyrinth (see how my own listing follows a sound pattern). Again another sequence could run: star/ sky/ light/ music. See also how the adjective "grey" infects Dublin, school, life, mind, culture. How do these chains work? In metaphoric language, I would say as kernels contaminating other signifiers or signifieds up to the last word, the globality giving the true meaning. Thus, Joyce's text is already a reflexive text, reflexive upon the language. Lowry's, on the other hand, is mainly reflexive of time and the self. The two major problematics of Language and Time running through their writing processes make of Lowry and Joyce real but quite distinct representatives of the twentieth-century mind.

Both Lowry and Joyce speak a language to twentieth-century readers who tend to fall into the same attitude to the texts as their writers do toward their respective materials. A contemporary reader tends to immerse himself in Lowry's text. He tends to identify with the hero Dana because the latter personifies the human condition of this century—the neuroses or psychoses of modern man, the fears and views of man as a child lost in the labyrinth of History and the maze of Language, an absurd world upon which he has hardly any hold. Therefore Dana never loses our sympathy. We are with and within him; we understand him, we use the same defining concepts and the same vocabulary to speak about the self and the world. In other terms, we can identify with him, and a Lowryan text belongs to all those texts working by sheer force of attraction: we, readers, founder head down in them. The pleasure derived from such text mainly consists in a recognition of the self.

Joyce's text also works upon the reader, just as his environment does upon the child Stephen. It works as a slow suffusion of the text through the reader's mind and heart. As with Leonardo's *Gioconda*, the text or portrait has to be slowly and repeatedly imbibed. Yet we keep at a distance. The pleasure consists in recognizing, not merging with, Stephen—in recognizing the power of words and images or rhetorics upon the mind, of recognizing the neuroses of the writer without really entering the hell of the cauldron of the Word made Flesh that was Joyce's plight. Why so? Because we recognize the well-oiled functioning of an intellectual mind, the endless process of the working of the mind upon words to re-create the world in terms of life, not of death. In our reading, anabolism, not catabolism, is the process at work. Dana, and the Consul later, will walk down to suicidal death, whereas Stephen and Finnegan resurge to life, while the river goes on running.

Notes

1. See Brivic 20 and 218, note 3, on Hans Walter Gabler's contention that Freud and Jones directly influenced Joyce's "extensive" revision of the first three chapters of *Portrait*, beginning in 1911.

2. Lowry in his schooldays suffered at the hands of his comrades for the feminine innuendoes attached to his first name, Clarence, which he soon dropped. Later, he also pretended to have been harassed on the wharfs of Cho Lon.

3. Lowry kept pretending that Aiken, his father substitute, asked him to share Jan Gabrial with him in Spain.

4. Later in the first chapter, Dana remembers how, at school, "the mathematics teacher [had] once actually given permission for the whole form to crowd around to watch his pathetic attempts . . . to create a regular hexagon" (*Ult* 41). In chapter 2 he is sitting on the number 6 hatch. For a discussion of such an interpretation of numbers, see Chevalier and Gheerbrant 3:282 and 4:213.

5. Furthermore, the title is an affirmation of Lowry's quest for a voice as a writer against Aiken's, Lowry's first proposition for the title being "Purple Passage" as counter-title to Aiken's *Blue Voyage*.

6. These worlds include the nursery and family ties at home, Cork and the family past, Nighttown's experience of sex and prostitutes, the Church and its pressure, and Ireland with her political and cultural past, all of which he has to lay down for the artist to emerge.

7. I beg to differ here with Brivic's interpretation of the amusement Stephen's father and master have over the incident. Their laughter does not appear to me as derisive since the rector's final pronouncement about Stephen is "manly little chap" and the section ends with a reported peal of laughters— not sneers—on the Jesuits' side, which calls for no comment on Stephen's part.

8. The fact that the chosen patronymic name of Icarus, Dedalus, might appear mostly as ironic due to the misfortune of Icarus and the dark memories attached to the labyrinth, does not fundamentally alter the structuring pattern of a subject toward a mythic ideal representation of the self.

9. Lowry will come to a full realization of this coalescence later, in *Dark as the Grave*, where his hero has an impression of living in a book whose author he is not. This study was drafted for a seminar in Antwerp in December 1993. I came across Deane's introduction to the 1992 Penguin edition of *Portrait* only later, when I decided to publish this. The similarity in thought here with Deane's introduction is purely coincidental.

10. The more so as both Joyce and Lowry were writers interested in one of the major problems in the first third of the twentieth century: that of the representation of the real in arts, together with how the mind apprehends it. In *Ultramarine* Proust is referred to as a writer of past things remembered.

Works Cited

Brivic, Sheldon R. *Joyce between Freud and Jung*. Port Washington, N.Y.: Kenrikat Press, 1980.

Chevalier, Jean, and Alain Gheerbrant, eds. *Dictionnaire des symboles*. 4 vols. Paris: Seghers, 1974.

Deane, Seamus. Introduction to *A Portrait of the Artist as a Young Man*, by James Joyce. Harmondsworth, England: Penguin Books, 1993.

eight

Syphilisation and Its Discontents: Somatic Indications of Psychological Ills in Joyce and Lowry

Martin Bock

"Sickness," Dr. Vigil reflects at the beginning of *Under the Volcano*, "is not only in body, but in that part used to be call: soul" (*UV* 5, 144). The connection between bodily disease and mental affliction preoccupied Malcolm Lowry and James Joyce throughout their writing lives, in part because they were inclined to drink—and shared what Delmore Schwartz calls a "withness of the body"—and in part because they lived with the fear of syphilis, a disease that first manifests itself in bodily lesions and was thought by the medical community of the early twentieth century to be a leading cause of mental insanity. The fiction of Joyce and Lowry thus attends closely to the figure of the syphilitic body as an index to ill health.[1] This literal body in their work has as its correlative a rhetorical or figurative body, which expresses the syphilophobe's fear of mental in-sanity. Foucault's *Madness and Civilization* provides a useful scheme for reading the relation between the literal disfigurement of the body and conventional tropes that express the horrors of mental disease. Foucault suggests that rhetorical figures such as animality, blindness, and death—all of which are common tropes in the work of Lowry and Joyce—convey a fear of madness because they are metonymies for the reduction of one's being toward that which is nonhuman. Moreover, in an age when insanity was thought to be caused in part by a sexually transmitted disease, the connection between mental insanity and moral impropriety became a focus for the remorseful conscience of both Joyce and Lowry, who were raised in cultural and familial environments that exploited the power of psychological guilt.

The Body as Literal Figure

While Joyce was studying medicine and shortly afterwards writing *Dubliners*, the medical profession was sharply divided about the causes of insanity and whether research in the field of mental disease should focus on a somatic or a psychological etiology. The mental scientists of the day were largely pathologists and neurologists who advanced theories of parallelism, concomitance, and synchronism, which posited varying degrees of necessity in the connection between the mind and the body, and who thus embraced a fundamentally somatic rather than psychological etiology for mental disease.[2] Writing in 1899 in the *Alienist and Neurologist*, the leading American journal in its field, Rudolf Arndt suggested that virtually any serious somatic disorder could cause insanity: "All diseases of the body, whether more of a general or more of a local nature . . . can be . . . the cause of a mental disease, of insanity. Rheumatism, gout, typhoid, cholera, influenza, malaria, every pulmonary inflammation, cardiac inflammation, every disorder of the stomach, intestines, liver and kidneys, the diseases of the bladder and genital organs, of the subcutaneous cellular tissue and also periosteal inflammations, tenosynitis, so-called paronychia and dental abscess, can in this way be the cause of a disease of the ego, of insanity" (32). The resistance to a psychological etiology of mental illness remained strong into the first decade of the twentieth century, well after Joyce abandoned his medical career and began writing *Dubliners*. I do not suggest that Joyce attended to the debate between psychologists and pathologists. But Joyce's interest in the physicality of the human body would have comprehended a wider range of medical issues than might be supposed by those of us who, after Freud, often link mental disease with a psychology of the unconscious. Joyce's ability to "read the lineaments of disease . . . on the faces and the bodies of the crowd" (Lyons, *James Joyce and Medicine*, 29) would provide him with literal and rhetorical figures of Ireland's ill health, a moral insanity closely linked in Joyce's time to madness.

Waisbren and Walzl in "Paresis and the Priest" long ago suggested that Joyce used somatic indications of mental disease in his portrait of Father Flynn, whose death, they argue, is due to paresis, or general paralysis of the insane (GPI), a disorder that was thought in Joyce's time to be caused by, or associated with, syphilis.[3] J.B. Lyons has argued against such an interpretation and "diagnosis" of Father Flynn, citing the differences between the priest's general symptoms and those of GPI, which is caused by cerebral syphilis ("Animadversions on Paralysis," 262-63). I believe that one reason for the confusion or debate over Joyce's intentions in "The Sisters" lies in misidentifying, as Waisbren and Walzl do, Osler's *Principles and Practice of Medicine* as the exclusive textual "source" that Joyce may have consulted in the Library of the Royal College of Physicians of Ireland. Another common source of medical information owned by that library was D. Hack Tuke's *Dictionary of Psychological Medicine*, likewise a standard reference tool in the medical community of Joyce's day.[4] Tuke's *Dictionary*, first published in 1892, is a comprehensive two-volume collection of essays and definitions written by 128 international experts in the field of mental science. Though Tuke's *Dictionary* received only a descriptive review in the *Journal of Mental Science* (which Tuke coedited), a review in the American *Journal of Nervous and Mental Disease* (after complaining about the lack of American contributors) gave the dictionary grudgingly high praise:

> The work is a strong one, rich in its suggestiveness, forming an elaborate and valuable contribution to the literature of medical psychology. It commends itself especially on account of its terminology which is thoroughly modern, and also because of its clear definitions. It is very reliable as a work of reference, not only to experts in mental diseases but to the student of psychology in any of its branches, and also to the profession generally. It certainly fills a want long felt . . . [and] brings into focus the widespread literature of the subject in a manner that betokens the editor's zeal, ability and broad learning. [Review of *A Dictionary*, 657]

Tuke's *Dictionary* was clearly the definitive pre-Freudian reference tool and would have been in use during Joyce's two years as an on-again-off-again medical student. The apparent reverberations throughout *Dubliners* of Tuke's *Dictionary* entry on GPI suggest that we need to modify Waisbren and Walzl's theory, though not reject it. While Joyce probably revised "The Sisters" in 1906 with the specific intent of adding descriptions of Father Flynn consistent with a medical diagnosis of paresis, he incorporated such descriptions throughout the *Dubliners* stories after his stint as a medical student in 1902-3. As Stanislaus Joyce's diary notation of August 13, 1904, indicates, his brother was doing a *"series of studies in it* ["syphilitic contagion"] in Dublin" (*Dublin Diary*, 51, my italics), which suggests that early in the composition of *Dubliners* syphilis and paralysis were projected to be important motifs in a series of *Dubliners* stories, not just "The Sisters." As Joyce wrote the studies, I suggest that he used materials commonly known to the medical community through Tuke's *Dictionary*; and having used the motif of GPI in many of the *Dubliners* stories, Joyce returned to "The Sisters" to make it consistent with and the inaugural story for the collection.

A case could be made that Joyce, in his revision of "The Sisters," consulted Tuke rather than Osler, for some of Tuke's descriptions of GPI are more verbally proximate to Joyce's text than are those of Osler. But what may be more useful is to show how the medical indications of GPI found in Tuke's *Dictionary* coincide with some of the most memorable distinguishing characteristics of the physical appearances and verbal lives of various Dubliners who appear after "The Sisters." Like Father Flynn, whose distinguishing physical characteristic is "his big discoloured teeth" that he laid bare when he "let his tongue lie upon his lower lip" (*D* 13), the exhibitionist of "An Encounter" is most memorable for his facial description: "I . . . involuntarily glanced up at his face. As I did so I met the gaze of a pair of bottle-green eyes peering at me from under a twitching forehead" (*D* 27). The *Dictionary of Psychological Medicine* mentions facial twitching at least six times in its entry on GPI, including a specific indication that "the occipito-frontalis is often gathered together or twitching" (Tuke 527). Moreover, the old man, who "shivered once or twice as if he feared something or felt a sudden chill" (*D* 25–26), illustrates the "quasi-shivering, not from fever or external cold" noted in Tuke (527). Tuke's *Dictionary* also suggests that the general paralytic may evidence a decline in sexual morality manifest in "open indecencies, attempt[ed] paederasty" (Tuke 529), acts that Joyce's young narrator respectively witnesses and fears.

If the moral failure of Joyce's Dubliners mirrors their mental illness, so too does the poverty of their verbal lives, though such a connection between language and insanity is anything but unique to Joyce. In *Madness and Civilization*, Foucault cites a conventional, indexical relation, during the classical age in Europe, between madness and language, which he calls the *"first and last structure of madness*, its constituent form. . . . [This structure exercises] a hold over the totality of soul and body; such discourse is both the silent language by which the mind speaks to itself in the truth proper to it, and the visible articulation in the movements of the body" (Foucault 100). In the age of Joyce, Tuke confirms the traditional close connection between language and madness: "When general paralysis has become established, the speech more clearly betrays the mental state" (Tuke 526) in various forms of aphasia and articular disorders (Tuke 527). The general paralytic of "The Sisters" spreads his syphilitic contagion throughout Joyce's collection, infecting the verbal lives of characters in at least one-third of the stories, beginning with his relatives and friends. The most notable attribute of adult characters in "The Sisters" is their verbal poverty. Generally read as part of the gnomonic rhetoric of *Dubliners* (Friedrich, Herring), "articular disorders" are also symptomatic of GPI: "Ellipses of syllables may occur, as well as of words" (Tuke 526) and "consonants afford the chief difficulty" (Tuke 527) in matters of simple pronunciation. Old Cotter's unfinished sentences and Eliza's malapropisms may thus be read as subtle bodily indications of mental ill health. The verbal life of the old man of "An Encounter" is likewise consistent with some of the possible indications of GPI as indicated in Tuke's *Dictionary:*

Dubliners	*Dictionary*
He gave me the impression that he was *repeating* something which he had learned by heart or that, magnetised by some words of his own speech, his mind was slowly circling round and round in the same orbit. . . . At times he *lowered* his *voice* and spoke mysteriously. . . . He *repeated* his *phrases* over and over again, varying them and surrounding them with his *monotonous* voice	Thence come . . . incapacity for storing up and combining new mental acquisitions. . . .

Symptoms of Dementia [may include] childish rhythmic *repetition* of a few fragmentary *phrases*. . . . The voice becoming weak, *monotonous, low*-pitched . . . . |
| [26, my italics] | [521, 524, 527-28, my italics] |

Mr. Duffy of "A Painful Case"—who consciously "abhorred anything which betokened physical or mental disorder" (*D* 108)—displays what Foucault calls "the mind speak[ing] to itself" and what Tuke's *Dictionary* cites as one of the *"anomalies of self-consciousness"* experienced by the general paralytic, who "may speak of himself in the third person" (Tuke 529). This anomaly corresponds precisely to Mr. Duffy's only endearing, most characteristic quality, the "odd autobiographical habit which led him to compose in his mind from time to time a short sentence about himself containing a subject in the third person and a predicate in the past tense" (*D* 108).[5] Like the old man in "An Encounter," Duffy habitually repeats short sentences in a kind of ritual that betrays the orbital mind of the paralytic. In "The Dead" Mrs. Malins and her son, Freddy, exhibit a different sort of halting articular disorder. "Her voice had a catch in it like her son's and she stuttered slightly" (*D* 190). In the paralytic, according to Tuke's *Dictionary*, one may observe "a stoppage, a faint stuttering . . . as of one somewhat in liquor" (Tuke 527). Freddy and Mrs. Malins are like the gnomonic talkers of "The Sisters," whose ellipses disrupt communication; and Aunt Julia, who has the priest's "large flaccid face" and whose "slow eyes and parted lips gave her the appearance of a woman who did not know where she was or where she was going" (*D* 179), is given to conversational pausing and murmuring (*D* 180-81) due to her progressive dementia.

Of all Dubliners after "The Sisters," Eveline shows the most obvious signs of bodily paralysis in her failed attempt to escape Dublin. The clinical disorder that might account for Eveline's hesitation again includes general paralysis, which may bring on what were called "epileptiform seizures" (Tuke 530) of varying severity.

Dubliners	*Dictionary*
She answered nothing. She felt her cheek *pale* and *cold* and, out of a *maze of distress,* she prayed to God to direct her. . . . Her distress awoke a nausea in her body and she *kept moving her lips* in silent fervent prayer.	sudden *pallor . . .* with *cold* perspiration . . . *mental confusion . . .* muttered automatic repetition of coherent or of incoherent phrases . . .
She set her white face to him, passive, like a helpless animal. *Her eyes gave him no sign of* love or farewell or *recognition.*	sudden pallor . . . *dilatation of the pupils; . . . sudden fixation of the lineaments, or an expression as of shock.*
[40-41, my italics]	[530, my italics]

Eveline also had the classic symptoms of hysteria, a condition thought in the early years of the twentieth century to be brought on variously by "unsatisfied sexual desire" (Tuke 620) or "great and sudden emotions, such as fear in all its forms" (Tuke 625). Moreover, "palpitation is very common" (Tuke 624) and "heredity plays an all important part in its production" (Tuke 625). Eveline complains of having "palpitations" when she "felt herself in danger of her father's violence" (*D* 38) and is struck with terror when she recalls her

> mother's . . . life of common-place sacrifices closing in final craziness. She trembled as she heard again her mother's voice saying constantly with foolish insistence:
> —Derevaun Seraun! Derevaun Seraun! [*D* 40]

If, as is sometimes argued, the mother's dying words are corrupted Gaelic for "the end of pleasure is pain," the phrase may be read as an encoded confession or the insistent admonition of a syphilitic Irish mother, warning her daughter about the consequences of sexual love.

Was Joyce, like Cranly in *Portrait*, "sitting over near the dictionaries" (*P* 226) and reading about disease as he conceived and plotted the moral insanity of Dublin, or did he learn of the many somatic indications of GPI less systematically and more gradually from his medical student friends? Was Joyce studying the indications and cyclical progress of the disease in fear of his own health? These questions will inevitably remain unanswered, but the medical precision of Joyce's literary portrayal of Ireland's ill health is clearly evident throughout *Dubliners*. The human bodies and moral beings of Joyce's various characters are connected inextricably and with clinical specificity, the body's appearance and operation an index to moral insanity or psychological illness. This connection between mind and body was no less interesting to Malcolm Lowry, who makes passing reference to general paralysis of the insane in *Dark as the Grave Wherein My Friend Is Laid* (39-43). The evanescence of Lowry's allusion suggests that he did not bring to his writing the medical knowledge available to Joyce, a possible exception being Lowry's acquaintance with depth psychology, for Lowry is clearly post-Freudian. In the gallery of Joyce's characters, it is difficult to imagine any would utter, as Lowry's Bill Plantagenet reportedly does in the hospital, "Hullo, father, return to the presexual revives the necessity for nutrition" (*LC* 266). A fallen, unhappy Dubliner, such as Mr. Kernan, bites his tongue rather than echo Freud, whom Joyce called "Viennese Tweedledee" (*LJJ* 1:166).

For Lowry, as for the Joyce of *Dubliners*, psychological ills are connected rather intimately with the physical indications of syphilis. Douglas Day tells us that Lowry, under sodium pentothal at Atkinson Morley's neuropsychiatric hospital, told his doctors that he had been syphilophobic since the age of five, when his older brother, Stuart, took him to the Anatomical Museum of Liverpool, whose collection included "a large number of pallid, plaster casts [depicting] the ravages of venereal diseases" (Day 25). Although even under the drug Lowry was not always truthful, syphilophobia is consistent with Lowry's "severe guilt over sexual experiences and impulses" (Dr. Ian Stevenson, quoted in Day 26n). And, not surprisingly, the real or imagined somatic indications of syphilis are closely allied with the Consul's psychological problems in *Under the Volcano*.

The Consul's psychological susceptibility to syphilophobia is obliquely referred to when he removes his sunglasses and Yvonne notices the "glare" in his eyes. Alluding to the traditional Freudian association between eyes and the male genitalia, the Consul replies with dark humor, "A touch of the goujeers . . . Just a touch" (*UV* 73). As Ackerley and Clipper note, "goujeers" contains a multilingual pun associated with "the French disease" (114)—English slang for venereal disease—which in turn is associated in the Consul's mind with other symbolic bodily indications of disease. The Consul's feet are "swollen and sore" (*UV* 73-74) "because his whole frame was so neuritic with alcohol" (*UV* 73).[6] (The Consul finds it impossible to bear the pain of wearing socks.) The bodily indications of alcoholism are thus associated in the Consul's mind with syphilis, disorders of the nervous system, and the sexual problems that plague him throughout the Day of the Dead, from his impotence with Yvonne in the morning (*UV* 90) to his "unprophylactic rejection" (*UV* 348) of Yvonne's love in the Farolito that evening.

Other incidental references to syphilis in *Under the Volcano* offer rather classic examples of Freudian displacement. Clipper and Ackerley pinpoint a dozen allusions to venereal disease, including Dr. Vigil's *mingitorio* notices (*UV* 23, 352); multilingual malapropisms and puns on "pepped petroot" (*UV* 290), "poxy eggs" (*UV* 291), "pricked peetroot" (*UV* 352), and "half past sick by the cock" (*UV* 352); the Consul's epithet "poxbox" (*UV* 275); and the "noseless peon" (*UV* 228). Most of these references connect a literal, slang, or common symbolic reference to a body part—root, egg, cock, box, nose—with venereal disease, and these references are further embedded with bodily indicators of alcohol abuse: the "pickled" and "sick" phallus and the peon's suggestively absent nose, a traditional phallic symbol here missing due to the final stages of syphilitic disfigurement. These body references are thus double indicators of mental disease: the neurological damage and eventual insanity that can result from syphilis, and the psychological illness manifest in syphilophobia and its concomitant feelings of guilt and sexual maladjustment.

It is interesting that while Lowry had no basis in medical training or reading for making an association between syphilitic insanity and the deformity of language, he nonetheless does so in both the Salón Ofélia and Señora Gregorio episodes and repeatedly through the character of Dr. Vigil. In the Salón Ofélia episode, Cervantes and his menu provide the Consul with sexual puns on genitalia and venereal disease, puns that begin as teasing banter and end, with the Consul's increasing intoxication, in the ugliest scene in the novel. The protean language of the Consul culminates with an accusation of sibling cuckoldry and the Consul's tortured, self-destructive prophecy: "Mummy, let me go back to the beautiful brothel!" (*UV* 313). The Salón Ofélia episode thus draws to an awful close with the Consul linking sexuality with self-destruction and insanity. This complex of associations is also apparent in the earlier scene with Señora Gregorio, who appears in the darkness, her hair done "into a Psyche knot. Her face, which was beaded with perspiration, evinced the most extraordinary waxen pallor" (*UV* 226). The visage of death and namesake of the Consul's soul, the Señora serves raw alcohol to a "noseless peon who had entered silently and was standing in a corner" (*UV* 228). This image of death and syphilitic deformity materializes during the Señora's confusing talk of life, love, and how to prevent losing one's mind, a phrase reminiscent of Dr. Vigil, whom the Consul nearly stumbles over as he leaves the cantina. Dr. Vigil, whose several medical specialties include the treatment of venereal diseases and who tells the Consul he is "very much interested in insanes" (*UV* 145), counsels his friends and patients to throw away their minds (*UV* 6).

The Body as Rhetorical Figure

Given the cultural admonishments about syphilis and the moral / religious conservatism of Joyce's and Lowry's families, it is little wonder that rhetorical figures for insanity are pervasive in their fiction. If we read the work of Joyce and Lowry attending to their use of the body as rhetorical figure, we see that their use of tropes is consistent with and extends the European cultural attitudes toward madness as defined in Foucault's reading of the social history of insanity. Foucault argues that insanity filled a cultural void created by the disappearance, at the end of the Middle Ages, of leprosy, a disease characterized in the human imagination by various forms of metaphorical disfigurement. Madness was thus associated in literature, folklore, social discourse, and practice with a variety of bodily and figurative deformities, since "the madman's body was regarded as the visible and solid presence of his disease" (Foucault 159). That presence is variously represented according to Foucault by animality, blindness, and that ultimate disfigurement, death.

These tropes are common in the work of Joyce and Lowry and have each received ample critical attention. They are born, I would argue, of the central figure of the body that becomes a kind of *archetrope:* a central, governing trope that serves as a matrix for the rise of associated figures within the work of a single author, and, at the same time, that can serve as a kind of primordial and intertextual figure that connects the work of more than one author. While considerations of space make it impossible here to explore all the associated Foucauldian disfigurements of madness that are common to both Joyce and Lowry, a brief discussion of animality, blindness, and the corpse will suggest how the various tropological manifestations contribute to the extended prose conceit of the body that forms the connective tissue of Joyce's and Lowry's work, their corpus, and their confraternity.

Perhaps the best place to begin is with the end: the corpse. Foucault identifies a traditional association in Western literature between death and madness: "From the discovery of that necessity which inevitably reduces man to nothing, we have shifted to the scornful contemplation of that nothing which is existence itself" (15-16). Madness, then, is a metalepsis of death; madness becomes a kind of death-in-life. Indeed, Joyce's Dublin is strewn with corpses, the bodies of those who lived a kind of psychological death-in-life: the "queer" and "peculiar case" of Father Flynn, whose mind was "affected"—who'd have dreamed "he'd make such a beautiful corpse"? (D 10, 17, 15); the "painful case" of Mrs. Sinico—not a "normal" person—who died of "sudden failure of the heart's action" (D 114); Eveline Hill's mother, who died in "final craziness" (D 40); the memory of the delicate Michael Furey, who did not want to live for love of Gretta (D 221); and, of course, the many cadavers-soon-to-be, beginning with Old Cotter, continuing with Mr. Mooney, Maria, Mr. Duffy, and Mr. Kernan, and ending with Aunt Julia.

The corpse, contemplated by both Stephen and Bloom, is also an important motif in *Ulysses* and serves as an index to the mental health of the two leading men. Bloom's contemplation in "Hades" is vividly and concretely conceived and is appropriate to the setting of a funeral procession and Prospect Cemetery:

> I daresay the soil would be quite fat with corpsemanure, bones, flesh, nails. Charnelhouses. Dreadful. Turning green and pink decomposing. Rot quick in damp earth. . . .
> But they must breed a devil of a lot of maggots. Soil must be simply swirling with them. Your head it simply swurls. Those pretty little seaside gurls. [U 6.776-85]

The metonymic trace between the corpse and madness—"Your head it simply swurls"—is clipped short; and, characteristically, Bloom's focus on the quasi-scientific notion of process leads him from death back to life again—"Those pretty little seaside gurls." Bloom may contemplate a "case I read of to get at fresh buried females or even putrefied with running gravesores" (U 6.998-99), but such grotesque contemplations of death lead him to a renewed and sane embrace of life. "Plenty to see and hear and feel yet. Feel live warm beings near you. Let them sleep in their maggoty beds. They are not going to get me this innings. Warm beds: warm fullblooded life" (U 6.1003-5). In "Proteus" Stephen also thinks about the process of life and death, which is also appropriate to the setting of Sandymount strand, where he can see both "seaspawn and seawrack" (U 3.2-3). There, like Bloom, he thinks about things to see, hear, and feel. But unlike Bloom he tests them by a process of sensate negation and focuses not on life but on seawrack, concluding his contemplation not with the warmth of a healthy, loving bed but with the solitary, disfigured body: "Bag of corpsegas sopping in foul brine. A quiver of minnows, fat of a spongy titbit, flash through the slits of his buttoned trouserfly. God becomes man becomes fish becomes barnacle goose becomes featherbed mountain. Dead breaths I living breathe, tread dead dust, devour a urinous offal from all dead. Hauled stark over the gunwale he breathes upward the stench of his green grave, his leprous nosehole snoring to the sun" (U 3.476-81). Stephen articulates his vision of life in terms of death, experiencing Foucault's "nothingness of existence from within." He breathes pestilential air, treads the desiccated streets, and consumes a "urinous offal from all dead," unlike Bloom, who relishes the "fine tang of faintly scented urine" (U 4.4-5) on the palate. And significantly unlike Bloom, who reflects that "drowning they say is the pleasantest" (U 6.988), Stephen closes his vision of death by water with the image of a "leprous nosehole" that in Foucauldian terms is squarely in line with the Western European trope for the disfiguring power of madness-death. Mentally, Bloom is healthier than Stephen.

Like Joyce's entire oeuvre, the main action of Lowry's *Under the Volcano* begins and ends with references to dead bodies. On the Day of the Dead, the first words we hear uttered by the Consul and the final sentence of the novel's action, describing his final transportation, refer to corpses: "A corpse will be transported by express!" (UV 43), and "Somebody threw a dead dog after him down the ravine" (UV 375). Lowry identified an encounter with death as "the germ of the book" (SC 1:519), a personal roadside incident that would serve as the inspiration for chapter 8, which describes the death of an Indian, the "compañero." The eeriness of this encounter and the Consul's unusual tension suggest that we must read it as more than a political allegory, as Lowry indicates we should in his letter to Jonathan Cape. The sequence is both a chance and an inevitable encounter. The compañero is, in Lowry's words, "mankind dying" (SC 1:518), but he is also the bodily figure in a scenario that *transports* the Consul, who becomes lost in introspective reflection: "God, I feel terrible" (UV 243) is all the Consul can manage. After Hugh places the Consul's handkerchief on the compañero's wound and tussles briefly with the vigilantes, the Firmins reboard the bus, which is "wait[ing] still as death, as a hearse" (UV 247), and begin the long, final descent of the novel. It is significant, I think, that the compañero's "cruel wound" is caused by, and in turn inflicts, a fatal violence to the mind.

The compañero—who is thus a symbol of mankind dying and a metonymic manifestation of the fear of madness—appears bodily in the novel twice before this scene, once in chapter 4, with "his broad hat half down over his face" (UV 109), and once in chapter 7, singing on horseback (UV 213). But he also appears figuratively as ghost and animal. If as Foucault suggests "the substitution of the theme of madness for that of death does not mark a break, but rather a torsion within the same anxiety" (16), then the same may be said of the ghostly and the animal. "The animality that rages in madness," Foucault argues, "dispossesses man of what is specifically human in him; not in order to deliver him over to other powers, but simply to establish him at the zero degree of his own nature" (74). Death, animality, and madness are likewise closely allied in the Consul's mind and, depending on his state of intoxication, sometimes confused. On the day of his death, the Consul hallucinates an "object shaped like a dead man and which seemed to be lying flat on its back . . . with a large sombrero over its face." The Consul reflects, "So the 'other' had come again" (*UV* 91). This psychic phenomenon, the appearance of a human-like presage of death, is apparently rather routine for the Consul and, though he accepts it calmly, suggests an underlying psychological anxiety. Conversely, near the end of the novel, the Consul believes he sees a soldier sleeping under a tree (*UV* 339) when the shape is that of the body of the pariah dog that will be thrown into the barranca after him (Markson 193, quoted in Ackerley and Clipper 421). The pariah dogs, at once "hideous" and "familiar" (*UV* 64, 127), that seem, in Hugh's mind, "to shadow his brother" (*UV* 106), are "torsions within the same anxiety," metonymic anxieties over death and madness.

The compañero's horse, like the pariah dog, is associated with death or the negation of being; and it is also associated with the mental panic of mortal terror. At the roadside in chapter 8, the horse is described as "looking innocent as only one of its species can when under mortal suspicion. Its eyes, that had shut blandly at their approach, now opened, wicked and plausible" (*UV* 246). In his letter to Jonathan Cape, Lowry volunteered that the horse, once thought of as a supernatural being by the indigenous Indians, is "the evil force that the Consul has released" (*SC* 1:523) and that will kill Yvonne. It must be remembered that Yvonne has been threatened by horses before. She was once terrorized by a herd of 200 stampeding horses in a ravine (*UV* 260), and that fear assumes a filmic reality as the "shadowy horse, gigantic" (*UV* 266) that seems to leap out at her on the screen. And Geoffrey, as Hugh ironically remarks early in the novel, is "as strong as a horse" (*UV* 122). The simile is horribly apt with regard to Yvonne's fate, for she imagines the Consul mounted on the riderless horse that kills her (*UV* 335-36); and it is pathetically wrongheaded with regard to the Consul's fate, for though he defies death, a dingy death is his fate.

The psychological ills of panic, mortal terror, and death are more comedically associated with animality in Joyce's *Ulysses*. Buck Mulligan is quick to remind Stephen (and us) that death is "a beastly thing and nothing else" (*U* 1.206-7). That is, death is the province of the animal body and of nothingness. In "Proteus" Stephen contemplates beastly death in the "bloated carcass of a dog" (*U* 3.286), "poor dogsbody" (*U* 3.351). Since dogs are Stephen's enemies, beastly death is something Stephen psychologically fears. In a moment of panic: "Lord, is he going to attack me?" (*U* 3.295). The dogsbody trope reappears numerous times (Epstein 81-82), but most notably in "Circe," which is named after the Homeric being whose mythological business is to transform men into beasts. Here, the ghost of Paddy Dignam, in the form of a beagle, materializes to corroborate Bloom's testimony: "(*The beagle lifts his snout, showing the grey scorbutic face of Paddy Dignam. He has gnawed all. He exhales a putrid carcasefed breath. He grows to human size and shape. His dachshund coat becomes a brown mortuary habit. His green eye flashes bloodshot. Half of one ear, all the nose and both thumbs are ghouleaten.*)" (*U* 15.1204-8). If Lowry's corpses are transported, Joyce's soul-corpses are metonymically transmigrated: death's disfigurement transforms the human (Paddy Dignam) to animal (beagle), to anthropomorph, and finally to ghoul. The "carcasefed breath" of the beagle recalls the breath of "wetted ashes" that characterizes the ghost of Stephen's mother, the "chewer of corpses" about whom he apparently dreams (*U* 1.270-79).

The mother-ghost's hallucinated appearance, leading to the climax of "Circe," is prepared carefully as a kind of inversion of the pastoral elegy: lament and grief are transformed into accusation; praise and idealization are transformed into repulsion; and consolation is transformed into remorse and flight. The mourning of nature and profusion of floral imagery is replaced by a menagerie of animals (including a "dark horse, riderless" [*U* 15.3974]) that grow increasing exotic and grotesque as the ghost's appearance draws near: "(*Stephen's mother, emaciated, rises stark through the floor, in leper grey . . . her face worn and noseless, green with gravemould. Her hair is scant and lank. She fixes her bluecircled hollow eyesockets on Stephen and opens her toothless mouth uttering a silent word.*)" (*U* 15.4157-61). Virtually all the Foucauldian metonymies for madness are present: the analogy to leprosy, the skull image of noseless death, the "hollow eyesockets" suggesting blindness, the linguistic registry of madness ("silent word"), and the animality, affirmed by Buck Mulligan: "dogsbody killed her bitchbody" (*U* 15.4178-79). The message she bears to Stephen is not a message of love and life, but the chilling news that "all must go through it. . . . You too" (*U* 15.4182-83).

The blindness indicated by the ghost's hollow eyesockets suggests a trope rich in metonymic meanings, for blindness is associated not only with madness but also with moral guilt experienced by the vulnerable sensibility. In *Madness and Civilization*, Foucault concludes his chapter

"Aspects of Madness" with a discussion of the metaphorical blindness
that is madness, for "once the mind becomes blind through the very
excess of sensibility—then madness appears" (158). In the postclassical
age, Foucault argues, the man or woman with heightened sensibilities is
more vulnerable to the power of social conscience. "Such an identification" between sensibility, blindness, and madness "gives madness a new
content of guilt, of moral sanction. . . . It describes blindness, the blindness of madness, as *the psychological effect of a moral fault*" (158). The art-
ist-type is thus one who is deemed blind and mad in his excess of
sensibility, which, in the eyes of civilization, is a moral defect. These
character types in Joyce and Lowry—the boy in "Araby," the Consul,
Stephen Dedalus, Sigbjørn Wilderness—are all aware of the program of
civilization, and, as they inevitably run counter to it, are prone to the
discontent attendant to guilt, especially in matters of love and sexuality.
     In Stephen Dedalus's fictional life, his very earliest memories spe-
cifically link these powerful ideas with the added threat of blindness:

> When they were grown up he was going to marry Eileen. He hid un-
> der the table. His mother said:
> —O, Stephen will apologise.
> Dante said:
> —O, if not, the eagles will come and pull out his eyes. [*P* 8]

The maternal figures are not exponents of love but rather threatening
emissaries of guilt and psychological terror. Similarly, Lowry offers a
metonymic complex of love, guilt, and the associated threat of blindness. In a passage previously alluded to, Yvonne, who twists her wed-
ding ring in a gesture of displaced "marital" discomfort, reacts to the
Consul, who has just removed his sunglasses:

> "Your eyes, you poor darling—they've got such a glare," Yvonne burst out . . .
> "A touch of the goujeers . . . Just a touch." . . .
>   . . . Yvonne, it was clear to him, dreaded the approaching scene as
> much as he, and now felt under some compulsion to go on talking about
> anything until the perfect inappropriate moment arrived, that moment too
> when, unseen by her, the awful bell would actually touch the doomed child
> with giant protruding tongue and hellish Wesleyan breath. "There, on the
> hibiscus!"
>   The Consul closed one eye. "He's a coppery-tailed trogon I believe."
> [*UV* 73-74]

The Consul's extraordinary bell metaphor collates a rather grotesque
bodily (sexual) metonym with a fearful allusion to the guilt inspired by

his conservative Methodist education; and this complex of figures is placed within the context of visual inhibition in the form of bodily and figurative blindness.

If Lowry's or Joyce's preoccupations with syphilis, madness, and death seem morbid to contemporary readers, for whom syphilis is curable and perhaps less threatening than other sexually transmittable diseases, it must be remembered that both Joyce and Lowry were raised in a socio-medical context very different from our own, in a time when syphilis was incurable. In Lowry's case, syphilophobia was a powerful response to his conservative Methodist upbringing. In Joyce's case, syphilis—a disease that Dr. George Savage held responsible for at least 70 percent of the cases of general paralysis treated in private practice (Tuke 1257)—was a focal point of the public discussion on the increase or "progress of insanity." During the 1890s and first decade of the twentieth century, the Annual Reports of the Lunacy Commissioners of Great Britain recorded a steady increase in the absolute number of insane persons under offi-cial cognizance. Though the reports accounted for the "apparent increase" by such demographic considerations as the increase in general popula-tion and the life expectancy of the insane, public concern was aroused.

W.J. Corbet campaigned to alarm the public of the growing number of insane under official care and the rising costs associated with their treatment and confinement. A former statistician for the Irish Lunacy Commission and briefly a member of Parliament, Corbet published at least a dozen articles from 1893 to 1906 in the *Fortnightly Review* and the *Westminster Review* challenging the conclusions of the Commissioners' Reports. His articles, full of statistics and inflamed rhetoric, succeeded in stirring public debate that focused on lunacy, heredity, and marriage. By 1906, two years after Joyce left Ireland, quite possibly infected with syphilis, Corbet was able to quote the *Freeman's Journal* as "one of the leading organs of public opinion in Ireland," recognizing and validating his project: "The increase of insanity in Ireland gives grounds for the gravest apprehensions. When all explanations and excuses have been considered and discounted, the appalling fact remains that, with a de-creased and decreasing population, we have a large increase, not rela-tive but absolute, in the number of the insane, [sic] Worst of all, the increase is progressive, absorbing each year a larger proportion of the popula-tion" (1906b 410). While Joyce was still in Ireland, W.R. MacDermott, an Irish physician, affirmed the urgency of Corbet's campaign, reporting that he found "one or more cases of insanity had occurred in over 50 per cent. of the families" he treated "in a particular area in the north of Ire-land" (291). MacDermott blamed both "intermarriage of predisposed persons [and] the postponement of marriage" (293) as contributing factors, but also cited family life itself: "When insanity arises in a family[,] association fixes and increases it, both in the family and the group" (294). Insanity is increased, according to MacDermott, for "in marriage all restraint disappears" (295) and with sexual exhaustion comes mental degeneration. Poor Stephen Dedalus in *Portrait*! Prone to masturbation, which leads to lunacy; frequenting prostitutes, who may give him syphilis and finally general paralysis of the insane; no prospect of marriage anytime soon; surrounded by a large family that resides within earshot of "the nuns' madhouse" (*P* 175)—St. Vincent's Asylum. *What's a body to do?*

To such fears of sexuality and madness, Joyce and Lowry responded as they were taught to respond: with a keen sense of guilt. In *Civilization and Its Discontents*, Freud concludes his essay by stating his "intention to represent the sense of guilt as the most important problem in the development of civilization" (91), for it is guilt, he argues, inspired by the civilized conscience, that keeps us doing what we have been taught is morally right at the expense of our individual happiness. It is conscience that Dubliners, who deal "with moral problems as a cleaver deals with meat" (*D* 63), so conspicuously lack. It is conscience that Stephen Dedalus sets out to create for the Irish race. It is conscience—*Agenbite of Inwit*—that Stephen grapples with in *Ulysses.* So, too, it is conscience that plagues the Consul in *Under the Volcano*: guilt for his drinking, his failed marriage and writing; remorse for his unsamaritan-like treatment of the compañero and for his sexual betrayal of Yvonne. The exercise of such conscience and guilt is based, Freud argues, on the threat of loss of love (80), that word known to all men, that feeling we cannot live without: *no se puede vivir sin amar.*

Lowry's word play in this repeated phrase reveals a complex ambivalence in his attitude toward human love and sexuality. Though one cannot live without loving, "sin amar," (*amar*, from Latin *amare*, affection), one's affective life in adulthood is tainted by the "sin" of sexuality (vis-à-vis *amor*, from Latin *amor*, passion). The Consul, psychologically speaking, is thus a rather painful case, caught between the need of intimate affection and the fear of sexual union. In *Ulysses* Joyce, too, registers verbal ambivalence in the range of his allusions to love: "Love's Old Sweet Song," *Sweets of Sin*, and Stephen's Yeatsian refrain, "love's bitter mystery." Variously sweet, sinful, and bitter, natural human love in the fiction of Joyce and Lowry is often tainted by cultural guilt. For Joyce and Lowry *amour* and *amer* (French for bitter) thus form a kind of signature pun: odd lexical bedfellows, coupled by the psychological ills born of the guilt-ridden conscience of syphilisation.

Notes

The pun on "civilization" in the title is taken from the utterance of Joyce's citizen in *Ulysses* (12.1197).

1. Since the completion of this essay and while the essays in this volume were being assembled and edited, Kathleen Ferris published *James Joyce and the Burden of Disease*. Compiling what, in my view, is persuasive medical and literary evidence, Ferris argues that Joyce's late works confess his infection with syphilis and reveal his sense of guilt in an elaborate scheme of puns and metaphors. While my essay does not specifically address the question of whether Joyce contracted syphilis, it suggests in ways that complement Ferris's work that Joyce had very detailed knowledge of the symptoms of paresis and that those symptoms appear in a wide range of his Dubliners.

2. For contemporary discussions of the pathologist/psychologist debate, see Andriezen, Arndt, and Tanzi. Hart later discussed the debate. Michael J. Clark offers a recent interpretation of the late Victorian rejection of psychological approaches to mental disorders.

3. At the 1902 annual meeting of the British Medical Association, a Dr. Mott presented one of the five papers delivered; his paper was entitled "Syphilis as a Cause of Insanity." *The Journal of Mental Science* noted: "Dr. Mott, in opening the discussion, said that the poison of syphilis was remarkable for its persistency, its potency, and its prevalence, and that it acted in many ways as a cause of insanity. . . . The relation of general paralysis to syphilis was now an established fact of great importance. . . . Acquired or congenital syphilis was equally potent to cause general paralysis. The occurrence of syphilitic infections could by careful investigation be traced in from 70 to 80 per cent. of cases of general paralysis. The symptoms of general paralysis, however, began to be apparent only several years after infection, the average interval being fifteen years. . . . Dr. Mott concluded by adopting, for the purpose of raising a discussion, the thesis, 'No syphilis, no general paralysis'" (808).

4. Both the Library of the Royal College of Physicians of Ireland and Trinity College Library own copies of Tuke's *Dictionary*, but neither library can establish an acquisition date. I wish to thank Paul Murphy, Assistant Librarian at University College Dublin, for providing me with this information.

5. This "odd autobiographical habit" is generally assumed to be based on Stanislaus Joyce, who claims in *My Brother's Keeper* (159-60) that a number of Duffy's idiosyncracies are based on his own.

6. Ackerley and Clipper gloss neuritis as "any inflammatory or degenerative condition of the nerves; it is accompanied by pain, the loss of reflexes, disturbances of the senses (such as hallucinations), and, in extreme cases, paralysis" (114).

Works Cited

Ackerley, Chris, and Lawrence J. Clipper. *A Companion to "Under the Volcano."* Vancouver: Univ. of British Columbia Press, 1984.

Andriezen, W. Lloyd. "On the Bases and Possibilities of a Scientific Psychology and Classification in Mental Disease." *Journal of Mental Science* 45 (1899): 257-90.

Arndt, Rudolf. "What Are Mental Diseases?" *Alienist and Neurologist* 20 (1899): 1-34.

Clark, Michael J. "The Rejection of Psychological Approaches to Mental Disorder in Late Nineteenth-Century British Psychiatry." In *Madhouses, Mad-Doctors, and Madmen: The Social History of Psychiatry in the Victorian Era,* edited by Andrew Scull. Philadelphia: Univ. of Pennsylvania Press, 1981

Corbet, W.J. "The Increase of Insanity." *Fortnightly Review* 59 (1893): 7-19.

———. "Ought Private Lunatic Asylums to Be Abolished?" *Westminster Review* 142 (1894): 369-80.

———. "The Increase of Insanity." *Fortnightly Review* 65 (1896): 431-42.

———. "Is Insanity Increasing?" *Fortnightly Review* 67 (1897): 321-24.

———. "Is the Increase of Insanity Real or Only 'Apparent'?" *Westminster Review* 147 (1897): 539-50.

———. "Lunacy Reform." *Westminster Review* 147 (1897): 200-210.

———. "Plain Speaking about Lunacy." *Westminster Review* 148 (1897): 117-25.

———. "The Holocaust at Colney Hatch." *Westminster Review* 159 (1903): 383-93.

———. "The Skeleton at the Feast." *Westminster Review* 159 (1903): 1-14.

———. "Progress of Insanity in Our Own Time." *Westminster Review* 163 (1905): 198-211.

———. "Progress of Insanity in Our Own Time." *Westminster Review* 165 (1906): 269-83.

———. "Progress of Insanity in Our Own Time." *Westminster Review* 166 (1906): 408-17.

Day, Douglas. *Malcolm Lowry: A Biography.* New York: Oxford Univ. Press, 1973.

Epstein, E.L. "James Joyce and the Body." In *A Starchamber Quiry: A James Joyce Centennial Volume, 1882-1982,* edited by E.L. Epstein. London: Methuen, 1982.

Ferris, Kathleen. *James Joyce and the Burden of Disease.* Lexington: Univ. Press of Kentucky, 1995.

Foucault, Michel. *Madness and Civilization,* translated by Richard Howard. New York: Random House, 1965.

Freud, Sigmund. *Civilization and Its Discontents,* translated and edited by James Strachey. New York: Norton, 1961.

Friedrich, Gerhard. "The Gnomonic Clue to James Joyce's *Dubliners.*" *Modern Language Notes* 72 (1957): 421-24.

Hart, Bernard. "A Philosophy of Psychiatry." *British Journal of Psychiatry* 54 (1908): 473-90.

Herring, Phillip. *Joyce's Uncertainty Principle*. Princeton: Princeton Univ. Press, 1987.

Joyce, Stanislaus. *My Brother's Keeper: James Joyce's Early Years*. New York: Viking, 1958.

———. *The Complete Dublin Diary of Stanislaus Joyce*, edited by George H. Healy. Ithaca: Cornell Univ. Press, 1962.

Lyons, J.B. *James Joyce and Medicine*. Dublin: Dolmen Press, 1973.

———. "Animadversions on Paralysis as a Symbol in 'The Sisters.'" *James Joyce Quarterly* 11 (1974): 257-65.

———. "Thrust Syphilis Down to Hell." In *James Joyce: The Centennial Symposium*, edited by Morris Beja et al. Urbana: Univ. of Illinois Press, 1986.

MacDermott, W.R. "Insanity and Morality." *Westminster Review* 159 (1903): 291-97.

Markson, David. *Malcolm Lowry's "Volcano": Myth, Symbol, Meaning*. New York: Times Books, 1978.

Osler, William. *The Principles and Practice of Medicine*. 4th ed. New York: D. Appleton, 1902.

Review of *A Dictionary of Psychological Medicine*, edited by D. Hack Tuke. *Journal of Nervous and Mental Disease* 20 (1893): 656-57.

"Syphilis as a Cause of Insanity." *Journal of Mental Science* 8 (1902): 808.

Tanzi, Eugenio. "The Limits of Psychology." *Alienist and Neurologist* 18 (1897): 340-58.

Tuke, D. Hack, ed. *A Dictionary of Psychological Medicine*. 2 vols. London: J. and A. Churchill, 1892.

Waisbren, Burton A., and Florence L. Walzl. "Paresis and the Priest: James Joyce's Symbolic Use of Syphilis in 'The Sisters.'" *Annals of Internal Medicine* 80 (1974): 758-62.

nine

The World as Book, the Book as Machine: Art and Life in Joyce and Lowry

Patrick A. McCarthy

> But the world, mind, is, was and will be writing its own wrunes for ever, man, on all matters that fall under the ban of our infrarational senses. . . .
> —Joyce, *Finnegans Wake*

In January 1946 Malcolm Lowry sent Jonathan Cape a remarkable document: a typed, single-spaced letter of twenty-two pages that explained the design of his unpublished novel, *Under the Volcano,* and defended it against a reader's recommendation that it be extensively revised and cut. At one point in the letter, Lowry conjured up the shade of James Joyce, only to dismiss Joyce's apparent relevance to his own work, contending that *Under the Volcano* involved "a simplyfying [*sic*] . . . of what originally suggested itself in far more baffling, complex and esoteric terms," while Joyce proceeded in the opposite way in his works (*SC* 1:506). The distinction was one that Joyce might well have approved, since he had told Frank Budgen that in his own writing "the thought is always simple" (Budgen 284), any complexities apparently resulting from his refashioning of an essentially simple concept into a complex literary artifact.

Even if the two authors composed their works in different ways, however, the final products often have much in common. Some of the more obvious comparisons involve *Ulysses* and *Under the Volcano,* encyclopedic and highly allusive modern epics that are each concerned primarily with a single day in one place. Both novels employ a wide array of structural devices apart from chronological narration, and both use changes in narrative perspective, and even in typography, that disrupt attempts to read either book as the expression of any single viewpoint.

Ultimately, too, *Ulysses* and *Under the Volcano*—not to mention *Finnegans Wake* and the series of fictions that Lowry planned to develop into *The Voyage That Never Ends*—are incessantly self-reflexive works, concerned with their own production and design, that resemble self-contained worlds and involve numerous interlocking planes of meaning.

Here, I want to comment on some aspects of Joyce's and Lowry's aesthetics, particularly the ideas of the book as a machine and the world as a book, both in *Ulysses* and *Under the Volcano* and in later works by the two writers. Joyce's later work, of course, was *Finnegans Wake*, a volume that he eventually completed, after sixteen years, under trying circumstances; Lowry's later productions resulted largely in a massive and rather confused "bolus" of manuscripts, most of which remained unfinished (and almost all of which were still unpublished) when he died in 1957. My purpose is to suggest that one of the problems Lowry faced, and one reason for his inability to complete *The Voyage That Never Ends*, was that he found the relationship between text and world, art and life, more complex, or at least more ambiguous, unresolvable, or unmanageable, than Joyce ever did.

Although Lowry tried to distinguish his work from Joyce's, another passage in the letter to Cape suggests that he conceived of *Under the Volcano* in a way that is suggestive of, yet significantly different from, the projects of Joyce and other modernist writers. After pointing to various ways his novel might be read—as "a prophecy, a political warning, a cryptogram, a preposterous movie, and a writing on the wall"—Lowry adds that it "can even be regarded as a sort of machine" (*SC* 1:506).[1] The description of his book as a "machine" could be interpreted as a Lowryan version of what José Ortega y Gasset called "the dehumanization of art": the "dehumanized" novel is not so much a realistic portrayal of events as a self-consciously literary work that creates its own world, operates according to its own laws, and to a large extent becomes its own subject. In *Ulysses*, not all of the language can be directly related to an immediate human situation: often the language seems to be about itself. Examples include Joyce's numerous stylistic parodies, beginning with the bold-faced headings of the "Aeolus" chapter, as well as the complex intertextuality implied by the many allusions and parallels to other works. From here, the way lies open to a reversal, or at least a complication, of the traditional distinction between life and art.

For Lowry, however, the idea of the book as a "machine" seems inevitably sinister, especially since one of the central symbols of *Under the Volcano* is a loop-the-loop machine known as La Máquina Infernal (*UV* 221), an infernal machine in which the Consul finds himself at one point suspended upside down over the world, where he regards his situation as "undoubtedly symbolic" (*UV* 222). The idea that both Lowry's book and the world it describes are machines is also implied a few pages before the Consul's ride on La Máquina Infernal, when the Consul picks up a copy of Jean Cocteau's play *La machine infernale*—a version of the Oedipus story in which the universe is explicitly described as an infernal cosmic mechanism—and opens it to a passage that emphasizes the insignificance of human lives and values in comparison to the gods' designs (*UV* 209).

What I find most interesting is the way Lowry substitutes terror and entanglement for the ironic distance that we normally expect in a modernist, and particularly in a Joycean, work. For modernists generally, the concept of the book as a kind of machine is a means of "dehumanizing" it; for Joyce, with his schemata and his range of styles, it is also a means of experimenting with artistic design and placing his work within a literary, historical, and cultural matrix. Joyce's descriptions of *Finnegans Wake* in mechanical terms—as "an engine with only one wheel" or "my old flying machine," for example (*LJJ* 1:251, 300)—might be regarded as a means of debunking romantic ideas of organic form and of the work of art as an extension of the author's life, related concepts that lie at the heart of much of Lowry's work. Once designed and set in motion by Joyce, *Finnegans Wake* is a machine that can be operated by any reader and whose generation of meaning is no longer susceptible to Joyce's control.[2] Joyce thus resembles an inventor or engineer in his concern with intricate design and his willingness to relinquish control once the design is complete, but Lowry found it virtually impossible to disengage himself from his "machine." The difference between Joyce and Lowry, in this regard, may be illustrated by a comparison of Joyce's mock-serious complaint about the "amount of reading . . . necessary before my old flying machine grumbles up" with Lowry's use of the same image in *La Mordida*, where his autobiographical persona Sigbjørn Wilderness recalls watching a newsreel about an inventor of a flying machine who lost control of his machine and crashed. Sigbjørn's interpretation, of course, is that he is the inventor and his novel is the machine, spinning dangerously out of control and even threatening his life (*LM* 169-70).

Unlike Joyce, Lowry and his protagonists inevitably see both the book and the world as infernal, and even personally threatening, machines. In *Dark as the Grave*, Lowry said, Sigbjørn "becomes ever more and more trapped in the machinery of his own work" ("Work in Progress," 83). Likewise, in "Through the Panama," Sigbjørn writes in his diary that his book *The Valley of the Shadow of Death (Under the Volcano)* "worked like an infernal machine" on his life (*HL* 36). That machine in turn manifests itself as the Panama Canal locks that Sigbjørn sees both as a kind of serial universe and as a fictional world presided over by an unseen lock operator, the supposed author of the fictional world-machine, "who, by the way, is myself, and who would feel perfectly comfortable if only he did not know that there was yet another man sitting yet higher above him in *his* invisible control tower" (*HL* 63). To distinguish between Joyce's confidence and Lowry's anxiety about their status as authors we need only contrast this passage, in which Sigbjørn sees himself as just one in an infinite regress of authorial figures, with Stephen Dedalus's description of the godlike artist who "remains within or behind or beyond or above his handiwork, invisible, refined out of existence, indifferent, paring his fingernails" (*P* 215).[3]

Lowry's inability to set himself apart from his work and to see a clear distinction between his life and his art became especially apparent when he returned to Mexico in 1945-46 and began to see meanings in his work that he had never seen before. By the time he wrote to Cape, for example, he had again encountered a sign that read "*¿Le gusta este jardín que es suyo? ¡Evite que sus hijos lo destruyan!*" and had learned that he had misunderstood the sign in much the same way as the Consul, in the novel, misreads it; still, he told Cape, "the real translation can be in a certain sense even more more horrifying" than the threat of eviction that the Consul mistakenly believes the sign represents (*SC* 1:514). Just as every encounter with the book produces new and unexpected meanings, Lowry's return to Mexico changed his relationship to his own work in a fundamental way, leading him to believe that he was fatally entangled with the world he had created in his novel or, at other times, that he was a character in a book being written by his demon. That book is the set of his experiences, just as, on a larger scale, the world itself is a book—God's "strange dark manuscript" from which, according to Sigbjørn Wilderness, we could be deleted "at any moment" (*DG* 142).

The line I have just quoted derives from *Dark as the Grave*, in which Sigbjørn also sees the world as comparable to "a rejected play" or to his own rejected novel (*DG* 12-13). A similar idea underlies the passage in which Sigbjørn imagines that his airplane flight to Mexico "was like sailing into the pages of Shelley—or was it perhaps ultimately sailing into the pages of one's own book?" (*DG* 69). The comparison of the world to a book or manuscript also appears frequently in Lowry's other works. In "The gentleness of rain is in the wind," a poem written in the mid-1930s, for example, Lowry imagines the world as a phrase in one of God's rough drafts:

> It is my joy to core the world as such
> A rounded phrase in God's black manuscript
> Remembered, but abandoned for a fairer,

> As such, mankind's alternative of God,
> Yet claimed by us, and thoughtfully conserved. [CP 67]

Related images may be found in such poems as "I wrote: In the dark cavern of our birth," in which Lowry speculates that the world could be the result of a printer's misreading of God's handwriting, and "The Plagiarist," whose speaker's pilgrimage through life is made meaningful by his discovery and appropriation of "certain pamphlets" (CP 185, 204-5).

The concept of the world as a book is fundamental to *Under the Volcano*, where Lowry sets up a parallel between the burning manuscript that Yvonne imagines at the end of chapter 11 and the burning world that the Consul envisions a chapter later. In chapter 1 Jacques Laruelle burns the Consul's unposted letter to Yvonne, but in Yvonne's imagination that letter becomes the Consul's unwritten book manuscript and is burned once more; the burning world, meanwhile, becomes not only the manuscript whose function would have been to restore the lost harmony between the material and spiritual worlds but also the contemporary world itself, poised on the verge of World War II. A similar analogy underlies Geoffrey's obsessive concern, throughout the novel, with the idea that the world around him is inevitably symbolic of his situation and that one of his functions is to "read" or interpret the world in its true sense.

That the world is a book and we are all its readers is also one of Joyce's recurrent tropes in the "fictionable world" (FW 345.36) of *Finnegans Wake*: "(Stoop) if you are abcedminded, to this claybook, what curios of signs (please stoop), in this allaphbed! Can you rede . . . its world?" (FW 18.17-19). Even Issy may be glimpsed "reading her Evening World," the world having become indistinguishable from a daily newspaper (FW 28.20). Joyce's most famous expression of the idea, however, occurs in *Ulysses*, when Stephen Dedalus walks along Sandymount Strand in search of "signatures of all things I am here to read, seaspawn and seawrack, the nearing tide, that rusty boot" (U 3.2-3). Stephen is alluding directly to Jacob Boehme's *Signature of All Things*, a book owned and consulted by both Joyce and Lowry,[4] but as Hugh Kenner long ago noted, the idea of "signatures" in nature comes from an even older tradition, "the so-called hylomorphic doctrine that created things are composed of signate matter plus substantial form." Kenner associates the concept of signate matter, which distinguishes clearly between the perceiving mind and the external world whose "signatures" the mind reads, with what Stephen Daedalus, in *Stephen Hero*, calls "the classical temper"; its antithesis, "the romantic temper," blurs the distinction between self and world, projecting the soul's desire onto external reality (*Dublin's*

Joyce, 138-41; *SH* 78). Such a blurring may be found in Stephen's shocked discovery, in the word *"Foetus,"* of "what he had deemed till then a brutish and individual malady of his own mind" (*P* 89-90).

In her study of *Ulysses,* Marilyn French notes that the Catholic Church traditionally divided God's creation into two "books," nature and scripture, both of which "had to be read if man were to discover truth" (French 25). But as Gabriel Josipovici observes in *The World and the Book,* the idea that we can read the world as the word of God depends on "the medieval notion of analogy," which has largely disappeared, leaving us with a universe that seems "an enigma without a key" (Josipovici 47). For modern writers, he says, "to discover correspondences in the world around us does not lead to the sensation that we are inhabiting a meaningful universe [but] to the feeling that what we have taken to be 'the world' is only the projection of our private compulsions: *analogy* becomes a sign of *dementia*" (Josipovici 299). This statement is certainly true of Lowry, whose reading of the external world inevitably bordered on solipsism, but it is not so clearly true of Joyce. Indeed, as Weldon Thornton has demonstrated in a recent study of Joyce's "antimodernism," Joyce takes care to undermine Stephen's naïve faith in the autonomy of the self, insisting instead on a complex involvement of mind(s) and matter.

The belief that the universe can be read only as an extension of ourselves has implications for Joyce, who found it a useful literary device, and for Lowry, who took it more seriously. Chris Ackerley has described Lowry as a "true analogist," one who "believed fervently that analogy was the key to all of Nature's secrets and the sole fundamental principle behind all revelations" (Ackerley 119, 116). Because Joyce tends to rationalize what might otherwise seem coincidental, Ackerley argues that Joyce was not really an analogist but a "'forger' of correspondences" who believed that our minds are predisposed to latch onto coincidence and analogy as a means of imposing order on our otherwise chaotic experiences (Ackerley 118-19). I believe that this is basically a valid distinction, although with both writers—especially Lowry—it is often hard to tell whether coincidences and analogies originate in the individual mind, in the external world, or in the artist's presentation of the relationship between the two.

Take, for example, the question of mythic or literary analogies for the characters and their situations. Joyce locates some of these parallels within the mind of Stephen Dedalus, who compares himself to the Count of Monte Cristo in *Portrait* and to Hamlet in *Ulysses,* but never thinks of himself as Telemachus, nor is Bloom aware that he is a modern Ulysses. The principles of order that we see in *Ulysses* are often quite different from what the characters recognize, since not only the parallels but also the book's styles suggest ways of interpreting the novel that are independent of the characters' knowledge or understanding. With Lowry, however, the reverse is true: virtually all the significant parallels exist in the text at least partly because they occur to the characters. Literary paradigms exist everywhere in *Under the Volcano,* and they are not merely part of the book's design but aspects of the characters' minds and, ultimately, of the worldview endorsed by the novel.

Lowry makes it virtually impossible to determine, finally, whether his characters merely perceive or create the reality that they find around them. As Stephen Tifft has observed, "When events ratify [the Consul's] tragic apprehensions, he is incapable of determining whether those events are self-fulfilling prophecies or confirmations of a transcendent necessity" (Tifft 67-68), and the reader finds it equally difficult to make this judgment. In theory, the same can be said of *Ulysses:* Marilyn French even argues that *Ulysses* incorporates "the tension between humans' sense that there is a reality, and their hovering terror that in fact they create it" (French 26). One difference between the two writers is that Lowry never really attempts to refute the paranoid notion that the world is a giant book written about us and containing our destiny, while Joyce fully subscribes to that idea only within the dream vision of *Finnegans Wake,* where the dreamer's solipsistic extension of himself throughout the world provides a rationale for the idea.

The contrast between Joyce and Lowry, in this regard, may be illustrated by a consideration of the ways in which Leopold Bloom and Geoffrey Firmin engage in random acts of reading. It would be difficult to think of two characters more fundamentally different than Bloom and the Consul: Bloom is rational, practical, temperate, and altruistic, the Consul none of these. Even a comparison of the arcane lore contained in the Consul's books (*UV* 174-75, 185) with the historical and scientific contents of many of Bloom's volumes (*U* 17.1361-407) indicates that the two men have very different interests and temperaments, although somewhat predictably both collections include an edition of Shakespeare. Yet what I have said elsewhere of Bloom—that whenever he reads something, he "almost inevitably discovers some relationship between himself and the text at hand" (*"Ulysses": Portals,* 97)—is even more obviously true of the Consul, whose readings verge on solipsistic acts.[5] A typical example of Bloom's reading occurs at the outset of the "Lestrygonians" episode, when Bloom is handed a "throwaway" announcing the coming of Dr. John Alexander Dowie and initially misreads the first word in the phrase "Blood of the Lamb" as his own name (*U* 8.7-16). The confusion is cleared up quickly (indeed, by the time he finishes the first word), but the momentary fusion of "Bloom" and "Blood of the Lamb" helps to

establish Bloom's symbolic role as sacrificial victim, a "throwaway" of
another sort, as well as to illustrate the self-involvement of his reading.

In a parallel passage in *Under the Volcano*, the Consul momentarily
misreads a newspaper headline as an announcement that he will die:
"Es inevitable la muerte del Papa. The Consul started; this time, an in-
stant, he had thought the headlines referred to himself. But of course it
was only the poor Pope whose death was inevitable. As if everyone else's
death were not inevitable too!" (*UV* 213). On the surface, this seems a
more paranoid reading than Bloom's: after all, the Consul is not a father,
although Hugh sometimes calls him Papa (*UV* 117, 257). The fact that he
is drunk might be used to explain his misreading, but the book does not
endorse such a simple solution: instead, Lowry repeats the phrase "Es
inevitable la muerte del Papa" at the end of the chapter (*UV* 230), where
it appears, ominously, without quotation marks or any other indication
of its source, thereby giving the phrase an authority akin to that claimed
by the portentous sign in the garden, especially when it is repeated at
the end of the novel. And if we think that the Consul's premonition of
his death has no more meaning than Bloom's momentary confusion of
himself with the Blood of the Lamb, we should remember that Bloom is
only a symbolic Christ figure, while a good deal more than symbolism is
involved in the Consul's premonition of his death.

Kenner observes that in "Wandering Rocks," when Bloom opens
Sweets of Sin and begins reading "where his finger opened," he inadvert-
ently practices *Sortes Virgilianae*, or Virgilian lots, the use of randomly
selected passages to divine the future (Kenner, "*Ulysses*," 53; *U* 10.607).
The game that Bloom unwittingly plays is played more seriously by the
Consul, who calls it *sortes Shakespeareanae*, and Lowry introduces such
prophetic readings in places where even the Consul's paranoia cannot
adequately explain why his fate seems so often to be inscribed in the
texts that he reads. When he opens a telephone book to look for Dr.
Guzmán's number, the Consul finds other significant names and numbers "starting out of the book at him" (*UV* 208). We might imagine that
he fastens on the number 666 because he recognizes its apocalyptic implications and on Cafeaspirina because this aspirin-caffeine compound
might be effective against hangovers, but how do we explain the fact
that names that are presumably unknown to him at this point, but that
will turn out to belong to two of the fascist "chiefs" who will be involved
in his murder a few hours later, virtually leap off the page at him? And
we can hardly blame the Consul's mind for what happens a year after
his death, when Jacques Laruelle opens the Consul's book of Elizabe-
than plays randomly to passages from *Doctor Faustus* that appear singu-
larly applicable to the Consul's situation, and then discovers in the book

an unposted letter in which the Consul portrays himself as a doomed Faustian figure.

The circular relationship between mind and world is reinforced by the cyclic form of *Under the Volcano*: chapter 1 occurs exactly a year after the rest of the book, so that the prologue is also an epilogue, and what the reader sees as a foreshadowing of a later event is, from another perspective, a memory. This technique continues past the opening chapter, blurring the distinction between prolepsis and analepsis and contributing to our difficulty in deciding just how the Consul's mind is related to the world around him. In this sense, *Under the Volcano* resembles *Finnegans Wake* more than *Ulysses*. Each backwards revolution of the luminous wheel at the end of chapter 1 sets in motion a machine-like sequence of events that will end once again with Laruelle's (re)discovery, (re)reading, and (re)burning of Geoffrey's letter, a sequence parallel to the repeated burial and retrieval of ALP's letter in *Finnegans Wake*.

Near the end of his letter to Cape, Lowry emphasized his book's "essentially *trochal*" shape: *Under the Volcano* takes "the form of . . . a wheel so that, when you get to the end, if you have read carefully, you should want to turn back to the beginning again. . . . For the book was so designed, counterdesigned and interwelded that it could be read an indefinite number of times and still not have yielded all its meanings or its drama or its poetry" (*SC* 1:527). This is no idle claim, any more than it is when it is made for *Ulysses* or *Finnegans Wake*, and in each case the point is not merely that the book is rich and complex but that what Joseph Frank called the work's "spatial form" requires a very active reader who is willing to read forwards and backwards, above all to reread, in order to understand the book in terms of its interplay of related elements rather than just as a chronological progression of events.[6] Like life itself, *Under the Volcano*, *Ulysses*, or *Finnegans Wake* initially might appear to be "a strange assembly of apparently incongruous parts," to cite Lowry's misappropriation of D.H. Lawrence in "Through the Panama" (*HL* 34; see also 97).[7] Only after repeated readings, and interpretations from varying perspectives, will it begin to assume clear form.

That form is never final, however, for reasons that Joyce celebrates, especially in *Finnegans Wake*. "Her birth is uncontrollable," says the narrator of Anna Livia (*FW* 11.33), and a similarly uncontrollable generation occurs on the linguistic level. Meanings proliferate, accumulate, resonate throughout the book, where "if you can spot fifty I spy four more" (*FW* 10.31). Contributing to this fecundity of meaning is the semantic and referential ambiguity that makes it impossible to interpret passages according to a clear and consistent level of meaning. Thus "the point of eschatology our book of kills reaches for now in soandso many counterpoint words" (*FW* 482.33-34) is always deferred, never quite reached, as Joyce's semantic excess overwhelms any attempt to bring the process of signification to an end.

The point is made explicitly in chapter 3 of the *Wake*, where the narrator, alluding to the mysterious "park incident," tells us that the individuals in the case cannot be identified "since in this scherzarade of one's thousand one nightinesses that sword of certainty which would indentifide the body never falls" (*FW* 51.4-6). Here, Joyce's readers are somewhat in the position of Shahriyar, Scheherazade's husband in the *Arabian Nights*: we are unable to put an end to the sequence of Wakean stories that continually run into one another because we cannot identify the body, nor define it, divide it, even make an indentation on it, all of which erodes our faith (Latin *fide*) in our ability to distinguish what is significant from what is trivial or arbitrary. The reader of *Finnegans Wake* is denied the luxury of a "sword of certainty" that, falling, would put an end to the stories and characters that multiply and merge with one another. Nor can we end the play of meanings, which I assume is another implication of the same passage, so that problems of narrative form become essentially indistinguishable from those of interpretation.

Joyce seems to have been perfectly comfortable with this situation, even to have regarded it as a highly desirable aspect of his art. Certainly the fact that his works generally, and especially *Ulysses* and *Finnegans Wake*, force us to recognize "the impossibility of closing off the processes of signification [and] the incessant shifting and opening-out of meaning in the act of reading and re-reading" (Attridge and Ferrer 7-8) is a major source of their continuing attraction for readers. Frances Restuccia, who cites the passage from Attridge and Ferrer that I have just quoted, even argues that Joyce deliberately "sets loose the chain of [typological] figures and fulfillments (which in the orthodox system finally refer to God) to the point that they no longer refer 'up' to him but seem self-propelled. The figural system traditionally closed by God is pried open by Joyce, thus enabling Joyce critics to generate unending commentary" (Restuccia 71).

For Lowry, however, this endless production of analogies and symbolic meanings had a sinister side, one implied in a passage from the 1940 draft of *Under the Volcano*. Recalling that Baudelaire, in "Correspondances," had described the world as "a forest of symbols," the Consul thinks, "Life was indeed what you made of the symbols and, the less you made of life the more symbols you got. And the more you tried to comprehend them, confusing what life was, with the necessity for this comprehension, the more they multiplied" (*UV* [1940] 346). Here the symbolic reading of the world becomes a source of terror by constantly generating new meanings and making it impossible for the Consul to see himself or his life clearly.

In Lowry's posthumously published story "Ghostkeeper" a similar idea underlies Tom Goodheart's meditations on the dilemma facing an artist who attempts to mold personal experience into an aesthetically coherent form: "Perhaps what happens is something like this. The minute an artist begins to try and shape his material—the more especially if that material is his own life-some sort of magic lever is thrown into gear, setting some celestial machinery in motion producing events or coincidences that show him that this shaping of his is absurd, that nothing is static or can be pinned down, that everything is evolving or developing into other meanings, or cancellations of meanings quite beyond his comprehension. There is something mechanical about this process, symbolized by the watch" (PS 223). Once again the mechanical process, although initiated by the writer-protagonist in his role as a kind of engineer, quickly leads to an overproduction of meaning that is both inevitable (and fundamentally true) and frightening.

As I argue in Forests of Symbols, Lowry shared his protagonists' anxiety about the proliferation of symbolic meaning and correspondences, which tended to undermine his sense of his individual identity, but he also found the continual expansion of symbolic meaning virtually irresistible. Douglas Day comments perceptively that Lowry "had in him that which prohibited him from stopping at the thing in itself; the thing had to *mean*, had to relate to another thing, and so on until order and symmetry were lost in a maze of arcane correspondences and brilliant conceits" (Day 274). Through years of painstaking revisions the "maze of arcane correspondences" in Under the Volcano was slowly brought under control, but the attempt to repeat, and indeed exceed, this achievement in his post-Volcano works failed—in part, I believe, because Lowry was never willing to grant his work the independence from his own life that Joyce granted Ulysses and Finnegans Wake.

Lowry planned his most ambitious post-Volcano project, The Voyage That Never Ends, as a multivolume series of works, beginning and ending in a hospital, where the protagonist, under anesthesia, would dream the remaining works. According to Lowry's 1951 "Work in Progress" statement, the sequence was to have involved "a sort of battle between life and delirium, in which life ... is fighting to give that delirium a form, a meaning" before death, which Lowry calls "the accepted manuscript of one's life" ("Work in Progress," 74). Although the title of the "Work in Progress" statement, the form of the cyclic dream-vision, and the virtual impossibility within the dream of distinguishing between "life and delirium" all suggest the example of Finnegans Wake, I suspect that

Proust's *Remembrance of Things Past* was actually a more important model for this series of works. Still, it is interesting to compare the *Voyage* with the *Wake*, keeping in mind Andreas Höfele's observation that whereas Joyce chose Daedalus as his image of the artist, suggesting intricate craftsmanship and freedom from the created work, Lowry associated himself with the Laocoön, which implies the artist's "entanglement, frustrated effort, agony" (Höfele 195-96).[8]

The difference between Joyce's detachment and Lowry's entanglement may also be seen in the striking contrast between what Lowry did after *Under the Volcano* and what Joyce did not do after *Ulysses*. Joyce did not return, in person, to Dublin; and although he began *Finnegans Wake* by sorting through unused notes for his earlier work, he did not see the *Wake* as inseparable from *Ulysses* but regarded it as a distinct project. On the other hand, Lowry's return to Mexico, where he was ultimately arrested and deported, parallels his continuing imaginative involvement with *Under the Volcano*: not only was this book to have been the center of *The Voyage That Never Ends*, but much of the later work involves either an imaginative return to the *Volcano* or an attempt to free its author from the book. Joyce achieved a sense of detachment from his own work far more easily, even saying, "*Ulysses*! Who wrote it? I've forgotten it" (Ellmann 590n). Lowry was never able to forget who wrote *Under the Volcano*, any more than he was fully able to believe that he had actually written such a marvelous book; instead, he was trapped by the book, written by it, or written into it by a daemon over whom he had no control. In "Through the Panama," Lowry's protagonist even speculates about the possibility that an author can be not merely "enmeshed by, but *killed* by his own book and the malign forces it arouses" (*HL* 38). If we believe (as I do) that Lowry's complex entanglement of world, text, and self in *Under the Volcano* is one of its greatest strengths, we should also recognize that that aspect of his art is inseparable from the decade-long effort to overcome or escape from his own work, to be its creator rather than its creation, that ended only with Malcolm Lowry's death.[9]

Notes

1. Lowry's mock-catalogue of *Under the Volcano*'s genres resembles Joyce's 1920 statement to Carlo Linati that *Ulysses* "is an epic of two races (Israelite-Irish) and at the same time the cycle of the human body as well as a little story of a day (life). . . . It is also a sort of encyclopaedia" (*LJJ* 1:146).

2. On *Finnegans Wake* as word-machine see Rabaté.

3. A related distinction may be made between Joyce's dismissal of questions of originality and Lowry's anxiety about the same issue. Joyce, who told George Antheil, "I am quite content to go down to posterity as a scissors and paste man" (*LJJ* 1:297), parodied the idea of plagiarism in *Finnegans Wake* by calling Shem a forger and plagiarist and the Letter that represents *Finnegans Wake* "the last word in stolentelling" (*FW* 424.35). On Lowry's recurrent fear of being charged with plagiarism see my *Forests of Symbols* and Grace, "Respecting Plagiarism."

4. Joyce owned the 1912 J.M. Dent/E.P. Dutton edition (Gillespie, app. B); Lowry owned the 1926 reprint of the same volume, according to the inventory of Lowry's books at the University of British Columbia.

5. On acts of reading in *Ulysses* and *Under the Volcano*, see chapter 8 of my *"Ulysses": Portals of Discovery* and chapter 3 of my *Forests of Symbols*.

6. For a consideration of *Under the Volcano* in terms of Frank's "spatial form," see Doyen.

7. Sigbjørn Wilderness implies that Lawrence was commenting negatively on *Ulysses*, but as Sherrill Grace has pointed out, the line referred to Lawrence's "concepts of being and cosmos"—in short, to our experience in the world—rather than to Joyce's book (Grace, "A strange assembly," 187, 221-22 n. 2). For the original citation see Lawrence's "Why the Novel Matters" (106). Lowry's creative misuse of Lawrence undoubtedly reveals his anxiety about Joyce's influence on his own work, but the ease with which he translated Lawrence's description of the world into a description of a book is also an indication of how closely he identified art with life.

8. The Laocoön image appears in a 1949 letter to Frank Taylor in which Lowry described *Dark as the Grave*, as well as in the novel itself (*SC* 2:165; *DG* 43, 165).

9. I want to thank Michael Wutz for sending me a draft of his article "Archaic Mechanics, Anarchic Meaning," which I read after writing the present essay. His article demonstrates in full and convincing detail the complex relationship between Lowry's romantic distrust of technology and his modernist concept of his own role as textual engineer, a relationship that Wutz represents as Lowry's "personal *barranca* between allegiance and resistance to the Machine" (31). In my own essay I have emphasized the romantic side of this divide, in part to sharpen the contrast with Joyce's more securely modernist aesthetic.

Works Cited

Ackerley, Chris. "'After Lowry's Lights': Coincidence in *Ulysses* and *Under the Volcano*." In *The Interpretative Power: Essays on Literature in Honour of Margaret Dalziel*, edited by C.A. Gibson. Dunedin, New Zealand: Univ. of Otago Press, 1980.

Attridge, Derek, and Daniel Ferrer. Introduction to *Post-Structuralist Joyce: Essays from the French*, edited by Derek Attridge and Daniel Ferrer. Cambridge: Cambridge Univ. Press, 1984.

Budgen, Frank. *James Joyce and the Making of "Ulysses."* 1934. Reprint, Bloomington: Indiana Univ. Press, 1960.

Day, Douglas. *Malcolm Lowry: A Biography.* New York: Oxford Univ. Press, 1973.

Doyen, Victor. "Elements Towards a Spatial Reading of Malcolm Lowry's *Under the Volcano.*" *English Studies* 50 (Feb. 1969): 65-74.

Ellmann, Richard. *James Joyce.* 1959. Rev. ed., New York: Oxford Univ. Press, 1982.

Frank, Joseph. "Spatial Form in Modern Literature." In *The Widening Gyre: Crisis and Mastery in Modern Literature.* New Brunswick: Rutgers Univ. Press, 1963.

French, Marilyn. *The Book as World: James Joyce's "Ulysses."* Cambridge: Harvard Univ. Press, 1976.

Gillespie, Michael Patrick. *Inverted Volumes Improperly Arranged: James Joyce and His Trieste Library.* Ann Arbor, Mich.: UMI Research Press, 1983.

Grace, Sherrill. "'A strange assembly of apparently incongruous parts': Intertextuality in Malcolm Lowry's 'Through the Panama.'" In *Apparently Incongruous Parts: The Worlds of Malcolm Lowry,* edited by Paul Tiessen. Metuchen, N.J.: Scarecrow Press, 1990.

———. "Respecting Plagiarism: Tradition, Guilt, and Malcolm Lowry's 'Pelagiarist Pen.'" *English Studies in Canada* 18 (Dec. 1992): 461-81.

Höfele, Andreas. "Daedalus-Laocoön: Self-Representing in Joyce and Lowry." In *Anglistentag 1989 Würzburg: Proceedings,* edited by Rüdiger Ahrens. Tübingen: Max Niemeyer Verlag, 1990.

Josipovici, Gabriel. *The World and the Book: A Study of Modern Fiction.* Stanford: Stanford Univ. Press, 1971.

Kenner, Hugh. *Dublin's Joyce.* Bloomington: Indiana Univ. Press, 1956.

———. *"Ulysses."* London: George Allen & Unwin, 1980.

Lawrence, D.H. "Why the Novel Matters." In Lawrence, *Selected Literary Criticism,* edited by Anthony Beal. New York: Viking Press, 1956.

Lowry, Malcolm. "Work in Progress: The Voyage That Never Ends." *Malcolm Lowry Review* nos. 21 and 22 (Fall 1987 and Spring 1988): 72-99.

McCarthy, Patrick A. *"Ulysses": Portals of Discovery.* Boston: Twayne, 1990.

———. *Forests of Symbols: World, Text, and Self in Malcolm Lowry's Fiction.* Athens: Univ. of Georgia Press, 1994.

Ortega y Gasset, José. "The Dehumanization of Art." In *The Dehumanization of Art and Other Essays on Art, Culture, and Literature.* Princeton: Princeton Univ. Press, 1968.

Rabaté, Jean-Michel. "Lapsus ex machina." In *Post-Structuralist Joyce: Essays from the French,* edited by Derek Attridge and Daniel Ferrer. Cambridge: Cambridge Univ. Press, 1984.

Restuccia, Frances L. *Joyce and the Law of the Father.* New Haven: Yale Univ. Press, 1989.

Thornton, Weldon. *The Antimodernism of Joyce's "Portrait of the Artist as a Young Man."* Syracuse: Syracuse Univ. Press, 1994.

Tifft, Stephen. "Tragedy as a Meditation on Itself: Reflexiveness in *Under the Volcano.*" In *The Art of Malcolm Lowry,* edited by Anne Smith. London: Vision Press, 1978.

Wutz, Michael. "Archaic Mechanics, Anarchic Meaning: Malcolm Lowry and the Technology of Narrative." Typescript, 1995.

ten

Literary Modernism and Cinema: Two Approaches

Paul Tiessen

Works by both Joyce and Lowry are often cited by scholars in terms of film technique. Among the many stylistic elements in novels such as *Ulysses* and *Under the Volcano* that invite references to cinema are the interior-monologue idiom suggesting cinematic montage and imagery suggesting photographic perspective. With the enormous growth of literature-and-film criticism in the 1960s and 1970s, Joyce's work more than any other writer's came into the foreground in study after study, often with particular elaborations of modernist literary techniques on the one hand, and a combination of modernist and conventional film techniques on the other. During those two decades, when the academic interest in Joyce and also in film was vastly enlarged, scholars simply looked to Joyce's *Ulysses,* modernism's most important and influential text, to find some ground on which to establish a basis for exploring shared relationships between literary modernism and the new medium of cinema. They found in Joyce's parodies and puns allusive plays either on details of the movie world or on elements of film technique, and they found in Joyce's structures and rhythms some acknowledgment of film form in general or some anticipation of 1920s movies by directors such as Sergei Eisenstein or Walter Ruttmann (to take two of whom Joyce spoke in the early 1930s) in particular.[1]

Robert Richardson in 1969 in his *Literature and Film* bluntly invited scholars to acknowledge "the obvious" about literature's relationship with cinema: Joyce's place as "the great master" of the montage technique (Robert Richardson 42). Edward Murray, in his *Cinematic Imagination: Writers and the Motion Picture* (1973), similarly helped to lock Joyce in place: "With James Joyce as a guide, a new breed of fiction writer would soon attempt to find out the extent to which [the novel] could accommodate the technique of the film without sacrificing its own unique powers. The history of the novel after 1922—the year *Ulysses* appeared—is to a large extent that of the development of a cinematic imagination in novelists and their frequently ambivalent attempt to come to grips with the 'liveliest art' of the twentieth century" (Murray 4-5). Keith Cohen, in the introduction to his *Film and Fiction: The Dynamics of Exchange* (1979), also legitimized the view that our picture of a literature / film exchange in the 1920s ought to rely on our acceptance of technique in *Ulysses* as offering the normative entry-point to discussions of literature-and-film: "The demonstration of the cinematic quality of the modern novel has been available ever since the first reader of *Ulysses* noted the montage technique of 'The Wandering Rocks.' . . . Certain modern novels proclaim themselves cinematic" (Cohen 2).

Not surprisingly, perhaps, studies in the 1960s and 1970s of Lowry's "cinematic technique" came close to linking *Ulysses* and silent cinema as joint forerunners. In his 1965 introduction to a new edition of *Under the Volcano*, Stephen Spender, discussing Lowry's style, virtually blended Joyce with cinema: "Lowry has borrowed from Joyce. . . . But the most direct influence on this extraordinary book is not, I would suggest, from other novelists, but from films, most of all perhaps those of Eisenstein" (Spender xiii). Anthony Kilgallin, interested since the early 1960s in Lowry's debt to Joyce, became interested also in Lowry's debt to cinema, and in his 1973 book, *Lowry*, suggested that *Under the Volcano* was "one of this century's most cinematographic novels" (Kilgallin 131).

Of course, scholars' discovery that Eisenstein since the 1920s had stressed connections between *Ulysses* and his own work[2] only had the effect of strengthening their suggestions and conclusions about Joyce's work. The 1929 meeting in Paris between Joyce and Eisenstein provided symbolic support for their attempts, but we might find in it other significance, too. What literature-and-film scholars have tended not to notice is Joyce's own subsequent absence from the vigorous debates concerning not only his and Eisenstein's work of the 1920s, but literature and film more generally. As Gösta Werner recently put it: "A remarkable meeting took place one November day in 1929 in Paris between two famous innovators, one in literature, the other in film: James Joyce (1882-1941) and Sergej Eisenstein (1898-1948). . . . The historical meeting . . . took place on November 30, 1929, at 2 Square Robiac, 192 rue de Grenelle, Paris 7e, where Joyce had a flat. . . . As far as is known, Joyce never mentioned this meeting in writing. . . . Joyce . . . does not seem to have been deeply impressed by Eisenstein" (Werner 491, 494, 495, 503).[3] Joyce's relative silence about cinema in his nonfictional writing is a feature of his career that stands in strong contrast to the work of his literary contemporaries such as Wyndham Lewis and Dorothy Richardson, for example, and the much younger Malcolm Lowry. In and around 1929 Lewis and Richardson spent considerable energy analyzing the relationships of film and literature to each other and the impact of popular cinema on literary and other cultural values.[4] Joyce's silence actually anticipated the failure of any broad intellectual discussion to develop around issues of literature-and-film from the 1930s to the 1960s. In part it was because the "talkie" took film in the "wrong" direction around 1930 that so little serious discussion developed; in part, a little later, it was "New Criticism"[5] that drew literature away from dialogue with a world that seemed only to be vulgarizing the place of the word itself. And when a literature-film analysis began to develop widely in the late 1960s and 1970s, it was a technique-based analysis that could be absorbed readily enough by scholars familiar with New Criticism; it was not a study of modernism expanded by modernists' multifaceted debates about literature, cinema, and their respective audiences.

Like Lewis and Richardson did around 1929, Lowry spent a great deal of time writing about cinema around 1949. To be sure, he picked up those earlier writers' discussions of literature's role in relation to cinema just when the literary world had effected a great distance from cinema. What Lowry seems to have been trying to do was to find and promote the historic moment that he, as an undergraduate student twenty years old in 1929, felt might seriously have developed in what he saw around 1929 as the mutually engaged worlds of literature and film.

Lowry in the 1940s and 1950s recalled those few brief but crucial years when cinema—in particular certain variants of art cinema, avant-garde cinema, and auteur cinema—looked expectantly to a lively and enlightened reception from literary modernism, the practitioners and supporters and manifesto writers of which had headily thrust themselves forward as among the most powerful artistic/cultural trendsetters and arbiters and lobbyists of the twentieth century. He had experienced the late 1920s as a period when short film scripts and experimental literary fiction both found themselves on the exciting staging ground of the little magazines, and it was this recollection of inter-artistic attentiveness that defined his attitudes about the potential for renewing a positive literary reception of cinema.[6]

Lowry was aware that there was much that was outrageously provocative about his arguments and efforts in the 1940s and 1950s concerning film, not least about his hoping actually to write for film himself (a "talkie" for Hollywood at that), first in a feature-length adaptation of a novel by another writer, F. Scott Fitzgerald, then in a feature-length adaptation of his own novel, *Under the Volcano*.[7] He wanted to make his film-script version of *Under the Volcano* in a style inspired by the German expressionist cinema of the 1920s. Finding in Joyce not only the word as culmination but also the word as cul-de-sac, Lowry felt the limitations of what had become the modernist literary tradition and was prepared to renew it by opening the word as text to the audiovisual image as text.[8]

Today, by examining Lowry's posthumously published writing in particular, we can remind ourselves that it is a relatively specialized literary reception of cinema that we inherit from the Joyce-inspired scholars of the 1960s and 1970s, one that favors questions of technique and is peculiarly shorn of literary modernism's many subtle arguments and blunt broadsides concerning cinema, shorn of the presence of Wyndham Lewis, Dorothy Richardson, and many other literary intellectuals of the 1920s who were in varying degrees and in complicated ways openly and sometimes aggressively addressing the idea of cinema. Lowry, though he came along later, takes his place as a writer who around 1950 offers new ways of thinking about literature-and-film twenty years earlier, and hence about modernism in general. In his interest in linking texts to the emancipation of the audience, we see in Lowry an interest in "cultural studies" not ordinarily evident in the thinking of modernists. Much like Dorothy Richardson in the period 1927-33, Lowry—simultaneously subversive and idealistic—saw in cinema a means to fulfill his search for a universal audience.[9]

Joyce, of course, was not primarily in search of a universal audience that included the average movie-goer, and so his career hardly prompts our thinking along those lines. We even get the sense of a Joycean such as Richard Ellmann protecting readers from the vulgar world of movie-goers: when Ellmann moves rapidly from a fleeting film reference to less transgressive areas, such as the literary translation of *Ulysses* into foreign languages, he assures readers that such a shift of focus, from film to literary concerns, "was more certainly to [Joyce's] taste" (Ellmann 654).

In the early 1930s Joyce, who actually liked talking with friends about the cinema and who had thought of modernist directors such as Eisenstein or Ruttmann when he thought about a film of *Ulysses*, "officially . . . discountenanced the idea" when Warner Brothers contacted him about movie rights for *Ulysses*, "on the ground that the book could not be made into a film with"—here again a fear, whether Joyce's or Ellmann's—"artistic propriety" (Ellmann 654).[10] On October 26, 1932, Paul Léon wrote on behalf of Joyce to the agent Ralph Pinker about Warners' having approached Joyce concerning the filming of *Ulysses:* "I have taken the matter up with Mr Joyce who in fact tells me that he is in principle opposed to the filming of *Ulysses*. . . . Mr Joyce . . . takes the literary point of view and is therefore opposed to the filming as irrealisable" (*LJJ* 3:263).

Of course, Lowry shuddered, too, when he considered the risks of

bringing literary interests into the realm of film. Lowry's own quite conventional perception of himself as a novelist, along with the similar perception of him by his publishers, readers, friends, and critics, forced him
to hold any open articulation of his love for cinema discreetly in abey-
ance. But with the help of certain literary friends (from Gerald Noxon to
Conrad Aiken to Earle Birney) he could from time to time overcome or
subvert conventional opposition to film. Certainly the film societies at
Cambridge in 1929-32 and in Vancouver in the 1940s offered gratefully
accepted shelter, not to mention respectable protective cover.

Lowry's private correspondence with Frank Taylor, then a producer
at MGM, reveals that in the late 1940s he was ready to position himself
deliberately as a movie-loving writer ranged against a hostile literary
opposition:

> An enormous number of writers have learned, though not half enough,
> from the film: comparatively few have given anything back. It may be that
> there are some writers who have learned absolutely everything that they
> know about writing from the film but who if given a film to do would still
> turn in a stereotyped job: why? ((Even writers who are not professional
> writers for the screen cannot help being members of the *audience,* and as
> writers could scarcely help, one would have thought, even should they
> pretend to be putting their critical faculties in their pocket, being creative
> members of that audience in a sense that members of many other profes-
> sions are not: the novel, of all the arts, is the one most allied to the film, yet
> novelists use their talents to complain, and little else.)) Should their works
> be bought by the movies, they continue to complain: should they be given
> a free hand they very often make a mess of it. ["A Few Items," 4][11]

In knowingly breaking rank with his fellows, in rejecting what he took
to be their often arrogant and patronizing presuppositions, he deliciously
added a touch of tension or daring to his essentially ideological enter-
prise by playing on the well-known clichés of taboo mouthed by his
more conservative contemporaries:

> Most of the writers we have known personally whose works have been,
> say, bought by Hollywood, or have gone there themselves, seem to have
> failed, and then blamed the failure on Hollywood. Or even when they have
> succeeded, they have blamed the success on Hollywood. Very often—in
> fact above all—they blame it on the ethics of Hollywood. . . . They say a
> good many complicated things, but what it all boils down to is (1) the eth-
> ics of Hollywood are vile, because they wish to sell only sex; (2) the ethics
> of Hollywood are vile because it is impossible to write of sex, ergo, to tell
> the truth. You may substitute "aesthetics," "artistic standards" or even "poli-
> tics" for ethics—but it seems to amount to much the same thing in the end.

Yet should one look at the scripts responsible for these failures there is often only one reaction possible: they love not the film. Mysteriously, despite their protests, they love it not. They may have learned from it, they may even be able to tell you what a good film is, and write intelligently about it, but at bottom they feel superior to it—or to everything except the money to be made by it. ["A Few Items," 6]

For Lowry, it was irresponsible for writers to attack the cinema simply as cinema, without differentiating between cinema and its individual achievements, whether in the corpus of a director or even in a fragment of a specific film. Indeed, he felt that a great film, even a "Hollywood" film, like a great poem, strove against and simultaneously utilized a set of conventions, that in its very greatness it stood as testimony against entrenched practices, and that it sometimes explicitly criticized those practices.

For nearly a year in 1949-50, Lowry, inspired increasingly by the project, worked secretly and quickly on his film-script adaptation of *Tender Is the Night*. He deliberately kept this project very much "in the family" (as he put it), by which he meant fellow transgressors Margerie Lowry and Frank Taylor. Margerie Lowry, his wife, was a cowriter of the script, as in another sense she had been of the post-1940 version of *Under the Volcano*;[12] Frank Taylor, one of the former Reynal and Hitchcock editors of *Under the Volcano* (1947), was the producer at MGM for whom Lowry was writing. Significantly, the project was officially "on the shelf," and Lowry—determined to achieve the superhuman, to out-Hollywood Hollywood—was writing it "against" the wishes or requests of the studio.

In a way, Lowry saw his "Tender Is the Night" contribution to Hollywood, a project linked to many expressionist and other stylistic motifs of cinema in the 1920s, as prologue to his proposed "Under the Volcano" contribution to German cinema. He seemed to think that Clemens ten Holder, who was his German translator, and ten Holder's German colleagues might offer him a haven in which to create cinema safely, as he had seen the Germans create cinema in the 1920s. It had been in the late 1920s in Germany that he had observed the acceptance of film at least in pockets of the literary and other artistic communities. When the Germans in the 1950s declared their love for his novel *Under the Volcano*, he felt he had found in Germany the congenial ground for exerting and exercising himself in terms of his filmmaking intentions, and for trying to pressure his publishers to open for him film-connected contractual options.

We can get an historically organized view of Lowry's interests as late as the 1950s by paying some attention to what Lowry might have seen in the late 1920s, if not already in Germany when he studied there in 1928,

then beginning in 1929 at Cambridge. And we see how some of his experiences compare with some of Joyce's. In the fall of 1929, when Eisenstein
was paying his visit to Joyce and, subsequently, to Cambridge, Lowry
entered Cambridge University, where some literary and other intellectual figures had developed a lively engagement with the international
cinema of the preceding four or five years. Thus, handily exposing the
colorlessly conventional but stiffly blunt resistance among those at Cambridge who dully kept insisting that "cinema [has] killed each art in turn"
(Reynolds 3), there was in the Fall 1929 issue of *Experiment* William
Empson's "Ufa Nightmare," a poem at once drawing attention to UFA,
the German film-production giant of the 1920s, and exploring aspects of
the implications of visual images in literature and in film. There was in
Experiment, too, J.H. Whyte's essay on the film director (in this case Dziga
Vertov) as author or artist, and the bold, full-page announcement that
the program of Cambridge University's film society, strategically named
the Cambridge Film Guild, was under way. Basil Wright, who was at
Cambridge from 1924 to 1929, has recalled (in a letter to me) that "the
intellectual students were taking film as a very serious aspect of art. It
was regarded as *the* art form."[13]

The 1929-30 film society's program at Cambridge included G.W.
Pabst's *The Loves of Jeanne Ney* (first released in Germany in 1927), Jean
Epstein's *Finis terrae* (France, 1928), Alberto Cavalcanti's *En rade* (France,
1927), Jacques Feyder's *Thérèse Raquin* (France, 1928), René Clair's *Les
deux timides* (France, 1928), Eisenstein's *The General Line* (USSR, 1929),
Grigori Kozinstev and Leonid Trauberg's *CBD* (USSR, 1927), V.I.
Pudovkin's *The End of St. Petersburg* (USSR, 1927) and *Storm Over Asia*
(USSR, 1928), and Viktor Turin's *Turk-Sib* (USSR, 1928). With such silent
films as these Lowry spiritually closeted himself on a lifelong basis. In
1949-50 he observed to Frank Taylor that "one single very short sequence
of moonlight" at the opening of F.W. Murnau's *Sunrise* (United States,
1927) had stayed with him "for over twenty years" (*CML* 60). It had
been in Bonn in 1928 that Lowry had seen *Sunrise*, and to Clemens ten
Holder he claimed in 1951 that the opening of that film, along with the
opening and closing shots of Karl Grune's *The Street* (Germany, 1923),
influenced his writing "personally" more than anything he had ever read.
When he was in correspondence in the early 1950s with ten Holder, Lowry
also brought to mind other silent films of the 1920s, from early work
such as Robert Wiene's *The Cabinet of Dr. Caligari* (Germany, 1919-20)
and Fritz Lang's *Destiny* (Germany, 1921) to Henrik Galeen's *The Student
of Prague* (Germany, 1926), all of Murnau's "wonderful things," including *The Last Laugh* (Germany, 1924), and "all the films of the great Ufa
days" (*CML* 4). In 1946 he drew animated attention to other silent films

of the 1920s in his conversations with Noxon, including Erich von Stroheim's *Greed* (United States, 1923-24), Clair's *The Italian Straw Hat* (France, 1927), Epstein's *The Fall of the House of Usher* (France, 1928), and Carl-Theodor Dreyer's *The Passion of Joan of Arc* (France, 1928), as well as *The Loves of Jeanne Ney*, *The Last Laugh*, and *Sunrise* (*LN* 127).

In a few intellectual circles literary modernism's ambivalent flirtation with cinema in the 1920s developed in the 1930s with the film-society community's fairly positive response to the documentary film movement of the 1930s, a movement that drew in artists (such as writers and composers) from disciplines other than film. For example, Auden, as a 1930s late-modernist, teamed up with John Grierson to make *Night Mail* (1936), for which Benjamin Britten wrote the music. Joyce, according to Maria Jolas (Hutchins 245), appeared to have liked Robert Flaherty's *Man of Aran* (1933-34); and when Joyce attended a screening of Pare Lorentz's *The River* (1937), with its musical score by Virgil Thomson, he declared its poetic script (narrated by Thomas Chalmers) "the most beautiful [prose] I have heard in ten years" (Rabinowitz 96). In 1940—in a letter sent to Noxon from "the Cabinet of Dr. Caliglowry" and bursting with reference to Len Lye and the genius of Karl Grune—Lowry fondly recalled Grierson's film, the 1929 documentary that signaled the British strain of socially committed (and Eisenstein-inspired) filmmaking documentary: "It seems a long time since I saw *Drifters*" (*LN* 34).

Unlike Joyce (Rabinowitz 100), whose interest in Lorentz's film was linked to the narrator's recitation of words—long lists of names of rivers, streams, rivulets, and towns—Lowry (with his growing interest in reaching and ennobling a large public) was prepared to consider what Paula Rabinowitz reminds us was a key dictum for Lorentz: "Good art is good propaganda" (Rabinowitz 97). In September 1940 Lowry offered Noxon a portrait of himself as one who saw that socially argumentative Soviet realism, like documentary realism, might very well be a vehicle for great artistic production: "Good propaganda, for whatever cause, is good art," he said, though perhaps not without a little self-consciousness (*LN* 32). To be sure, he did insert into that self-portrait his assumption about artistic brilliance, itself the primary condition for spiritual and moral ennoblement through art:

> Knowing nothing even though I had been a fireman at sea and through a Chinese Revolution at the time I first saw *The End of St. Petersburg* [probably at the often empty "home of unusual films" in Liverpool, where Lowry practically lived for a time in 1928 (*CML* 7)], I did not recognize it as [Soviet] propaganda at all. I merely thought, responding to it emotionally, that

it was marvellous, the best I had ever seen (etc.) up to that point: the opening sequence of windmills on the steppes made me weep, as it were "from
the sheer beauty of it." In the same way, I was moved—or misled—by . . .
Room's *The Ghost That Never Returns* [USSR, 1929; screened at Cambridge
University's film society in the 1930-31 season], of which I can, though I
saw it only once and that eleven years ago, remember every detail. [*LN* 32]

But Lowry also knew enough to comically debunk himself yet further,
calling himself a Canadian "Pudovkin in the Outhouse" and toasting
Noxon's "Thunder over Canada" with a "Que viva—life!" (*LN* 33).

Lowry, unlike almost all other leading figures active within late modernism, accepted the members of a mass audience as legitimate readers
of literary and nonliterary texts alike. If Joyce invited the literary community into a new reading of the increasingly esoteric word, Lowry invited the literary community to break out of its worship exclusively of
the written word. In effect, Lowry argued in favor of a kind of artistic
eclecticism that has something in common with postmodernism's ignor-
ing of traditional disciplinary boundaries, and that includes the com-
mercially made product.
    Lowry coveted in 1949-50 the prospect of making a great work that
would be not only "uplifting" but also on at least one level absolutely
obvious to "a five-year-old messenger boy" (*NS* 69). And he wanted to
utter his position in public terms, in a public voice. He observed that
"when Chaplin . . . lets forth a blast [of intelligent critical breath about
Hollywood] one listens indeed" ("A Few Items," 7). Lowry almost hinted
that he too wanted to enter the public debating space in which Chaplin
moved about and spoke to the world.
    Of course, for Lowry, as for Joyce, a narrative text always held lay-
ers within layers of meaning, and it was here, Lowry argued (again in
opposition to conventional wisdom, though very much in keeping with
Eisenstein), that the potential for film should match the potential for
literature. Lowry—in his search for an artistic model that would offer a
standard helpful in his idea for an artistically influential cinema—found
it precisely in Joyce. In argument that suggests surprising parallels with
Eisenstein's, Lowry, in search of a cultural, intellectual, and artistic defense of cinema, turned to *Ulysses*. Both Lowry and Eisenstein used that
revolutionary piece of 1922 art as a standard of measurement to explain
or justify their own experimentation in and hopes for innovative cinematic work that would reach artistically sophisticated and general audiences alike. But it was in ways quite different from Eisenstein's that
Lowry proposed a cinema reminiscent of *Ulysses*:

Let us look at what happened in literature. The ban on *Ulysses*, whatever anyone says, was not really lifted because it was not intentionally obscene or an aphrodisiac and so on but because of the passion and scholarship and artistic devotion Joyce had put into it, so much more passion and scholarship and artistic devotion indeed was there in Joyce's work than in almost any other contemporary production . . . that it gave one the illusion that the conventional resources of nobility or ennoblement in literature right up to their highest expression were exhausted, and the thing became a noble achievement in itself: nor, if we are being somewhat incomplete, are we wholly joking. It was the very best there was, and so we had to have it, and not to have it would have been a grave impairment of our freedom, and that of other writers. ["A Few Items," 9]

Lowry delighted in registering his recognition that such an analysis, as his of Joyce, would put him "at the risk of heresy to our own profession as writers" if he applied it to the movies; but the movies, he insisted, were typically "approached from the wrong direction" ("A Few Items," 9). Reversing the usual arguments about greatness in art, and opposing the typical vulgarization and sentimentality of the "fifth rate" writer, he conjectured that film was an appropriate place to "correct" the contemporary artistic malaise ("A Few Items," 8), even (or especially) when that malaise was reinforced by such opposition as censorship by law:

> Now however that may be about literature [i.e., the lifting of the ban in the case of *Ulysses*], one has often thought it might be just the other way round with the film ((or at least the sound film)). "The resources of nobility" (for lack of a better phrase) seem not really to have been tapped [in the sound film]. . . . Yet a man should be able to write nobly ((and we are speaking of some hypothetical bird who probably exists here and there, in fact—who is writing with the whole film and its direction and its effect in view, not just for the pleasure of listening to his own words—should be able to write nobly)) and even greatly, even within such limitations as Hollywood provides, even those of the Catholic church. . . . The way to break your bonds . . . is . . . by straining upward. ["A Few Items," 9-10]

With this nod to his *Under the Volcano*, where one of the epigraphs is from Goethe—*Wer immer strebend sich bemüht, den können wir erlösen.* (Whosoever unceasingly strives upward . . . him can we save.)—Lowry developed his audacious vision of a great Hollywood cinema matched by a great Hollywood public: "Actually if you go really high enough [even] the censorship won't be able to see you. (Though the public will, you having carried them part of the way with you, while the censorship and the League of Decency are still down below with their noses stuck in the mud.)" ("A Few Items," 10). Having posited a cinema of genius that (as Joyce had done in *Ulysses*) would prove itself immune to the legalistic arguments of the censor, Lowry extended his "risk of heresy" to his profession as a writer by articulating his faith in the massive movie-going public, a public whose yearning for great things Lowry had come to understand by keeping a keen watch on them in the egalitarian light of the public spaces of cinema lobbies:

> Grandmama would like to see *Intolerance* again; not only Grandmama, but millions of her grandsons, one feels would like to see *Intolerance* again, or "films of that kind." . . . This is not something we are just making up but something we have heard implied thousands of times. Nor is the yearning for the excellent satisfied, we suggest, whatever the financial returns, or their merits, by most of the great pseudo-serious hits that immediately come to mind: there is a sense of frustration one has seen expressed in a thousand gestures of impatience in cinema lobbies, a thousand exclamations of "after all" or "well, you know it's Hollywood" or that it's "just another movie," a thousand interruptions by people . . . with no train to catch, and who have not seen the film through, but yet who go out before the end. ["A Few Items," 11]

In 1965 Stephen Spender was insisting on *Under the Volcano*'s resemblance to cinema as technique. But already in *Under the Volcano* Lowry was conducting not only a kind of Joycean appropriation and transformation of cinema, but also an intertextual conversation with texts that had lives of their own and that in many cases he admired and respected. Joyce turns his cinema notes in *Ulysses* and *Finnegans Wake* into a kind of hilarious revenge on a popular but commercialized world conspiring to take over modern life and art; Lowry, like Dorothy Richardson in the late 1920s, though fearful enough about the technologies and mass media of that commercial world, tried to get its best exemplars to speak. Feeling that corrective action was necessary, he declared himself a friend of Hollywood. "What Hollywood does is of importance in the world," argued Lowry, noting that he, like other "youth of the world," had been shaped by its "colossal" power. Insisting that "most everyone has a stake in it" ("A Few Items," 7), he decided to enter its orbit rather than boycott it. Thus he hoped to fulfill his dangerous ambition to inspire the creation of a vigorous commercial cinema more than two decades after the safely fashionable silent era had ended. Joyce might have been amused, or alarmed, at Lowry's fraternizing with the enemy; but Lowry's action and analysis involving film give literary and film scholars new ways to think about writers such as Joyce and Lowry in particular, and about modernism in general.

Notes

1. By the late 1960s and early 1970s—as represented by the publication of *Literature/Film Quarterly* (ed. Thomas L. Erskine; first issue, January 1973); Harry Geduld's edition *Authors on Film* (1972); Edward Murray's *Cinematic Imagination: Writers and the Motion Pictures* (1972); and Robert Richardson's *Literature and Film* (1969)—North American scholars began in large numbers to pay attention to literature-film associations, especially apparent connections found in formal aspects of technique.

Austin Briggs, in "'Roll Away the Reel World, the Reel World': 'Circe' and Cinema," draws attention not only to Edward Murray's and Keith Cohen's analyses of Joyce and cinema in *The Cinematic Imagination* and *Film and Fiction*, respectively, but also to Alan Spiegel's *Fiction and the Camera Eye: Visual Consciousness in Film and the Modern Novel*, R. Baron Palmer's "Eisensteinian Montage and Joyce's *Ulysses*: The Analogy Reconsidered," Susan Bazargan's "Headings in 'Aeolous': A Cinematographic View," Craig Wallace Barrow's *Montage in James Joyce's "Ulysses,"* and Richard Pearce's *Novel in Motion: An Approach to Modern Fiction*. In "Joyce, modernism, and post-modernism" (1990), Christopher Butler suggests that Joyce's influence in the "Wandering Rocks" chapter of *Ulysses* may have been "directly cinematic, and influenced by concepts of montage as we find them in Eisenstein (with whom he discussed the possibility of turning *Ulysses* into a film. . . .)" (270). Butler was in part extending earlier suggestions such as that of Patricia Hutchins, who in her *James Joyce's World* (1957) argued, "By the thirties, *Ulysses* had influenced much contemporary writing and it would be interesting to trace the use of the interior monologue in early sound films." She added: "Sergei Eisenstein greatly admired the book" (245). Similarly, Erwin R. Steinberg has drawn attention to connections between Joyce's and Eisenstein's techniques (Steinberg 274). Robert Gessner wrote in 1970 in his *Moving Image: A Guide to Cinematic Literacy*: "Joyce, that fountainhead of original waters, was the legitimate father of the cinematic novel" (265). For a discussion partly related to our present concerns, see Terence Brown's "Joyce's Magic Lantern." In his *Film and the Narrative Tradition*, John L. Fell firmly and helpfully moves beyond a focus exclusively on Joyce to draw also Dorothy Richardson and Virginia Woolf into his discussion of "two ways to consider the relation of the modern novel to film techniques" in the teens (68-69).

Associations drawn between the 1950s world of Jean-Luc Godard and the 1920s world of Joyce have often worked against our seeing the arguments that (as I shall note) Lowry was trying to make in 1949-50. In *The New Wave* (1976) James Monaco eloquently—but, I think, too narrowly—fits the Godard of the late 1950s rather than the early avant-garde movement in film with modernists such as Joyce (and Schoenberg, and Picasso); he argues that the early avant-garde movement, which would include Hans Richter, Viking Eggeling, and Fernand Léger, was isolated from the mainstream (Monaco, *The New Wave*, 99-100). Fell, too, stresses that the film of the 1950s (such as Kurosawa's *Rashomon*, released in 1950) draws on novels (such as *Ulysses*) rather than on novels *and* films of the 1920s, although he does allow that there are parallels in narrative structure between *Rashomon* and such early "city documentaries" as *Rien que les heures*—which was made in 1926 by Cavalcanti, whom Lowry's friend Noxon met in Paris (Fell, *Film: An Introduction*, 77-78). And in 1988, for Robert Lapsley and Michael Westlake, it is these two, Joyce and Godard, who are linked by their production of an "alternative to the classic realist text, and that was the revolutionary text" (Lapsley and Westlake 173). More recently, Thomas E. Valasek, too, in effect erases earlier modernist film's place within a broader modernism when he ties Godard's *Breathless* (1959) primarily to work by writers such as Joyce, as well as Beckett (Valasek 102). But Charles Eidsvik provides a more nuanced reading of shifts from the 1920s to the 1950s (see, for example, Eidsvik 168-69); and Monaco offers a helpful linkage of, among others, early Mack Sennett with dadaism and surrealism (and, more tentatively, early Griffith with Joyce, as well as Conrad and Dreiser, Strindberg, Chekhov, Shaw, and Picasso) in his *How to Read a Film* (236).

2. Eisenstein's essay "Dickens, Griffith, and the Film Today," published in his *Film Form*, has been a touchstone for many other elaborations of cinema's apparent roots in literature. An overview of Eisenstein's assessment of Joyce is provided by Neil Cornwell in his 1992 monograph *James Joyce and the Russians* (see especially "Sergei Eisenstein," 79-87). For example, early on, in 1928, Eisenstein "wrote of his familiarity with Joyce's writings, of *Ulysses* as 'the most interesting phenomenon in the West for cinematography. I don't know about it from the literary point of view, but I think the same goes'" (Cornwell 80). See also Aleksandar Flaker's "Russian Joyce," especially pp. 205-9: "*Ulysses* as a Model for the Film of the Future."

3. For drawing Werner's essay to my attention, I am grateful to Paul Salmon.

4. For discussions of Lewis and cinema, see my essays "A New Year One: Film as Metaphor in the Writings of Wyndham Lewis," "The Critic, the Film, and the Astonished Eye," and "Wyndham Lewis's *The Childermass* (1928): The Slaughter of the Innocents in the Age of Cinema." In his writings, Lewis derided Joyce for his cinematic style. For example, in the first part of *The Childermass* Lewis's Joyceans, Pullman and Satterthwaite, are hopelessly lost in an environment where a television or film medium determines the fluctuating coordinates of space and time. For one of the more recent of many readings of Joyce's responses to Lewis, see "Jellyfish and Treacle: Lewis, Joyce, Gender, and Modernism," by Bonnie Kime Scott.

Some of Dorothy Richardson's arguments about film were prompted by H.G. Wells's view that critics should acknowledge the demise of conventional literature and the inevitable ascendancy of cinema. Wells produced his argument in "Film, the Art Form of the Future," the introduction to his *King Who Was a King*, in 1929. Richardson gently rebuked Wells in her 1929 essays "Talkies, Plays, and Books: Thoughts on the Approaching Battle between the Spoken Pictures, Literature, and the Stage" and "Continuous Performance, [XIV]: Almost Persuaded." Many of her essays appeared in the "little magazine" called *Close Up*, which was devoted to cinema. Although Richardson herself did not contribute to each issue, *Close Up* appeared monthly from July 1927 to December 1930. From 1931 to 1933 it was published only quarterly, but in a format enlarged and more profusely illustrated with photographs. See also my essay "A Comparative Approach to the Form and Function of Novel and Film: Dorothy Richardson's Theory of Art."

In her anthology *The Gender of Modernism* (1990), Bonnie Kime Scott makes available for the first time, from Virginia Woolf's private reading notes, a quotation of Woolf admiringly saying, as early as 1919, of Joyce's *Ulysses:* "Possibly like a cinema that shows you very slowly, how a hare does jump" (643). For a discussion of Woolf on cinema, Joyce, and the traditional novelists of the 1920s, see my essay "The Shadow in 'Caligari': Virginia Woolf and the 'Materialists'" Responses to Film." Woolf, generally, offers a reading of Joyce-and-cinema that would surely have resisted Lewis's. See Lewis's chapters "Mr. Jingle and Mr. Bloom" in *The Art of Being Ruled* and "An Analysis of the Mind of James Joyce" in *Time and Western Man.*

5. With reference to the impact of such critics as I.A. Richards (who in 1931 was teaching *Ulysses* to undergraduates at Cambridge, where Noxon was a student until 1931 and Lowry until 1932), John Crowe Ransom, and Allen Tate, Kevin J.H. Dettmar explores Joyce's selling of *Ulysses* to the reading public "by way of the academics." Joyce's art, suggests Dettmar, is "the art of the universities" (Dettmar 805, 806, 807); it was in the universities that New Critics and their contemporaries for some decades from the 1930s on in effect blocked the recuperation of literary modernism's earlier rapprochement (rooted in avant-garde activities and attitudes) with cinema.

6. Lowry himself was offering only rudimentary statements about film around 1929, however. For example, in *Ultramarine* (1933), on which Lowry began work in the late 1920s, the protagonist outrageously declares, amongst his pronouncements on and descriptions of the movies, "In Moscow I was a camera man under Pudovkin" (*Ult* 100). In breaking rank with literary culture's general sanctions against film, Lowry did in 1949-50 muster support from the likes of Christopher Isherwood and James Agee. Stanley Fox has recently recalled Lowry's admiration for the opening scene of Alexander Dovzhenko's *Aerograd* (1935) and other works by this Soviet filmmaker, whose famous film *Arsenal* was released in 1929. Lowry, for some reason, according to Fox (who met Lowry in Vancouver in 1951), referred to Eisenstein "as 'an ass'" (Fox 27-28).

Lowry, helped along by his friend Gerald Noxon's strong interest, would have been aware of the short film scripts that had developed into a kind of avant-garde genre from the end of World War I to the early 1930s, especially in Paris (where Noxon had lived—and observed the world of the avant-garde—from 1926 to 1928). Philippe Soupault, according to Richard Abel (1:113, 123, 143), "was the first of the young Dada-Surrealists to become interested in the cinema" and by 1918 was writing short scenarios and a hybrid form of cinematic poetry. By 1927, *Nouvelle revue française* was showing strong interest in cinema and had published Antonin Artaud's scenario for *La coquille et le clergyman* (Abel 1:322, 341). Running historically parallel to *Close Up*, French journals such as *Photo-Ciné, Cinégraphie*, and *On tourne* in 1927-28 "especially supported the work of the French narrative avant-garde" (Abel 1:322, 341). Until the early 1930s Artaud, Luis Buñuel, and many others associated with the avant-garde, often surrealism, wrote scenarios that "found their way into the burgeoning ranks of published 'scenario' literature" (Abel 2:23, 36). In his private exercises, Lowry occasionally sketched out brief scenario versions of portions of his fiction.

7. Lowry completed only the first of these when he adapted F. Scott Fitzgerald's *Tender Is the Night*; however, it is a script that, in many of its parts, suggests that really Lowry was already adapting his own work, including pieces of *Under the Volcano*, and was also exploring ways of extending *Under the Volcano* and other of his texts by transforming them into a blueprint for his proposed connections of all his prose fiction in "The Voyage That Never Ends." For a discussion of the connections between Malcolm (and Margerie) Lowry's film script "Tender Is the Night" and Lowry's proposed "The Voyage That Never Ends," see Miguel Mota's and my introduction to *The Cinema of Malcolm Lowry*, especially pp. 36-38.

8. Even before Lowry made his 455-page "Tender Is the Night" proposal to Hollywood in 1949-50, or his subsequent overtures to potential German film personnel, he looked forward in 1940-41 to the possibility of work with the National Film Board of Canada, where John Grierson was commissioner and where his Cambridge University associates of the late 1920s—Gerald Noxon and Stuart Legg—were working, though Noxon only for a short period in 1940-41. See also *LN* 29-36.

9. Gerald Noxon kept copies of *Close Up*—which included Richardson's essays on film—in his rooms at Cambridge, and (as Noxon himself suggested to me) it is likely that Lowry glanced at them there during his visits with Noxon from 1929 to 1931.

10. Patrick McCarthy, to whom I am grateful for his reading of this study as a whole, has added the following comment: "But Ellmann also reports that Joyce didn't discourage others from writing scenarios, suggesting perhaps that Joyce was mainly opposed to having the film done by a Hollywood studio. His keeping Hollywood at arm's length reflected perhaps (a) an aversion to commercialism, which inevitably meant artistic compromises, and (b) the fact that Joyce would lose control over the process. Maybe he also realized that this would distract him from his work on *Finnegans Wake*." See also Patricia Hutchins's reference to Joyce's connection with a Hungarian director in 1934-35 (Hutchins 245).

11. The portions in double parentheses here and below are marked "cut" in Lowry's little-known and posthumously published "A Few Items" manuscript. However, they seem to reflect both his thinking and his practice.

12. Although Margerie Bonner Lowry is identified in the manuscripts as having been a cowriter of the "Tender Is the Night" film script, the 1995 "Moby Dick" radio script, and texts such as "A Few Items," the dominant voice in these works is always Malcolm Lowry's. Patrick McCarthy, citing Hugh Kenner, has reminded me that on an important level there are at least distant parallels in Joyce, who once said to a "party of friends": "Really, it is not I who am writing this crazy book [*Finnegans Wake*]. . . . It is you, and you, and you, and that man over there, and that girl at the next table" (Kenner 327).

13. Gerald Noxon indicated to me in an interview that Lowry considered the work of serious filmmakers "as on a par with the kind of work he was

doing" in literary fiction. Noxon did not know whether Lowry had seen or heard Eisenstein when the Soviet director and theorist spoke at Cambridge in 1929. As publishing-editor, Noxon brought out seven issues of the avant-garde magazine *Experiment* from November 1928 to Spring 1931. In his article "How Humphrey Jennings Came to Film," Noxon recalled: "*Experiment* rapidly became a focal point of intellectual interest in the University. Its editorial board included J. Bronowski, William Empson, and Hugh Sykes-Davies, and among other resident contributors were Basil Wright, Richard Eberhart, John Davenport, Malcolm Lowry, George Reavey, James Reeves, Kathleen Raine, Timothy White, Julian Trevelyan, Henri Cartier-Bresson, and Jack Sweeney. From outside the University came contributions from Conrad Aiken, Richard Aldington, James Joyce, Mayakovsky, Boris Pasternak, and Paul Eluard. I give these names because they indicate, I think, the kind of intellectual and aesthetic climate which prevailed in Cambridge at the time" (Noxon 70). If Joyce happened to see his piece "from *Work in Progress*" in the seventh and final issue of *Experiment* (Spring 1931), followed by Stuart Gilbert's "A Footnote to *Work in Progress*," he might have seen there, too, Lowry's "Punctum Indifferens Skibet Gaar Videre." Indeed, on the front cover of the magazine (which appears in a photograph on page 89 of volume 1 of *Sursum Corda! The Collected Letters of Malcolm Lowry,* edited by Sherrill Grace), in a boldly typeset list of authors, the names James Joyce and Malcolm Lowry appear side by side.

Works Cited

Abel, Richard. *French Film Theory and Criticism: A History/Anthology.* Vol. 1, *1907-1929;* vol. 2, *1929-1939.* Princeton: Princeton Univ. Press, 1988.

Barrow, Craig Wallace. *Montage in James Joyce's "Ulysses."* Madrid: Studia Humanitatis, 1980.

Bazargan, Susan. "The Headings in 'Aeolous': A Cinematographic View." *James Joyce Quarterly* 23 (Spring 1986): 345-50.

Briggs, Austin. "'Roll Away the Reel World, the Reel World': 'Circe' and Cinema." In *Coping with Joyce,* edited by Morris Beja and Shari Benstock. Columbus: Ohio State Univ. Press, 1989.

Brown, Terence. "Joyce's Magic Lantern." *James Joyce Quarterly* 28.4 (Summer 1991): 791-98.

Butler, Christopher. "Joyce, modernism, and post-modernism." In *The Cambridge Companion to James Joyce,* edited by Derek Attridge. Cambridge: Cambridge Univ. Press, 1990.

Cohen, Keith. *Film and Fiction: The Dynamics of Exchange.* New Haven: Yale Univ. Press, 1979.

Cornwell, Neil. *James Joyce and the Russians.* London: Macmillan, 1992.

Dettmar, Kevin J.H. "Selling *Ulysses.*" *James Joyce Quarterly* 30.4 and 31.1 (Summer 1993 and Fall 1993): 795-812.

Eidsvik, Charles. *Cineliteracy: Film among the Arts.* New York: Random House, 1978.

Eisenstein, Sergei. *Film Form: Essays in Film Theory and the Film Sense.* Cleveland and New York: World Publishing Company, Meridian Books, 1967.

Ellmann, Richard. *James Joyce.* New and rev. ed. New York: Oxford Univ. Press, 1982.

Empson, William. "Ufa Nightmare." *Experiment* 4 (Nov. 1929): 28.

Fell, John L. *Film and the Narrative Tradition.* Norman: Univ. of Oklahoma Press, 1974.

———. *Film: An Introduction.* New York: Praeger, 1975.

Flaker, Aleksandar. "Russian Joyce." In *International Perspectives on James Joyce,* edited by Gottlieb Gaiser. Troy, N.Y.: Whitston, 1986.

Fox, Stanley. "Stanley Fox on Malcolm Lowry." *Malcolm Lowry Review* nos 29 and 30 (Fall 1991 and Spring 1992): 27-30.

Geduld, Harry M., ed. *Authors on Film.* Bloomington: Indiana Univ. Press, 1972.

Gessner, Robert. *The Moving Image: A Guide to Cinematic Literacy.* New York: E.P. Dutton, 1970.

Hutchins, Patricia. *James Joyce's World.* London: Methuen, 1957.

Kenner, Hugh. *Dublin's Joyce.* Bloomington: Indiana Univ. Press, 1956.

Kilgallin, Tony. *Lowry.* Erin, Ontario: Press Porcepic, 1973.

Lapsley, Robert, and Michael Westlake. *Film Theory: An Introduction.* Manchester, England: Manchester Univ. Press, 1988.

Lewis, Wyndham. *The Art of Being Ruled.* 1926. Reprint, Santa Rosa, Calif., Black Sparrow, 1989.

———. *Time and Western Man.* Boston: Beacon Press, 1957 (originally published London: Chatto and Windus, 1927).

———. *The Childermass.* London: Chatto and Windus, 1928.

Lowry, Malcolm, and Margerie Bonner Lowry. "A Few Items Culled from What Started Out to Be a Sort of Preface to a Film-script," edited by Paul Tiessen. *White Pelican* 4.2 (Spring 1974): 2-20.

———. *"Moby Dick* Adapted (1945)," with an introduction by Paul Tiessen. *Malcolm Lowry Review* nos. 36 and 37 (Spring 1995 and Fall 1995): 96-153.

Monaco, James. *The New Wave: Truffaut, Godard, Chabrol, Rohmer, Rivette.* New York: Oxford Univ. Press, 1976.

———. *How to Read a Film: The Art, Technology, Language, History, and Theory of Film and Media.* New York: Oxford Univ. Press, 1977.

Murray, Edward. *The Cinematic Imagination: Writers and the Motion Pictures.* New York: Frederick Ungar, 1972.

Noxon, Gerald. "How Humphrey Jennings Came to Film." In *"On Malcolm Lowry" and Other Writings by Gerald Noxon,* edited by Miguel Mota and Paul Tiessen. Waterloo, Ontario: MLR Editions Canada, 1987.

Palmer, R. Baron. "Eisensteinian Montage and Joyce's *Ulysses:* The Analogy Reconsidered." *Mosaic* 18 (1985): 73-85.

Pearce, Richard. *The Novel in Motion: An Approach to Modern Fiction.* Columbus: Ohio State Univ. Press, 1983.

Rabinowitz, Paula. *They Must Be Represented: The Politics of Documentary.* London and New York: Verso, 1994.

Reynolds, O.W. "Synopsis: Mirror to Introspection." *Experiment* 4 (Nov. 1919): 3.

Richardson, Dorothy. "Continuous Performance, [XIV]: Almost Persuaded." *Close Up* 4.6 (June 1929): 31-37.

————. "Talkies, Plays, and Books: Thoughts on the Approaching Battle between the Spoken Pictures, Literature, and the Stage." *Vanity Fair* 32 (Aug. 1929): 56.

Richardson, Robert. *Literature and Film.* Bloomington: Indiana Univ. Press, 1969.

Scott, Bonnie Kime, ed. "Jellyfish and Treacle: Lewis, Joyce, Gender, and Modernism." In *Coping with Joyce,* edited by Morris Beja and Shari Benstock. Columbus: Ohio State Univ. Press, 1989.

————. *The Gender of Modernism: A Critical Anthology.* Bloomington: Indiana Univ. Press, 1990.

Spender, Stephen. Introduction to *Under the Volcano.* Philadelphia: J.B. Lippincott, 1965.

Spiegel, Alan. *Fiction and the Camera Eye: Visual Consciousness in Film and the Modern Novel.* Charlottesville: Univ. Press of Virginia, 1976.

Steinberg, Erwin R. *The Stream of Consciousness and Beyond in "Ulysses."* Pittsburgh: Univ. of Pittsburgh Press, 1973.

Tiessen, Paul. "A Comparative Approach to the Form and Function of Novel and Film: Dorothy Richardson's Theory of Art." *Literature/Film Quarterly* 3.1 (Winter 1975): 83-90.

————. "The Critic, the Film, and the Astonished Eye." In *Figures in a Ground: Canadian Essays on Modern Literature Collected in Honour of Sheila Watson,* edited by Diane Bessai and David Jackel. Saskatoon: Western Producer Prairie Books, 1978.

————. "The Shadow in 'Caligari': Virginia Woolf and the 'Materialists" Responses to Film." *Film Criticism* 5.1 (Fall 1980): 1-9. Reprinted in *Film Criticism* 11.1-2 (Fall-Winter 1987): 75-83.

————. "A New Year One: Film as Metaphor in the Writings of Wyndham Lewis." In *Words and Moving Images: Essays on Verbal and Visual Expression in Film and Television,* edited by William C. Wees and Michael Dorland. Montreal: Mediatexte Publications, 1984.

————. "Wyndham Lewis's *The Childermass* (1928): The Slaughter of the Innocents in the Age of Cinema." In *Apocalyptic Visions Past and Present,* edited by JoAnn James and William J. Cloonan. Tallahassee: Florida State Univ. Press, 1988.

Valasek, Thomas E. *Frameworks: An Introduction to Film Studies.* Dubuque: William C. Brown, 1992.

Wells, H.G. *The King Who Was a King.* London: Ernest Benn, 1929.

Werner, Gösta. "James Joyce and Sergej Eisenstein," translated by Erik Gunnemark. *James Joyce Quarterly* 23.3 (Spring 1990): 491-507.

Whyte, J.H. "Werthoff and the *Kino-Auge.*" *Experiment* 4 (Nov. 1929): 38-40.

eleven

The Filmmaker as Critic: Huston's *Under the Volcano* and *The Dead*

Rebecca Hughes and Kieron O'Hara

In the last few years before he died, John Huston made films based on Malcolm Lowry's *Under the Volcano* (1984, Universal, with Albert Finney, Jacqueline Bisset, and Anthony Andrews) and James Joyce's story "The Dead" (1987, Vestron Pictures/Zenith, with Anjelica Huston and Donal McCann). Because these films were different in important ways from the original literary works, we can make discoveries about Joyce's and Lowry's works by comparing the originals with Huston's adaptations. First, we will need to have a view on the originals for the purpose of comparison. Second, we will argue that these Huston films are *critical* studies of the originals. Our main effort in this essay will be to reconstruct a critical argument based on the films.

Huston is portrayed as the man who made a mess of *Under the Volcano*. Guillermo Cabrera Infante wrote an ambitious screenplay for Joseph Losey, but was angered when Losey "lost his battle [to film *Volcano*] to John Huston (who, typically, after professing a love for the book for years, proceeded to make a turd of it—what's amazing is that some reviewers saw the turd as an urbane turkey)" (Infante, quoted in Binns, "Filming," 109). Ronald Binns notes that Huston's film pleased no one: "The film was too undramatic to satisfy cinema-goers unacquainted with the novel, and Lowryans were disappointed by Huston's feeble evocation of Mexico and by his ruthlessly compressed and oversimplified version of Lowry's dense, ambiguous multi-levelled text" ("Filming," 109-10). The conventional story, then, is that Huston was the wrong man for the job, that Joseph Losey, or perhaps Luis Buñuel, should have made the picture, because only a filmmaker of that style would be able to be faithful to the uncertainties, hallucinations, tragedies, comedies, horror, politics, and mystery of *Under the Volcano*.

In fact, it is even possible that luminaries such as these would not quite do. Lowry himself was very knowledgeable about the cinema, and his tastes are well known. *Volcano* is packed full of cinematic references, and both Yvonne and Laruelle have connections with the industry. Further, Lowry also wrote a screenplay for another "difficult" novel, *Tender Is the Night*. In it, there are many expressionistic tricks, montages, dream sequences—the full works. Many sequences in that screenplay are described highly visually, and the overall effect is relatively easy to anticipate. Hence, for many critics, the ideal director of the picture would be Lowry himself, and therefore, any *actual* director of the picture is to be judged as a Lowry-surrogate. "When a second *Under the Volcano* is made one can only hope that it will attract the talents of a director temperamentally akin to Lowry, with a willingness to take risks" (Binns, "Filming," 123).

Yet this critical consensus—the ready dismissal of Huston—is implausible, for two reasons. Huston is a giant of the cinema. His willingness to take risks is evident; such willingness has brought him both success (*The Maltese Falcon, The Asphalt Jungle*) and notorious failure (*Moby Dick, Annie*). Further, Huston colludes with his antagonistic critics in presenting himself as some sort of primal, styleless filmmaker. As Binns puts it: "Huston's sensibility was far removed from that of Joyce or Lowry or Nabokov, who relished oddity, the startling metaphor, the unusual angle, and his film-making style, lodged firmly in a mainstream American realist tradition, belonged to a different world to that of artful, highly self-conscious continental directors like Buñuel, Bergman, Godard, Fassbinder and Tarkovsky. As Huston cheerfully admitted in 1986, 'I have no style that I'm aware of. There's nothing self-conscious about it'" ("Filming," 122-23).

Huston's claim is implausible, but it is part of a tradition; John Ford—the director of a stylized masterpiece, *The Informer*—made similar claims. Huston is a very different director from the others that Binns lists, but the suggestion that there is nothing self-conscious about *The Maltese Falcon* or *The Treasure of the Sierra Madre* or *The List of Adrian Messenger* would appear on the face of it to be simply false. This then raises an obvious question as to how a vastly experienced, supremely talented filmmaker could make such a poor film as Huston is supposed to have made of *Under the Volcano*.

The claim that *Under the Volcano* is a turkey needs explanation that cannot be provided simply by the assertion of the undoubted fact that he made a realist film of an expressionist novel. As Victor Sage reminds us, Billy Wilder's *Lost Weekend*, a triumph of cinematic art and one of the high points in Wilder's career, is also a documentary treatment of a highly self-conscious, literary text, Charles Jackson's novella (which Lowry, at least, perhaps erroneously, thought was horribly close in style and content to his own). Indeed, despite his claim that Huston's sensibility was remote from that of Joyce, Binns is happy to agree that *The Dead* stands up as an example of impressive cinematic adaptations of literary classics. Hence the badness of Huston's version of *Under the Volcano* needs to be argued for; the mere observance of divergence from Lowry's own vision and style does not qualify as such an argument.

The second reason for the implausibility of the critical consensus is its implicit assumption that Lowry was a filmmaker manqué. Lowry was certainly a novelist who could be called "cinematic." But this does not imply that he could have made films successfully, any more than a computer programmer whose programming style is fairly called "elegant" could become a model on a catwalk, or a chess player whose chess is "aggressive" could go fifteen rounds with Muhammad Ali. Lowry did, to be sure, write a screenplay; the resulting film, it has been calculated, would have lasted six hours. This betrays an inability to grasp the constraints of the cinema. Six hours of the dazzling expressionism that Lowry was interested in could be fatal to an audience. Not surprisingly, no one was prepared to make the picture. Indeed, it is a defensible position that the screenplay isn't particularly good, at least in comparison to works similar in tone, such as *Under the Volcano* or "Through the Panama." It certainly is a lesser work than Fitzgerald's novel (see O'Hara).

In this paper, we wish to explore the dynamics of Binns's criticism that Huston's *Under the Volcano* was not dramatic enough to satisfy cinemagoers, while not Lowryesque enough to satisfy Lowryans. For the purposes of argument, we can accept that Binns's claim is true. The film was not a commercial success (although it was also relatively low budget); neither did the critics like it. Yet Binns and others imply that Huston should not have worried about satisfying cinema-goers, and should instead have made the film of *Volcano* that Lowry would have made. Hence their criticism would have been expressed just as forcibly had Huston made a commercial success, since the critical consensus is not that *Huston failed to make a successful movie* (though that may be true), but instead that *Huston failed to make a sufficiently Lowryesque movie*.

We certainly agree that Lowry is unlikely to have approved of the film as a whole—Binns quotes Lowry's disapproval of Huston's *Moby Dick* ("Filming," 122)—but the question of the interaction between director and author is surely not so simple, as *The Lost Weekend* and *The Dead* indicate. What we want to explore is how far the claim that Huston failed to make a sufficiently Lowryesque movie is a *genuine* criticism of a picture, and how far it is merely an expression of subjective regret and disappointment on the part of the critic. This discussion will also lead to new insight into the literary originals of Huston's films—in this case *Under the Volcano* and "The Dead." In particular, we contend that Huston's films are not attempts to reproduce literary works in a different medium, but instead are critical comments in tension with those literary works.

Huston's Films

Huston's own films provide one context in which his versions of *Under the Volcano* and *The Dead* may be examined. Huston was a major filmmaker, and his portrayal of himself as some sort of styleless journeyman should be seen as laconic reflexive mythmaking; it is certainly at odds with his annoyance at the rewriting of many of his early scripts (*Juarez*, for example, was extensively rewritten for star Paul Muni, radically altering what Huston considered to be some of his best writing).

Huston's point of view has been explored in several ways over the years, both in his early scripts and in films under his direction. This view of the workings of the world has been spelled out numerous times, not least by Huston himself. For a representative statement of the Huston creed, we can quote Truman Capote and Richard Avedon (Capote had worked with Huston and Bogart as writer on *Beat the Devil*):

> Consider the plot of the first, still best, Huston-directed film, *The Maltese Falcon*, in which the motivation is contributed by a valuable bijou in the shape of a falcon, a treasure for which the principal participants betray each other and murder and die—only to discover the falcon not to be the jewelled and genuine item but a solid lead fake, a cheat. This happens to be the theme, the dénouement, of most of Huston's films, of *The Treasure of the Sierra Madre*, in which the prospector's hoard of killed-over gold is blown away by the wind, of *The Asphalt Jungle*, *The Red Badge of Courage*, *Beat the Devil*, and, of course, of *Moby Dick*, that dead-end statement on man's defeat. Indeed, Huston seems seldom to have been attracted to material that did not accept human destiny as an unhappy joke, a confidence ploy with no pea under any pod; even the scripts he wrote as a young man—by example, *High Sierra* and *Juarez*—confirm his predilection. [Capote and Avedon 548-49]

Time and again this theme emerges in Huston's pictures. Yet it is important to note that the philosophy, in Huston's hands, is not mere cynicism, mere despair at the all-too-frequent undoing of man's hopes or dreams. In his description of the nature of the *Volcano* screenplay, producer Weiland Schulz-Keil notes, "He [the Consul], and we, must see his existence as determined by fate, which condemns the unfortunate to guilt because it does not recognize any difference between guilt and misfortune" (Schulz-Keil 134). The interplay between the inexorable workings of the world and the traits of a central figure were drawn out explicitly by Huston's team: "We [Schulz-Keil, Huston and screenplay writer Guy Gallo] chose to see the tension between fate and character as the constitutive gesture of Geoffrey Firmin's life and of Malcolm Lowry's novel" (Schulz-Keil 136). We certainly should not see in Huston's works a vision of man as the passive victim of fate or God. Huston's is a realist philosophy, a straightforward philosophy, but is nonetheless profound for that.

The Maltese Falcon is, as the above quotation implies, often taken as the archetypal Huston film (see also McCarty). That is a perfectly respectable point of view, but another film that might be regarded as a blueprint for subsequent Huston works is a comedy-thriller from 1938, for which Huston cowrote the script (with John Wexley, from Barré Lyndon's play), The Amazing Doctor Clitterhouse. This is a very early example of Huston's work; it is the fifth screenplay Huston worked on, and his second film for Warner Brothers (his first three films were scripted for Universal in 1932). And yet already the characteristic Huston plot has formed. The eponymous doctor, played by Edward G. Robinson with characteristic verve, is a criminologist researching psychological aspects of criminal activity. Frustrated by the difficulty of getting reliable subjects for his studies, he takes to crime, using himself as a subject for his own tests. He plans brilliant jewel robberies and records his own pulse rate and blood pressure afterwards. He soon has his own gang, played by the regular Warners gangsters (including Humphrey Bogart). However, his knowledge of the criminal mind, and his superior intelligence, which enable him to carry out audacious crimes and escape the law, are powerless to prevent his downfall because of a crucial lack of self-knowledge. Although his unfitness for a life of crime is recognized by Jo Keller (one of Claire Trevor's repertory of "tarts-with-a-heart"), Clitterhouse himself fails to see that he has become addicted to crime. His final academic coup, a study of his own physiological and psychological reactions as he commits a murder, leads to his downfall; as he is declared insane, his work is wasted.

The point is not that Clitterhouse is beaten by fate. Rather, his eclipse is the result of a theory, confidently held, and a method, carefully designed, failing to encompass or predict the likely course of events; once the plan goes into action, tragedy is virtually inevitable, since reality is likely to be too complex to be fully describable in theory. And since the cleverer the guy the more ambitious his plans and theories, it follows that it is the clever guys who fall farthest.

The theme we discern in Huston, then, is not man suffering from the workings of a malicious fate, but instead a view of man as creator and interpreter of his own destiny, unable to square that vision of himself with a world that is neither hostile nor sympathetic, but complex and reluctant to be summed up in a couple of sentences. The vision is ironic, not tragic or comedic.

For example, in *Across the Pacific*, Dr. Lorenz (Sydney Greenstreet), spy and admirer of all things Japanese, cannot bring himself to commit hara-kiri upon the collapse of his plans. In *The Asphalt Jungle*, Doc Riedenschneider's (Sam Jaffe) plans for the perfect heist fail because the villains eventually turn on each other after the robbery has succeeded; Riedenschneider himself is arrested when he lingers at a roadhouse to watch a sexy female teenager dancing. In *The Treasure of the Sierra Madre*, the prospectors Fred C. Dobbs (Bogart), Howard (Walter Huston), and Curtin (Tim Holt) succeed in mining gold from a Mexican mountain— luck had played a part in their success, when the expedition was financed by a winning lottery ticket—only to lose the gold in their greed and obsession.

This inability to understand or predict the way events will develop seems to imply that the sensible course is to be cautious and to curb ambition. But nowhere does Huston agree with the pessimistic view that the best we can do is keep our heads down. Huston's heroes all act, all attempt to be influential presences in the world. In fact, the ideal of retirement after action is the goal of many of Huston's protagonists, and the apparent possibility of withdrawal is one of the chief illusions, the bait on the end of the hook (Dobbs, Doc Riedenschneider, Dix Handley in *The Asphalt Jungle*, Roy Earle in *High Sierra*). What we see as admirable in these characters is their drivenness, their desire to succeed against the odds. This is the real theme of Huston's work—not the "missions" upon which the characters launch themselves, but their explorations of their own nature while doing so. It is almost part of their nature to battle and strive, not only against the odds, but crucially in circumstances where the odds are stacked against them thanks to misjudgment and misplaced ambition. In the case of the Consul as conceived by Schulz-Keil, Huston, and Gallo, the driving force is melancholy taken nearly to the point of self-indulgence: "He hates his despair, his dejection because they are uncommon, because they do not drive him into depression, but an— inevitably aristocratic—melancholy" (Schulz-Keil 140).

It would, of course, scarcely be rational for such characters to strive as they do were the possibility of success genuinely chimerical (see O'Hara). But Huston's view is very dependent on the neutrality of events, on the nonexistence of "fate," at least where fate is conceived as being some sort of consistent narrative. Fate, for Huston, has no such semantic charge; humans plan, and their plans sometimes work, sometimes don't. When the plans *do* work, it is usually for the wrong reasons, and when they don't, it is usually not because the plan itself was flawed, but because "unforeseen circumstances" wreck the assumptions upon which the plan was based.

It is perfectly consistent with Huston's philosophy that hopeful messages be sprinkled among the despair, and hope is what we find in a smallish number of his pictures. For example, in *The African Queen*, Charlie (Bogart) and Rosie (Katharine Hepburn) have a mission, to destroy a German battleship with Charlie's rusty old boat. Their plan to ram the battleship, using the *African Queen* as a floating torpedo, fails; the *African Queen* sinks. But as Charlie and Rosie are about to be executed by the German captain (who has just married them with the classic line "I now pronounce you man and wife; proceed with the execution"), the battleship runs into the explosive remains of the *African Queen* and is sunk after all. Though the plan failed, Charlie and Rosie are triumphant, and *would* have been triumphant even had they been executed and the battleship remained afloat. Through their marriage they overcome their own weaknesses in the face of overwhelming odds, unlike Clitterhouse or Riedenschneider, whose failure to transcend their own weaknesses dooms them. The fact that nothing goes according to plan does not mean that there is no point in action.

So it is not surprising that, at the end of his career (and his life), Huston should have been drawn to classic stories about characters whose personal philosophies are tested in adverse circumstances, and whose ultimate failures are ambiguous. In this context, we should examine Huston's realist critiques of "The Dead" and *Under the Volcano.*

Filming Joyce

The critical consensus that Huston's *Volcano* failed because it was not sufficiently faithful to Lowry's novel raises the question of what type of film *would* be faithful. It also raises the question of the critical success of his film of "The Dead," since Huston changed Joyce's story significantly. We will examine the differences between Joyce's and Huston's versions of "The Dead" to show that although the film superficially resembles the original story to a high degree, it is closer than Joyce's story to the preoccupations that we have outlined as guiding many of Huston's works. Such preoccupations, centered as they are on characters who dare to *act* and are brought down by unforeseen *events*, are by their nature suited to the cinema, since central players can be shown both striving and being overtaken by circumstances. It is those elements of the fiction that depict external actions and events, rather than inner thoughts and emotional responses, that are most easily portrayed in the visual text of the classical Hollywood picture (Bordwell, Staiger, and Thompson). Prose fiction, on the other hand, not only shows us people's actions and the events that overtake them, but also has the capacity to explicitly convey rich internal worlds, worlds that in the case of Lowry's Consul are rich to the point of sickness. The *details* of such aspects (for example, how a particular character perceives the actions or words of another), no matter how gifted the actor, cannot be established by visual means with any close faithfulness to the original author's text. Information normally conveyed by dialogue may be transferred to the new medium in various ways: an actor may be given new dialogue with which to speak of inner feelings or perceptions (but in so doing the nature of the dialogue is necessarily altered, and the character portrayed becomes the apparent author of the utterance); a written subtitle may be added (as Tiessen suggested would be a potential improvement to the film of *Volcano* to make the time reference explicit); or an authorial voice surrogate in the form of a "voiceover" may be added. However, each of these is unsatisfactory in some way—particularly in a film of the classical Hollywood style.

Bearing this in mind, we want to give particular emphasis to the translation of fictional dialogue from the page to the screen, and the additions to any screenplay version. Without the aid of authorial voice the dialogue must be convincing from the point of view of approximating real speech and, equally, must present the viewer with sufficient information about the context of the events taking place, the motivations of characters and their actions. Huston's alterations of Joyce's dialogue reveal something of the director's own interpretative slant.

Moreover, Joyce's story "The Dead" is itself centrally concerned with the impressions made on characters by speech-making, storytelling, joke-cracking, and singing. Two significant events in the story revolve around preparations for performance. Gabriel rehearses the speech he is to give at the supper during the first half of the story, and during the second he makes an internal rehearsal of the love scene he intends to act out with Gretta. From the opening of the story, where he finds he cannot speak comfortably with the maid Lily, Gabriel is presented as being painfully aware of the impression he makes as he speaks. Joyce's authorial presence makes a direct connection between his early faux pas and the big speech: "He would fail with them just as he had failed with the girl in the pantry. He had taken up a wrong tone. His whole speech was a mistake from first to last, an utter failure" (D 179).

Gabriel's sensitivity to audience response is related to our central concern. The surreal quality of *Under the Volcano* is in part due to the lack of authorial authority that would connect the internal workings to some stable "reality." This is an essential difference between the narrative style of the prose originals we are dealing with. Throughout *Under the Volcano* we are faced with the problem of how seriously to take the Consul's view of reality, a problem that becomes magnified for the director of a film, who must both interpret and reproduce. This interpretive problem is generated by the narrative style, which Frederick Asals, in his comparison of the 1940 *Volcano* with the later revisions, describes as a product of "a gradual confronting of the interior" (Asals 95). He notes the change from the omniscient author/reporter, who is by nature external to the events recorded, to the presentation of the narrative from within the consciousness of the protagonists and the ensuing problems of interpretation, together with richness and depth, that this change creates for the reader and, more pertinent to our argument, the film director. As readers we can "bathe" in the sea of ambiguities and marvel at the deft representation of the vagaries of human perception. We can admire the way the narrative devices mirror the limitations of our ability to comprehend life. As (realist) directors we must choose something to represent on film.

We will now look briefly at how these differences in narrative stance between "The Dead" and *Under the Volcano* manifest themselves, and suggest how the choices made by Huston as to what to represent reflect a realist critique of *both* works—the multiply centered narrative of the novel and the more traditional author-centered style of the short story.

Three extracts will serve to exemplify some of the key differences in style:

(A)   "Laruelle?" The Consul's voice came from far away. He was aware of vertigo; closing his eyes wearily he took hold of the fence to steady himself. Mr. Quincey's words knocked on his consciousness—or someone actually was knocking on a door—fell away, then knocked again, louder. [*UV* 136]

(B)   Gabriel coloured as if he felt he had made a mistake and, without looking at her, kicked off his goloshes and flicked actively with his muffler at his patent-leather shoes. [*D* 178]

(C)   He was trembling now with annoyance. Why did she seem so abstracted? He did not know how he could begin. Was she annoyed, too, about something? [*D* 217]

The first of these quotations is a short, but typical, example of the narrative device that lends an air of unsteady reality to Lowry's book. The

Consul echoes the name of his rival. It is stated that his "voice came from far away." However, it is not clear whose perspective this adverbial stance "far away" relates to. Is the voice far away from Quincey? From the reader? From the Consul? The last is the most likely choice, but this answer suggests a second problem of interpretation, for the Consul is himself named as the subject of the sentence, and the verb, "came," does not lend itself to a metaphoric interpretation. Lowry does not say the Consul's voice *seemed to him to come* from far away or *sounded as if it came* from far away. In choosing the "bare" verb phrase "came," together with a subject that presents the speaker's own voice as distanced from the body producing it, Lowry challenges us to make sense of the nonsensical. The point is not that one's own voice might seem distanced from oneself, but rather that as readers and interpreters we do not know where to place ourselves in relation to a simple declarative sentence. Lowry as author does not stand beyond the Consul and distinguish between what happened and what the Consul thought happened.

A similar and frequently used device is also apparent in the Lowry extract quoted above: the unexplained double interpretation of phenomena. In this case a potential metaphor, "Mr. Quincey's words knocked on his consciousness," is coordinated by means of "or" with a literal explanation, "someone actually was knocking on a door." This has the effect of raising the metaphor to the level of something that is to be taken more literally. The repetition of *knocked / was knocking / knocked again* makes us reinterpret the supposed metaphoric usages of the verb more physically. The representation of a literal knocking on a door raises the possibility that there is a real noise—something might really be "knocking" at the Consul's consciousness (a belief that is hard to justify in nonmetaphoric terms). Lowry presents us with two potential explanations of events that are given equal weight by being coordinated: words knocking on a consciousness; a person knocking on a door. Again the supposedly omniscient author is deliberately noncommittal as to which explanation is "true."

The two quotations taken from "The Dead" exemplify the very different narrative stance offered by Joyce. They demonstrate internal confusion of rather different kinds, the former embarrassment and the latter incomprehension. What is noticeable is that although the characters may be feeling doubt or confusion the actual presentation of their inner state does not reflect this. In extract (B) the relation between Gabriel's blushing and his feelings is made explicit by the subordinate clause "as if he felt he had made a mistake." In extract (C) doubt is presented by the most logical grammatical structures, question forms: "Why did she seem so abstracted? . . . Was she annoyed, too, about something?" Again, although we may not know the answers to these questions, in the process of reading we remain external to the actual state of bewilderment felt by the character. Clearly formulated questions such as these suggest clearly formulated thoughts, and the conventions of prose fiction in English mean that the thoughts are those of Gabriel. Unlike with the multiple and shifting referents and origins of extract (A), there is little cause for readerly unease or bemusement.

Furthermore, in the extracts from "The Dead," there is a close connection between physical actions and emotions. Gabriel colors because he is embarrassed and trembles because he is annoyed; when irritated he kicks and flicks. In *Under the Volcano* the relationship between individual movements and states of mind is less straightforward. The key image is that of the infernal machine. The import of the Consul's ride is one of acausality and uncontrol: when the Consul gives himself up to the machine, any link between his actions and our interpretation of his actions is broken. Fundamental to the book is the fact that it is not known why the Consul does what he does, and the ambiguity of action is a key way in which we are prevented from coming to many conclusions on this matter. In extract (A) the Consul feels vertigo and takes hold of the fence. If this were in "The Dead" we might expect to know precisely *why* he does this. However, in *Volcano* it is as if the mere mention of Laruelle's name is enough to debilitate the Consul physically. On the other hand, the nonauthoritative presentation of the narrative is such that parallel interpretations of the Consul's near-swoon are possible: he might be overwhelmed with memories, hatred, guilt, or the weariness of his own hell; he might simply be sloshed. For the realist filmmaker such causal ambiguity may be a problem (Bordwell, Staiger, and Thompson). The actions of characters must mean something; it is part of the grammar of the conventional cinema in which Huston was working that they do. Unfortunately, it is hard for them to mean more than one thing at a time, or for the less probable meaning to be conveyed. If a drunk leans on a fence for support, the first gloss people will put on the action, and one that the director and actor have to work to quash, is that he or she does this because inebriated. In this sense, writing of the style found in "The Dead" is more amenable to realist filmmaking than that in *Under the Volcano*. Actions link to local inner causes rather than indeterminate motives and/or inner states.

Even so, there are still crucial mismatches between Joyce's world and Huston's. Consider the two versions of "The Dead," which could be summarized as follows:

Joyce Version

A prig with a measure of social success, who is sensitive to all around him in as far as they respond to his own person, discovers that such self-centered success is meaningless in the face of his wife's capacity to grieve for an old love. In effect, his worldview is dealt a mortal blow from which it is hard to imagine him ever recovering. At the end of the story his soul appears to die.

Huston Version

A socially successful and quite sensitive man is made to realize, at the very moment that he thought he could overcome the troubles in his relationship with his wife, that his view of the world is sadly limited, and that they remain apart. At the end of the film he muses with bittersweet melancholy on the mortality of man, and in the very act of uttering a sustained poetic monologue, raises his stature near to that of tragic hero.

During the progress of the party that is the main event of the short story, many of the key relationships are portrayed through the characters' attempts at engaging with an audience and the reactions of others to these performances. The reshaping and repositioning of some of these events in the film version hint at Huston's concerns. In the Joyce version the story of Johnny, the horse that lets its master down, is told with great aplomb to an audience of the departing dance-goers in the hallway of the house. It is therefore a consolidation of Gabriel's success during the after-supper speech in this version; he is relaxed and in his element, his capacity to hold an audience proof to him of his own importance and security. Such success is in marked contrast to the downfall he is to suffer with Gretta, where all his bluff urbanity is shown to be no match for the final truths of life, love, and death. It is also in contrast to the treatment of the same funny story in the film. In the Huston version the anecdote is saved for the drive to the hotel, and here, rather than meeting with success, it is hardly noticed by the one listener present, Gretta. Gabriel's attempt at jolly communication is a singular failure, a precursor of the dénouement to come.

The point is that in the short story Gabriel thinks he has overcome all his difficulties (his worries about making a speech, his difficult conversations) and is filled with confidence, only to discover that the very stuff of such social success is both superficial and without lasting worth, that he and all socially grounded preoccupations of the living are worthless and meaningless. At the end of the Joyce story there is a sense of Gabriel as individual dissipating and disintegrating: "He was conscious of, but could not apprehend, their wayward and flickering existence ["the vast hosts of the dead"]. His own identity was fading out into a grey impalpable world: the solid world itself which these dead had one time reared and lived in was dissolving and dwindling" (*D* 223). As an individual and central character Gabriel no longer exists. The greatness of Joyce's ending is that it is neither happy nor sad; rather, there is a leveling out between the living and the dead to a point where they are indistinguishable.

In the film version, however, the relationship with Gretta takes center stage as a motivating force to the story. As in many a Huston film the main character is defeated at the point of triumph, and in this moment of being stymied his driving preoccupations take on universal and tragic weight. At the nadir of events a Huston film often kicks into a different gear, and it is this kick that seemed to preoccupy the director. The difference between Joyce's and Huston's versions of the story is a subtle one, but one that is fundamental to Huston's relations to the sources of his story lines. It can, perhaps, be further exemplified by the treatment of the performance metaphor.

The theme of performance is a strong one in "The Dead." The aunts whose party is being celebrated have a keen interest in the musical world of Dublin: Aunt Kate teaches music, Aunt Julia had a choir, their niece Mary Jane plays "the organ in Haddington Road." These facts act as a backdrop to a story that revolves around self-conscious utterance as Gabriel's driving characteristic and unselfconscious song as the purest state of human relations. The dichotomy between fear of failure and craving for worldly acknowledgment, in an atmosphere of spontaneous song and unrequited love, creates a complex matrix in which Gabriel's inner fears take on significance beyond mere stage fright. In the film version, where the explicit conveyance of internal states is problematic, rehearsal and performance become just that. We see Gabriel nervously handling the notes for his speech, and this nervousness has little universal significance. He catches his wife's eye, and a hint is made of the relationship between the public speech to come and his lack of direct verbal communication with his wife.

The social isolation of Freddy Malins is suggested in Joyce's story by the fact that the joke he tells is not presented in the text; rather, we see him laughing explosively at his own joke, a joke that no one present shares and that the reader cannot share. In the film version a whole joke about a piglet is created for Freddy, and he is seen with an appreciative audience listening to him. In the Joyce text Freddy's mother, too, has no attentive interlocutor, the problem being that she is talking to another performer who is internally rehearsing what he will say: "Gabriel hardly heard what she said. Now that supper was coming near he began to think again about his speech" (*D* 191). His fingers tremble, as they do when he starts to speak after supper, and he rehearses a barbed attack on Miss Ivors. This internal attack is similarly doomed to miss its intended recipient, Miss Ivors, who departs before the speech is given (in both versions). In the film the ramblings of Mrs. Malins and the discomfiture of Gabriel are played for laughs.

The Protestant Browne is marked out by a lack of audience approval, for example when he makes a verbal faux pas in his putting on of a "low" Dublin accent to tell a risqué joke to the musical young girls (D 183). In the film, however, the anecdote takes on no great weight. Mary Jane, too, performs to a largely uncaring audience: "The only persons who seemed to follow the music" are herself and her aunt. Although in the film hints are given of boredom and fidgeting, the "great applause" of the original text cannot carry quite its ironic shaft in the new medium. Also the treatment of Julia's elderly voice is altered somewhat. In the book there is little hint that the singing is not pure and, in its way, captivating, for it is described as "strong and clear in tone." In this context Freddy's enthusiasm appears good-hearted: the two characters share some common features, including an inability to appreciate the performances of more ordinary characters—the one from senility, the other from drunkenness. In the medium of the film, the old woman's voice can be little more than pathetic, and the enthusiasm of the drunken man seems ludicrous.

The unheeding audience motif in Joyce contrasts with two moments of great success on the part of performers, who seem to wholly captivate their listeners. The first of these moments is Gabriel's successful after-supper speech (a speech notable for its rhetorical sonority and lack of content); the second is the transcendental moment when Gretta stands on the stairs transfigured by the memories evoked by Bartell D'Arcy's singing. Gretta seems a stranger to Gabriel in this episode: he sees her initially as "a woman . . . standing near the top of the first flight," only realizing after this initial impression that "it was his wife" (D 209). In the film it is impossible to convey the moment of dislocation Gabriel experiences when he cannot recognize his wife. She is literally a stranger to him, as she will be again, more fundamentally, in the hotel room.

Nor is it possible for bad singing to be transcendental on film, so the moment is simplified. In the book, the tenor's voice is "hoarse" and it is the associations it has for the listener that make it so special. In the film, however, D'Arcy's voice is sweet and moving, Gretta remains Gretta, and Gabriel looks on as a humble husband who, quite understandably, given the emotional beauty of his wife, will attempt to secure their relationship. The "improvement" of the tenor's performance might be contrasted to the "downgrading" of Aunt Julia's singing, suggesting that neither change was made simply for reasons of cinematic practicality. It is more predictable that an old woman should sing pathetically and that a woman should be deeply moved by a lovely tenor voice, and, given the altered focus in the Huston version, the changes are not surprising. The film has no point to make about performance as a symbol for human relations in general. In order for the less predictable performances to be justified and explained, attention would need to be diverted from the Gabriel-Gretta story.

In addition to a social aspect, suggesting the shallowness of most of human interaction, songs and jokes and public utterance have a symbolic centrality in the story. The culminating blow to Gabriel is set in motion by his wife's hearing of "The Lass of Aughrim," a performance that echoes the tragically significant singing of the dead boy, Michael Furey, and symbolizes a capacity for sincere feeling and self-negation to which Gabriel cannot aspire. Furey had no interest in audience reaction, and here he is shadowed in the singing of the ancient Aunt Julia, and the uninhibited laughter of Freddy Malins, whose inner thoughts are never presented to us. It is perhaps significant that this boy is *not* primarily a performer: he took up singing "for his health," and, despite this, succeeds where the more self-conscious Gabriel fails. Through the performance motif Gabriel's falseness becomes more evident to the reader and, fatally, to Gabriel himself toward the end of the story.

Filming Lowry

We have seen that Huston's adaptation of Joyce's story is driven by two, in this case complementary, needs: the filmmaker's need to focus on actions and eschew the internal or seek other means of representing inner states, and Huston's personal need as an artist to shape the material according to his own view of life and the world. To recall, Huston's philosophical position, outlined above, has two components: an epistemological component, which states that even if life does have a purpose or grand pattern, mere humans do not possess the capacity for accurate grasp of that purpose or pattern; and an artistic component, which sees the driving force of human ambition as being, in the context of these epistemological imperfections, deeply ironic.

It might be said that this ironic, detached view of human endeavor is much less profound than that of Joyce and Lowry, both of whom resist strongly the Hustonian epistemological claim. When Gabriel realizes at the end of "The Dead" that all socially based significance is no significance at all, is meaningless, the result is certainly consistent with the implication behind Huston's epistemological claim, that we cannot reliably discern a grand pattern in events because there isn't one. However,

Joyce and Huston part company with respect to Gabriel's reaction to this discovery; Huston's Gabriel is raised as a result of this discovery, while Joyce's is crushed under the weight of his realization of his exclusion. Joyce's implied criticism of Gabriel is that he has relied complacently upon social success for direction in his life; Gabriel's malaise is not *epistemological*, but *spiritual*. But if the problem is spiritual, it follows that Gabriel is out of touch with "greater" truths.

As such, Joyce's view is arguably deeper than Huston's. However, Huston could resist this conclusion; his case is also arguable. What that argument would need to exploit is the realism with which Huston is associated. That realism could be allied to the epistemological claim, to make the case for the implication we introduced above; there can be no knowledge of a grand pattern, because there is no grand pattern. What we have, roughly speaking, is atoms and the void, and any governing laws that exist are to be found at the atomic level. Human society is an attempt to place significance on wider groupings of these atoms, but since there *is* no significance at this macro-level, that attempt is doomed. Nevertheless, this does not mean that such activity is pointless or absurd; indeed, such activity may even be seen ironically as heroic (as in the case of *Don Quixote*). But unless human significance is seen against the background of such cosmic randomness, it will be falsely presented. This is the view put forward by, for example, Camus in *The Myth of Sisyphus*. But note how this view is heavily influenced by the medium in which Huston works: whereas Joyce has the medium of prose in which to express a philosophical pattern, Huston, working within the film, faces a challenge in conveying any such ideas explicitly. Whereas Joyce has the resources of the authorial voice to "guide" the reader, Huston must first interpret and then seek some means of representing his interpretation through the medium of film. The ending of his film of "The Dead" turns to voiceover to replace the omniscient author whose presence is so evident in the short story. Alternatively, Huston can depart from his realism to "give" us some filmic metaphor—there is an example of this at the beginning of *Under the Volcano*, where the Consul is seen in close-up, with the toy skulls from the Day of the Dead celebrations reflected in his dark glasses. However, this is not a technical resource that Huston can exploit to any great extent, for as a realist, Huston cannot consistently break into what is in effect *surrealism* at the drop of a hat.

Huston's film of "The Dead" may be seen, then, not just as a realist (and therefore inaccurate) version of Joyce, but as a realist *critique* of Joyce. However accurately Joyce presents the world at the level of the story, at the meta-level he misrepresents it. Joyce is right to point out that the surface of human significance is precariously balanced on top of a random superstructure, and as such is liable to slip or fall without warning. The problem is Joyce's assumption of a greater level of significance from which such occurrences can be seen, predicted, and judged. Huston would resist the postulation of such a level of significance, whether it be spiritual, religious, or simply artistic, rooted in Joyce's vision of the world. Such a level can never be explanatory.

It is not our aim here to evaluate the Hustonian reply. Our aim is the more modest one of placing Huston's filming of the classics in the proper context, so that the quality of his films may be judged more reliably. Our remaining task is to develop the case that Huston, on top of producing a realist film of Lowry's expressionist novel, has also provided a realist *critique* of Lowry.

Lowry and Huston are actually closer with respect to the epistemological stance than Joyce and Huston. However, Lowry, by making subjective the epistemological crisis of absurdity, not only dramatizes it but also sacrifices realism by importing the crisis, via subjectivity, to a central role in the action. The inability to know the grand pattern, an inability that Huston exploits in his pictures, is certainly an important factor in Lowry's *Under the Volcano.* But Lowry explores the space by using as his central character the Consul, who has a strong sense of what metaphysical reality is (combined with a very tenuous grasp on *physical* reality); the problem arises because we as audience (and Lowry as author) cannot be sure that the Consul has got it right. Even the fact that the Consul's dire predictions and wish for death are fulfilled at the close of the book fails to convince; what we do not, and cannot, know is how much, if at all, the metaphysical forces adduced by the Consul are actually *responsible* for his death, or whether, on the other hand, he just picked a fight with the wrong people. After all, the Consul was convinced that he was on his way to hell, and that the Farolito was hell. He therefore went to the Farolito under his own steam. The causal agent here could equally well be Fate or the Consul. Given that he was in the Farolito, and drunk, and argumentative, and excited, the chances of his picking a fatal fight would, one supposes, be relatively high. Hence the Consul's beliefs certainly caused his death; what we don't know is in what sense. One possible interpretation is that the Consul was right about the world, about heaven and hell, and his death was inevitable, metaphysically necessary. One other interpretation is that the Consul died because of his beliefs: that because he believed as he did he behaved as he did, and because he behaved as he did he died as he did, but that his death itself has no extra significance. Doubtless there are many more interpretations in between. But the way that Lowry's *Volcano* dramatizes the epistemological crisis is to show us that there is no certainty about which of the interpretations of the Consul's death is right. This transferral of the crisis to center stage is the direct source of the multilayering described so effectively by Binns in his essay "Materialism and Magic in *Under the Volcano*." And so we can see that the fact that Lowry's *Volcano* fails to convince us totally of the Consul's interpretation of events is not a failure of Lowry as an author. Quite the opposite: the several layers of ambiguity are Lowry's authorial *strategy*.

But what this also shows us is why Lowry's work both attracted Huston and compelled him to simplify. For Huston's realism prevents him from wholeheartedly adopting the epistemological crisis as a central narrative element in the way that Lowry has, despite the fact that he endorses the claim that the truth is difficult to find. The central point of Huston's philosophy is the irony of human endeavor against God or nature. To raise human failure to the level of irony demands that that failure be inevitable; it should simply not be a possibility that Huston's agents get it right. Their partial successes, which spur them on to greater efforts, must be seen as random accidents to be ironic. The Lowryan tactic of leaving it open that the Consul may be right cannot serve Huston's project.

Note how this squares with Huston's realism. If all we are is arrangements of atoms in a void, then the significance that the Consul postulates is spurious. If we are merely whirling around on a small planet in the spiral arm of a small galaxy, then hell is not contained in a grotty bar in Parián. Hence the epistemological crisis is held at one remove. Whereas Lowry, by his subjective stance in the novel, actually puts us in the position of someone in that crisis (since the novel's conventions are such that metaphysical reality can be real), Huston, by his realist objectivism, makes us, the audience, the observers and judges of someone in that crisis.

Huston would firmly resist the claim that he has merely simplified Lowry, however. Contrast the behavior of a nonrealist critic and a biographer. The critic will take seriously, and describe, the many layers of Lowry's text, for example in the manner of Binns (in "Materialism and Magic"). Now suppose, for the sake of argument, that some expressionist sequences of *Under the Volcano*—the final scene, say—were semiautobiographical. How would the *biographer* deal with that? Lowry wrote up the scene as if the Farolito were hell, and as if the Consul—that is, Lowry himself by hypothesis—were reaching the nadir of his descent. The scene will be important for the biographer. But will he or she take this description seriously? Surely not; the biographer will see the Farolito as merely a bar in a small Mexican town, peopled by various more or less unsavory clients, a bar of great significance, one way or another, for

Lowry himself, but a bar nonetheless. It is not the biographer's job to see hell on earth, except purely figuratively.

So Huston's line must be that, in the realist view of things, the critic should be as tolerant of personal metaphor and subjective imagery as the biographer. In art, as in life, a man may be demonic, but may not be a demon. The result is a film that is a critique of *Under the Volcano*, with a concentration on the surface action, because every other layer lacks truth in some way. The truth lacked is objective; Huston clearly does not doubt the *subjective* truth of the Consul's private hell. The doubt is whether one can remain ambiguous about such an interpretation of events. Huston sees himself as an artist who presents the objective.

Much of the criticism of Huston appears to have been premised on the assumption that the filmmaker is primarily a mirror for reflection of literature. What we have tried to defend is the idea that the filmmaker is an artist, in an alien medium, and that any significant interaction between a filmmaker and an author will result, not merely in a "film-of-the-book," but in a separate artistic entity, with its own life. Huston's *Volcano*, like *The Dead*, is better seen as a commentary on the literary original from a realist perspective. This does not, of course, imply that *Volcano* is (or is not) a great film. Great novels can make mediocre films *(War and Peace)*, and mediocre novels can make great films *(To Have and Have Not)*. What it does imply is that it has to be taken on its own terms if a constructive critical dialogue is to result. A simple *comparison* between Lowry's original and Huston's interpretation is, of course, possible, but the relevance of *that* debate to judgments about the quality of the film needs to be shown.

Works Cited

Asals, Frederick. "Revision and Illusion in *Under the Volcano.*" In *Swinging the Maelstrom: New Perspectives on Malcolm Lowry*, edited by Sherrill Grace. Montreal and Kingston: McGill-Queen's Univ. Press, 1992.

Binns, Ronald. "Materialism and Magic in *Under the Volcano.*" *Critical Quarterly* 23 (Spring 1981): 21-33.

———. "Filming *Under the Volcano.*" In *Malcolm Lowry Eighty Years On*, edited by Sue Vice. London: Macmillan, 1989.

Bordwell, David, Janet Staiger, and Kristin Thompson. *The Classical Hollywood Cinema: Film Style and Mode of Production to 1960.* London: Routledge & Kegan Paul, 1985.

Capote, Truman, and Richard Avedon. "John Huston." In Truman Capote, *A Capote Reader.* London: Hamish Hamilton, 1987.

McCarty, John. *The Complete Films of John Huston*. Secaucus, N.J.: Citadel, 1987.

O'Hara, Kieron. "'You do not know *why* you dance': Comedy in *Under the Volcano*, 'Through the Panama,' and 'Tender Is the Night.'" *Malcolm Lowry Review* nos. 31 and 32 (Fall 1992 and Spring 1993): 68-84.

Sage, Victor. "The Art of Sinking in Prose: Charles Jackson, Joyce and *Under the Volcano*." In *Malcolm Lowry Eighty Years On*, edited by Sue Vice. London: Macmillan, 1989.

Schulz-Keil, Weiland. "The 67th Reading: *Under the Volcano* and Its Screenplays." In *Apparently Incongruous Parts: The Worlds of Malcolm Lowry*, edited by Paul Tiessen and Gordon Bowker. Metuchen, N.J.: Scarecrow Press, 1990.

Tiessen, Paul. "John Huston's *Under the Volcano*." *Malcolm Lowry Newsletter* 14 (Spring 1984): 43-48.

Contributors

CHRIS ACKERLEY is a Senior Lecturer in English at the University of Otago, Dunedin, New Zealand. He coauthored *A Companion to "Under the Volcano"* (1984), provided the explanatory annotation for *The Collected Poetry of Malcolm Lowry* (1992), and has been a frequent contributor to the *Malcolm Lowry Review*. His Toronto Ph.D. discussed aspects of ambiguity in *Ulysses*, both the comic and the cosmic. He wrote *A History of the Otago Bridge Club* and is currently working on a *Companion*-like annotation of Samuel Beckett's *Murphy*.

MARTIN BOCK is an Associate Professor of English at the University of Minnesota, Duluth. He is the author of *Crossing the Shadow-Line: The Literature of Estrangement* (1989) and of essays on Lowry or Joyce in the *Malcolm Lowry Review*, and *Modern Fiction Studies*. He is currently at work on a biographical essay about A.E. Tebb, the personal physician and friend of Joseph Conrad, Ford Madox Ford, and Violet Hunt.

RICHARD K. CROSS taught at Dartmouth and UCLA before moving, in 1983, to the University of Maryland at College Park, where he served for five years as Chair of the English Department. He is the author of *Flaubert and Joyce: The Rite of Fiction* (1971) and *Malcolm Lowry: A Preface to His Fiction* (1980) as well as articles and reviews on Lowry appearing in *Contemporary Literature, Modern Fiction Studies,* and *Modern Philology*. His most recent essays are "The Soul Is a Far Country: D.M. Thomas and *The White Hotel*" in the *Journal of Modern Literature* and "Climbing the Brocken," a piece drawn from his experiences in Germany during the year of unification, in *Modern Age*.

SHERRILL GRACE is a Professor of English at the University of British Columbia, where she teaches modern and Canadian literature and courses on comparative and interdisciplinary studies. She has published

197

books on Margaret Atwood, on literary expressionism, and on Malcolm Lowry, including *The Voyage That Never Ends* (1982), the edited collection *Swinging the Maelstrom* (1992), and *Sursum Corda! The Collected Letters of Malcolm Lowry* (1995-96). She is currently writing a book on Canadian culture titled *Canada and the Idea of North*.

REBECCA HUGHES is the Deputy Director of the Centre for English Language Education at the University of Nottingham. Her *English in Speech and Writing: Investigating Language and Literature*, one chapter of which deals largely with *Under the Volcano*, is being published by Routledge.

SUZANNE KIM taught English and American literature for many years at the Sorbonne-Université de Paris. She is now working as Associate Research Scholar at the Centre National de la Recherche Scientifique, Paris, where she is currently engaged in the collective transcription of Joyce's notebooks for *Finnegans Wake*. Her major articles on Joyce and Lowry are "Subjectivité et écriture: Malcolm Lowry ou la conscience de soi suicidaire" in *Genèse de la Conscience Moderne*, edited by R. Ellrodt (1983); "Imaginaire de l'espace" in *Genèse de Babel*, edited by Louis Hay (1985); and "Le récit piégé de *Under the Volcano*," in *Études anglaises* (1990).

PATRICK A. MCCARTHY is a Professor of English at the University of Miami, Coral Gables, Florida. His publications on Joyce and Lowry include *The Riddles of "Finnegans Wake"* (1980), *"Ulysses": Portals of Discovery* (1990), *Forests of Symbols: World, Text, and Self in Malcolm Lowry's Fiction* (1994), and *Malcolm Lowry's "La Mordida": A Scholarly Edition* (1996).

KIERON O'HARA is a researcher in the Artificial Intelligence Group, Department of Psychology, at the University of Nottingham. He is particularly interested in the connections between literature, film, philosophy, and science. He has published papers in a range of academic journals, including the *Malcolm Lowry Review*, the *Dickensian*, *Mind*, the *Notre Dame Journal of Formal Logic*, and the *International Journal for Human-Computer Studies*. He is the co-editor of *Advances in Knowledge Acquisition* (1996).

BRIAN W. SHAFFER is an Assistant Professor of English at Rhodes College and the author of *The Blinding Torch: Modern British Fiction and the Discourse of Civilization* (1993). He is also the author of essays in *PMLA, ELH, Journal of Modern Literature, James Joyce Quarterly, Joyce in Context,* edited by Vincent J. Cheng and Timothy Martin (1992), and *Molly Blooms: A Polylogue on "Penelope" and Cultural Studies,* edited by Richard Pearce (1994). He is presently at work on a book-length study of Kazuo Ishiguro.

PAUL TIESSEN is a Professor and Chair of English at Wilfrid Laurier University in Waterloo, Ontario, and editor of the *Malcolm Lowry Review*. Books he has edited or coedited in recent years include *The Letters of Malcolm Lowry and Gerald Noxon, 1940-1952* (1988), *The Cinema of Malcolm Lowry: A Scholarly Edition of Lowry's "Tender Is the Night"* (1990, with Miguel Mota), *Apparently Incongruous Parts: The Worlds of Malcolm Lowry* (1990), and *The 1940 "Under the Volcano"* (1994, with Miguel Mota).

SUE VICE is Lecturer in English literature at the University of Sheffield. She has edited *Malcolm Lowry Eighty Years On* (1989) and *Psychoanalytic Criticism: A Reader* (1995).

JOSEPH C. VOELKER has just completed his second term as Chair of the Franklin and Marshall College English Department. He is at work on a mystery novel entitled *Terminus*, set in Mauves sur Loire, France.

Index

Note: References to *Ulysses* and *Under the Volcano* are not indexed, but references to specific chapters of *Ulysses* (e.g., "Circe") and to the 1940 draft of *Under the Volcano* are listed.